SCOTTISH FOLK-LORE AND FOLK LIFE

STUDIES IN RACE, CULTURE AND TRADITION

BY

DONALD A. MACKENZIE

Author of "Scotland: The Ancient Kingdom"
"Wonder Tales from Scottish Myth and Legend", &c.

1935

PREFACE

In this volume the folk-lore of Scotland is given intensive study and its characteristic features brought into prominence. I have not only sifted and collated the recorded evidence, but provided fresh material as a collector of many years' experience and drawn upon my recollections of the persisting folk-beliefs in which I shared in my boyhood. Comparative notes are provided along with a historical summary which deals chiefly with intrusions, settlements or expulsions of aliens; and there is a study of the race question based upon reliable data, including those accumulated in many Scottish schools and during the recruiting period of the Great War.

Among the striking features of Scottish folk-lore are those afforded by the remarkable " pork taboo "; the " Blue Men of the Minch "; the widespread giant stories; the myths of the ferocious and benevolent goddesses; the beliefs regarding demons of rivers, lochs and mountains; the animal forms assumed by souls; the association of the dead with the fairies, and the haunting reverence of sacred stones, wells and trees.

In several instances there can be detected interesting links with the folk-lore of neighbouring countries—with England, especially in regard to giants and giantesses, a fact that appears to have a bearing upon the problem presented by the *Beowulf* epic; and with Wales and Ireland in this and other connexions. But there are also sharp differences that cannot be overlooked, and these tend to re-open the whole Celtic question by emphasizing that cultural contact was for considerable periods greatly hindered by the barriers of distinctive dialects. Withal, special complexes were produced by culture-blending in those localities in which intruders of Celtic speech fused with earlier settlers of different origin and different experiences. It will be found further that in the Scottish complexes there are traces of culture drifts from the Continent whence came, by various routes and at different periods, the peoples of the Bronze Age and those of Celtic speech who introduced the working of iron, the war chariot and other elements of *La Tène* civilization, itself veined with cultural elements emanating from the Near East. Cultural drifts did not cease, however, after the period of Celtic migrations. The " pork taboo ", for instance, suggests the operating influence of a religious cult which appears to have been imported. It is absent in England, Wales and Ireland, and it cannot be urged that in Scotland the early people could have had different experiences in connexion with the use of pork from those of neighbouring peoples. The archæological evidence indicates that this taboo was not a survival from the Bronze Age. Those who favour the theory of Biblical origin are met with the difficulty that it must therefore be concluded the taboo was introduced by the early Christian missionaries into Scotland alone, a view that cannot carry conviction.

The Continental Celts were pig-rearers and pork-eaters, and the only Celtic folk who tabooed the pig were the Galatians of Anatolia, who became converts to the Attis-Great Mother cult. That there was cultural contact between Galatia and the northern part of the Western Celtic area has been established by the discovery of the Gundestrup cauldron in Jutland, with its Asiatic and European flora and fauna and deities. The route of culture-drifting represented by this relic was directed across Europe and across the North Sea and continued to be used for centuries, as is made manifest by the existence of Byzantine art-motifs on the Pictish sculptured stones of Scotland and

PREFACE vii

the importation of Byzantine pigments for use in the Celtic illuminated manuscripts of the early Christian period.

Scottish folk-lore not only affords evidence with regard to diffusion, but also, as is shown in connexion with the "Blue Men of the Minch", of the independent origin of some myths and beliefs. It also provides rich material for the study of the problem of Tradition.

An outstanding characteristic of the Scottish lore is the prominence given to female supernatural beings like the ferocious, one-eyed, storm-raising Cailleach Bheur who resembles the primitive Artemis of Greece, and is associated mainly with wild animals and uncultivated flora, is the enemy of growth, and has connexions with megaliths or boulders; the glaistig who, on the other hand, is associated mainly with domesticated animals and with the agricultural mode of life, and is attached to certain families, but has a sinister aspect as a river fury; the benevolent Bride, the "aid woman" invoked at birth, the nourisher of the early lamb, the milk-giver and the bringer of luck and plenty; and the fairies who are mainly, although not entirely, of the female sex. Cailleach Bheur possesses a magic or druidic wand (also referred to as a hammer or beetle), which brings on frost and, as folk-tales show, kills human beings, or restores the dead to life, and transforms warriors into megaliths or megaliths into warriors. Similar magic wands are carried also by the glaistig and Bride.

In Scotland the male supernatural beings are not so prominent or always as sharply defined as those in the Irish Danann pantheon, or in the pantheons of Wales and ancient Gaul. Strong and powerful as the giants may be, they are less so than the ferocious, cunning and deceitful old Great mother, Cailleach Bheur.

Traces of the influence exercised by imported dragon lore are found in the stories regarding Cailleach Bheur and Bride. The former, when attacked, may be overcome and have her body cut up, but, as in the case of the "deathless snake", the parts may re-unite and she may then come to life again. A worm creeping out from one of her bones will on reaching water become a fierce dragon. This is a myth preserved in northern Ireland, which may help to explain her Scottish Lowland name "Nicnevein" ("daughter of the bone"). Bride has associated with her a serpent which sleeps all winter and awakes in the spring like the Asiatic serpent-dragons.

It is evident that Scotland has retained much that is archaic or, at any rate, uncommon, a fact which makes the study of its folk-lore and mythology of very special interest.

D. A. MACKENZIE.

CONTENTS

	Page
INTRODUCTORY: THE PEOPLE, THEIR ORIGINS AND HISTORY	
I. The Celtic Theory	1
II. Intrusions of Aliens	8
III. The Race Problem	16
IV. Language and Customs	30

CHAPTER		
I.	THE SCOTTISH PORK TABOO	41
II.	SWINE CULTS: SANCTITY AND ABHORRENCE OF PIG	56
III.	SCOTTISH MOUSE FEAST AND MORE TABOOS	75
IV.	THE BLUE MEN OF THE MINCH	85
V.	GIANT LORE OF SCOTLAND	99
VI.	A SCOTTISH BEOWULF	118
VII.	A SCOTTISH ARTEMIS	136
VIII.	ANCIENT GODDESS FORMS	156
IX.	THE GLAISTIG AND BRIDE	176
X.	FAIRIES AND FAIRYLAND	195
XI.	FAIRIES AS DEITIES	211
XII.	DEMONS OF LAND AND WATER	232
XIII.	SACRED ROCKS AND STONES	255
XIV.	SACRED WELLS AND TREES	267
XV.	FESTIVALS AND CEREMONIES	278
	INDEX	291

SCOTTISH FOLK-LORE AND FOLK LIFE

Introductory: The People, their Origins and History

I. THE CELTIC THEORY

National elements in tradition—Ancient forerunners of historical novelists—Gaelic annals and Icelandic sagas—Snowballs of confused narrative—Uses of the term Celtic—Scottish " non-Celtic " elements—No homogeneous Celtic religion—The original Celts—Differences in Celtic pantheons—Varying Celtic beliefs regarding the Otherworld—Plundering of Scottish folk-lore—Irish, Welsh and Norse claims.

The folk-lore of Scotland has some most distinctive features and is found to reveal interesting phases of Scottish life and character. It brings us, at the outset, into contact with the immemorial modes of thought of a long-settled people and therefore with the cumulative influences exercised by historical experiences throughout many centuries. These experiences were of varied character and not entirely products of forces that had origin in the environment in which they became operative. We find revealed in certain beliefs and customs and in some myths and legends indelible traces of alien cultures that were imported at different periods, leaving little or no trace of the carriers, and also evidence of the subtle process of culture blending. But, although foreign concepts may be discovered in the Scottish complexes, indications are not awanting of the antiquity of indigenous ideals of right thinking and right conduct according to a traditional code. These are enshrined in heroic folk-stories, in bardic eulogies of fair and gracious ladies and wise and brave men, and in traditional proverbial sayings like those still prevalent in the Highlands, including " Remember your ancestors and be worthy of them ", " It is a reputation for good deeds that ennobles a man ", " Keep up your honour ", " A good man is better than many men ", " None ever prevented his fate ".

A Scot combines with profound love of country and adherence to those inherited ideals that control and direct behaviour a haunting pride in the past. The once-upon-a-time type of folk-story has ever been in great demand around camp fires during hunting operations or campaigns and in rural house gatherings, called *céilidhs* (pronounced " kay'lees "), and has helped in no small measure to cultivate the historical spirit. That consciousness of ancestral times, which is still perpetuated along with ancient habits of life in lonely islands and glens, has been entirely obliterated in industrial centres, which are ever fretting with immediate concern regarding progress or change. The rural dweller may remember his forbears for several generations; the city dweller may confess ignorance of his grandmother's maiden name.

We must not, however, overrate the value of tradition from the viewpoint of sober history. In the popular folk-stories we can frequently detect the art and methods of the ancient forerunners of our historical novelists, who had audiences to entertain and even

INTRODUCTORY—THE CELTIC THEORY

flatter, and were under no compulsion to adhere in strict detail to the restrained relation of fact. At the same time, it must be recognized that many narratives preserved by oral tradition afford us illuminating glimpses of ancient life and the manners and customs and aspirations of the folk. The view of Lord Raglan that "historical facts never find their way into tradition" cannot therefore be accepted without qualification.[1] Gaelic annals and Icelandic sagas taken down from oral tradition contain genuine historical elements, as has been abundantly proved. It must, however, be frankly admitted that the value, as data for historians, of the heroic folk-tales varies as greatly as does a Gaelic or Icelandic saga from an Arthurian metrical romance in which fable and local and alien traditions have been inextricably blended. There are many Scottish folk-tales of heroic character in which the popular heroes are not only lauded for their own achievements, but credited with those of a predecessor or predecessors, and even with the attributes of supernatural beings. In such cases a rolling "snowball" of confused narrative was kept in motion, and, although the consequent preservation of archaic elements may greatly interest the folklorist, serious difficulties are presented to historians with regard to the sequence and reliability of events. In other cases a kernel of historical fact may emerge from material which appears to be wholly fabulous, but only after a clue has been afforded by a record of more or less reliable character. The "Blue Men of the Minch" chapter affords an

[1] His address "What is Tradition?" as president of the anthropology section of the British Association, 1933, in which he criticizes severely and deservedly those who have treated tradition as undiluted history.

interesting illustration of the value of tradition in this connexion.

One hesitates to characterize the folk-lore found in Scotland by applying to it, as a whole, the term " Celtic " (or the very modern " Keltic ", which is associated with some hazardous hypotheses) lest there should be confusion with the folk-lore of Ireland or Wales or Brittany, or to admit offhand that certain " non-Celtic " elements must be regarded as either " Norse " or " Anglo-Saxon ". Nor, unless strong confirmatory evidence is available, should one assume regarding certain " non-Celtic " elements which cannot possibly be attributed to a Teutonic source that they must necessarily be " pre-Celtic " and therefore a heritage from the archæological Bronze Age. Culture drifts, as is shown with regard to the Scottish pork taboo, have not been confined to any particular age.

" Celtic " is not a racial term. It applies to groups of peoples who spoke, or still speak, dialects of the Celtic language. The Continental " Celts ", according to Diodorus Siculus (V, 32), were those who dwelt above Marseilles, near the Alps and to the east of the Pyrenees. Beyond that area they were called Galatae, but the Romans included all the tribes under the name " Gauls ". There were migrations of peoples of Celtic speech to Great Britain and Ireland, but none of these groups of settlers ever called themselves " Celts " or " Kelts ".

Although the Celts were a branch of the northern, or Nordic, fair race, they possessed a distinctive and differentiated culture, an early phase of which is known to the archæologists as La Tène. This culture had a history rooted in late Mycenæan and has also revealed influences exercised by Greek colonists in the western Mediterranean area and the Etruscans who settled in Italy. The Celts were the pioneers of the early Iron Age in Western Europe, and at the beginning of the La Tène epoch were possessed of the war-chariot, which came, with much else, from the East. Their civilization so closely resembled that of the Achæans of Greece that it might be referred to as " Homeric ".

But, although culture and race have no necessary association, the term " Celtic " has been loosely applied, and especially by those who have sought to account for certain mental leanings alleged to be a common heritage of the Irish, the Welsh, the Bretons and the Scots, the so-called " Celtic fringe " of Victorian politicians, " the troublesome Celtic background " of Freeman. Yet the peoples of the " fringe " have had not only different historical experiences, but, as national groups, have reacted differently in similar circumstances. Their physical characters vary a good deal, and they are consequently less intimately related than is assumed by those who invest the term " Celtic " with a racial significance. Withal, although, as has been indicated, their native languages may be grouped as " Celtic ", these present marked differences, just as do the languages of the larger group designated " Aryan ", or " Indo-European ", or " Indo-Germanic ", in which they are included. No longer are theories regarding a distinctive and widespread Aryan religion or Aryan folk-lore seriously entertained, but there still remains the haunting theory of a definite " Celtic religion " and a characteristic " Celtic folk-lore ". There is, however, no real proof that the various peoples of Celtic speech ever attempted to systematize their beliefs and pantheons into a homogeneous religion. Even the ancient Egyptians in their restricted area never accomplished as much, as is emphasized by Dr. Wiedemann, who says that "it is open to us to speak of the religious ideas of the Egyptians but not of an Egyptian religion ".[1] We should similarly refer to " Celtic religious ideas ", rather than insist upon the term " Celtic religion ". On the Continent, as well as in Scotland, Ireland and Wales, we find differences in the pantheons and differences in ideas regarding the destiny of the soul. Some Gauls had embraced the doctrine of metempsychosis (the transmigration of souls), while others believed in a Paradise in some distant land, or in the " sky-world ", or in "Islands of the Blest", to which souls passed immediately after death. Valerius Maximus (II, vi, 10) informs us regarding those Gauls who lent one another money on promise of repayment in the next world.

Varied ideas regarding the Otherworld are found in Ireland, Scotland and Wales. As the "sky-world" was in ancient Egypt originally confined to Pharaohs and later to aristocrats, so were the "Islands of the Blest" confined in Ireland to great kings and heroes. There was an underworld for others, and in Scotland the dead were often associated with the fairies. Wales had an "upper world" (*elfydd* and *adfant*) and is distinctive in our group of islands in having had as gloomy an after-state as is referred to in the Babylonian epic of Gilgamesh—the Welsh *anghar*, " the loveless

---

[1] A. Wiedemann, *Religion of the Ancient Egyptians* (London, 1897), p. 3.

place ", which is also called " the cruel prison of earth ".[1] In Scotland, as will be shown, there are references to an underworld resembling that of the Egyptian god Osiris, in which the dead pluck fruit and reap fields of grain.

The modern habit of reconstructing, or rather of inventing, a homogeneous Celtic religion by selecting evidence at random from various " Celtic " areas is as hazardous as it is unscientific. The sins of omission are no less marked in this connexion than those of commission. Scotland is drawn upon for suitable material, but such distinctive evidence as that afforded by the " non-Celtic " pork taboo, the " Blue Men of the Minch ", and the widespread giant lore, is completely ignored. Even when links are found, distinctive local features are overlooked. The sins of commission include a general plundering of the Scottish material on behalf of Ireland, Wales and Norway. When all such claims are conceded, little is left for the modern Scots folklorist to credit to the ancestral Caledonians, Picts and others, who must surely have had an intellectual life as capable of survival in the accumulated stock of folk-lore as that of an ancient people in Ireland or Wales or Norway.

[1] Edward Anwyl, *Celtic Religion* (London, 1906), p. 61.

II. INTRUSIONS OF ALIENS

Race leanings and national temperaments—Culture and bilingualism—Cultural influences transformed Normans—Few alien intrusions in Scotland—Roman period—Resistance of Scotland—Invasion of Roman England—Northern and southern Picts—Change of dynasty—Picts and Dalriada—British kingdom of Strathclyde—Military and peaceful intrusions of Angles—First and second Anglian occupations—Gaelic kingdom of Malcolm II—Spread of English language—Norse element in Scotland—Lowlanders and Flemings in northern burghs—Norse claim to Hebrides—Norse surnames in Highlands—The Gall-Gael.

Skull shapes and the colours of eyes, hair and skin have as little connexion with mental characteristics and temperament as have the stars and planets whose movements or groupings involved the astrologers of old in so much painstaking research. A people are more influenced by tradition and group ideals formulated in particular localities than by that vague influence referred to as " racial leanings ". Temperament is an individual thing and differences of temperament may be detected among the members of a single family. When we refer to " national temperaments "—the French temperament, the German temperament, the English or Irish or Scottish temperament and so on—we are really endeavouring to account for mass behaviour, for a national reaction under certain circumstances that may have arisen. It is evidently the sense of nationality, with its particular economic and other interests and its traditions, that is made manifest and not really a group temperament. In all nations in Europe popularly credited with distinctive temperaments we find similar racial types, mixtures of broad heads and long heads, of dark and fair individuals, tall and short, heavy and light. There may be language barriers, but, as in the case of Switzerland, these may be overcome by the influence of nationality. The English language is spoken in the United States as well as throughout the British Empire, but the two great political groups are quite separate and independent. Germanic languages are spoken by nations that are similarly independent of one another, and when national interests are threatened hostilities may ensue.

The character of a long-settled people is shaped by the influences of environment and of their historical experiences—pressure both from without and within. Certain tendencies or leanings, certain mental habits become traditional, but it does not follow that these had originally a racial significance. Much appears to depend upon how a national group has reacted in times of crises caused by intrusions of aliens and whether or not their aspirations have been fulfilled. Loss of " morale " due to disaster and subsequent oppression may involve loss of individuality and national consciousness. When conquest involves complete loss of a native language the influence of tradition ceases to operate. On the other hand, if an intrusion has been partial and there follows a long bilingual period, traditions may flow from one language to another, or there may be, as happened in England after the Norman conquest, a renaissance of a language and of national aspirations.

Cultural influences may be found to have proved much more decisive in shaping the character of a people than language or racial tendencies. The Normans were conquerors in northern France, yet they not only lost their language and their sense of Teutonic origin, but acquired Franco-Latin civilization and culture. They were a very different people when they invaded England than when they first settled in France, and when in the course of some three centuries they lost in England their acquired language they became anglicized, having come under the influence of a prevailing sense of nationality.

In Scotland there have been fewer alien intrusions than in almost any other country in Europe. At the dawn of history the Romans, who as Tacitus [1] explains were successful in England mainly because the various tribes or nations failed to co-operate against a common enemy, found when they operated in Scotland that the nations there effected a union and fought as allies under the Caledonian general Galgacus (Calgacus). There was subsequently constant resistance to Roman aggression. Hadrian (A.D. 117–38) had erected a great fortified wall between the Solway and the Tyne to secure Roman Britain against the inroads of the people of Scotland. Antoninus Pius (138–61) found it necessary to erect another wall between the Forth and Clyde, where Agricola had previously had a line of fortified camps, but the advanced frontier was successfully assailed by the Highlanders. Ultimately Severus (193–211) undertook the conquest of Scotland north of the Forth and Clyde and succeeded in breaking the power of the Caledonians. He fought no great battle, but lost many thousands of men, and before he died in York in February, 211, Scotland was in open revolt again. His son Caracalla (211–7) withdrew his gar-

[1] *Agricola,* Chapters XII and XXVII.

INTRODUCTORY—INTRUSIONS OF ALIENS

risons from Scotland and Hadrian's wall again became the frontier. The hegemony in Scotland ultimately passed to the Picts, the northern seafaring and agricultural people, who continued the Caledonian policy of united action against the common enemy, but in doing so imposed their own system of government upon the other nations which became subject to them. They learned more from Rome than did the Caledonians, and especially the advantages of strong centralized government. Like the Romans, they also effected alliances and in the fourth century, co-operating with the Scots mercenaries from Ireland and the Saxon pirates, they breached and turned Hadrian's wall, conquered all the forts and overran England, breaking up the Roman military organization. Theodosius came from the Continent with an army of auxiliaries and recovered the lost province and subsequently conducted naval operations as far north as Orkney, striking at the naval bases of the allies. During the remaining period of the Roman occupation of Britain the Picts remained unconquered. They were not a numerous people. Like the later Normans, they formed a military aristocracy, and by the time of Bede (672 or 673–735) the peoples north of the Grampians were known as the " northern Picts " and those south of that mountain range as the " southern Picts ". The Pictish dynasty of high-kings can be given accurately from the time of Columba, the sixth century, till that of Kenneth mac Alpin in the ninth century.

The Scots who had fought against Rome as allies of the Picts settled in different areas in Scotland. In Angus they suffered loss of identity, becoming part of the "southern Picts", their aristocrats apparently having intermarried with the Pictish ruling caste.

Scots began to settle in Argyll (Dalriada) about A.D. 180, and by the beginning of the sixth century they had formed an independent kingdom. The Pictish king Brude I (*c.* 555–84) conquered Dalriada, and St. Columba had to obtain Brude's confirmation of the gift to him of the island of Iona from the subject Scots king of Dalriada. The Scots of Argyll subsequently regained their independence, but ultimately lost it finally in the eighth century when Angus, king of the Picts, subdued Argyll. Many Dalriadic nobles and their followers migrated to Galloway, and it was from that area Kenneth mac Alpin came to establish his claim to the throne as "King of the Picts". He displaced the Pictish nobles, substituting Gaelic nobles. His descendant Malcolm II (1005–34) ultimately united all Scotland from Shetland to the Tweed under his rule.

A British kingdom existed in Strathclyde from early Pictish times until the reign of Malcolm II. Its relations with the Picts had long been friendly, but there were frequent clashes with the Scots of Dalriada. Its influence appears to have extended to the Lothians in the east until the seventh century, when the first Anglian intrusion took place. King Aidan of Dalriada (*c.* 574–608), who began to reign as a subject of the Pictish king, fought and lost a battle in conflict with Ethelfrid, king of the Angles (593–617), in the vicinity of Jedburgh. It is known as the battle of Degsastan [1] and took place in 603. Edwin overthrew his kinsman

---

[1] Supposed to be the modern Dawstane.

Ethelfrid in 617, and Ethelfrid's children fled to Scotland and were reared as Christians by the Columbans. Two of them were subsequently kings of the Angles—Oswald (634–42) and Oswy (642–71). The Gaelic Christian mission was established at Lindisfarne in 634.

Owing apparently to the influence of the Columban church, which was hostile to the Dalriadic king Donald Brecc, grandson of King Aidan, Oswald and Oswy became politically influential in the Lowlands and part of Argyll. Oswy's son, King Egfrid, claimed tribute from the Picts, and when endeavouring to enforce his demand was lured with his army into Angus and disastrously defeated by the Pictish king Brude III in the battle of Nectansmere in 685. The Angles were thereafter driven out of the Lowlands, their military occupation of which, dating from the time of Ethelfrid's invasion, lasted for eighty-two years.

The next invasion of the Lowlands was that of King Ethelstane, the Saxon king, in A.D. 934. The military occupation that ensued lasted till A.D. 975, a period of forty-one years. In 1018 Malcolm II, who occupied Cumberland, shattered the Anglian power at the battle of Carham (Wark) in Northumberland, and he " planted " Gaelic colonies in the Lowlands, represented in our own day by the Scotts and others, who fused with the earlier Britons of Lothian and the Border counties. The subsequent spread of the " Ingliss " language into the east Lowlands was apparently due to trading connexions.

The extent of the Norse element in Scotland has been grossly exaggerated. On the mainland there were raids, but these left no permanent influence. Viking pirates and Norse refugees settled in Orkney and Shetland, mingling with the native Picts and ultimately absorbing them. They also had "pirate nests" in the Hebrides. But there were no wholesale conquests like those effected by the Danes in England and by Norsemen and Danes in Ireland. "The resistance of Scotland," as Professor MacNeill says, "is especially noteworthy."[1] When in 1018 Malcolm II won the battle of Carham, England and Norway had been included in the empire of Denmark. The Scandinavian hold upon Ireland was shattered two years earlier in the battle of Clontarf. Thorfinn, Earl of Orkney, was the grandson and subject of Malcolm II, and the Scottish suzerainty continued until the latter part of the eleventh century, when, owing to the growing influence of the Normans, Edgar, son of Malcolm Canmore and Queen Margaret, became king of Scotland, displacing the rightful heir, the grandson of Malcolm Canmore by his first wife, the widow of Earl Thorfinn.

King Magnus Bareleg of Norway, a relative of Thorfinn's widow, raided Orkney, displacing the earls who were subjects of the Scottish kings and laying claim to the Hebrides. He forced Edgar to acknowledge his right by treaty. During the twelfth century the Highlanders were in revolt against the Normanized kings of Scotland, and King William the Lyon had to operate against the rebels, who were aided by Norsemen. The rightful heirs to the throne, according to the northerners, were the MacWilliams, and it was not

[1] *Phases of Irish History* (Dublin, 1919), p. 205.

INTRODUCTORY—INTRUSIONS OF ALIENS 15

until during the reign of Alexander II (1214–49) that the last MacWilliam heir, a baby, was executed.[1]

William the Lyon established castles and burghs along the Moray Firth coast, and in these burghs planted colonies of Lowlanders and Flemings. The Norman lords and alien burghers introduced the "Ingliss" language. As traders, the settlers were more influential than ever were the Norsemen. They ultimately fused with the native peoples, and some Norman barons became the chiefs of clans.

The Norse claim upon the Hebrides came to an end after King Hakon's futile naval expedition and the skirmish at Largs in 1263. In 1266 Norwegian representatives signed the Treaty of Perth, which confirmed the right of the Scottish king to the Hebrides. Those islanders who claimed to be Norse or preferred Norse rule were permitted to proceed to Norway.

It does not follow that all Highland families which still retain Gaelicized Norse surnames were originally Norse. Scandinavian Christian names were adopted by Gaelic and Pictish peoples. Dugald (*Dùbhghall*), for instance, meaning "dark stranger", had become a Christian name, and Clan MacDougall (*M'Dhughaill*) perpetuates that of Dougald, the founder, uncle of Donald, whose Christian name is similarly perpetuated by the MacDonalds. In Galloway MacDougall became "MacDowell".[2]

There was a good deal of intermarrying between Norsemen and natives. Withal, Hebridean Christians

---

[1] My *Scotland: The Ancient Kingdom*, p. 314.

[2] Irish descendants of Hebridean mercenary soldiers surnamed MacDowel or MacDowell are known as Doyles and Coyles. MacDonalds are MacDonnells and MacConnells.

embraced Norse paganism and became allies of the Vikings. The " Gall-Gael " (*Gall Gháidhil*, "Foreign Gael ") were in the middle of the ninth century referred to as " Scots and foster-children of the Norsemen ", and sometimes as " Northmen ". Annalists state that they were men " who had renounced their baptism " and proved worse than " the real Northmen as plunderers of churches ".[1]

III. THE RACE PROBLEM

<small>Racial elements in Scotland—No Scottish race—A majority type—Evidence of survivals in France, Egypt and Crete—Intrusions of males—"Breeding-out" process—Angles and Britons—Norse intermarried with Highlanders—Tall, muscular Scots—War-time evidence regarding ethnics of Scotland—Head shapes—Hair and eye colours—Broad-heads of east and north—Bronze Age element—The tall Celts—Tall and dark Scots—Problem of pigmentation—Robert Burns tall and dark—Tall men of Galloway—Lowlanders and Highlanders—When Ayr men were Highlanders—Dunbar the poet—Gaels in Lothian and Border counties.</small>

Although cultural influences may have more to do with shaping the character of a people than those assumed to be of racial origin, the problem of race is still replete with interest, especially in relation to habits of life which have fostered and perpetuated certain habits of thought. A long-settled people, with traditions rooted in their environment, owe something to their physical qualities. In the course of time their area of occupation proves to be one of characterization, and a distinctive blend or " sub-race " may emerge.

In Scotland we do not expect to find absolute purity of race, for from early times there have been intrusions, in varying degrees, of the three main European races

[1] W. J. Watson, *History of the Celtic Place-Names of Scotland*, p. 172.

INTRODUCTORY—THE RACE PROBLEM

—the "Mediterranean race" of Sergi, renamed by Elliot Smith the "Brown race", a dark-haired, dark-eyed and short type; the "Alpine", or "Armenoid", race of hairy, muscular and "stocky" broad-heads, with brown or dark hair and light or hazel or "green" eyes; and the "Nordic", or "Northern", race (also called the "Teutonic race"), with light hair, light eyes, long heads and flat cheek bones. Perhaps, too, mention should be made of the Palæolithic peoples of the Pleistocene Age, including the Cro-Magnons, who had short, broad faces like the Armenoids, but long heads like the Nordics. They had also high cheek-bones, and these are fairly common in Scotland. Continental black-and-white artists invariably represent the Scot with very high cheek-bones indeed, thus distinguishing him from the typical flat-cheeked Scandinavian. If, however, we do not find racial purity in Scotland, the fact that we meet, as will be shown, with comparative permanence of type among a majority is of very special interest. There may be no such thing as a "Scottish race", but apparently there is a majority type, which, in the physical sense, has been influential, both fair and dark varieties partaking of its characters.

At the outset it will prove helpful, in undertaking an investigation of the Scottish race question, to receive guidance from the data, accumulated in various other countries, with regard to the persistence of ancient types, despite intrusions and settlements of aliens, and the resulting process of ethnic fusions in different degrees. Apparently much depends upon the character of an intrusion, and whether it has happened to be either gradual or sudden. The law of reversion to type may, in the course of time, tend to modify or even nullify it.

Proofs of survivals in various areas have been made available for us by several ethnologists, who have conducted investigations independently of one another, and these are found to be helpful when the Scottish evidence is given consideration. Dr. Colignon, the French ethnologist, has, in the Dordogne valley in France, detected peasants who retain the physical characters of the Cro-Magnons of the Pleistocene period. In Egypt Professor G. Elliot Smith has met with similar evidence, after examining many mummies of different periods and dissecting pre-dynastic bodies that had been naturally dried and preserved in the warm, dry sand. In this connexion he writes:

" Although alien elements from north and south have been coming into upper Egypt for fifty centuries, it has been a process of percolation and not an overwhelming rush; the population has been able to assimilate the alien minority and retain its own distinctive features and customs with only slight change; and however large a proportion of the population has taken on hybrid traits, resulting from Negro, Arab or Armenoid admixture, there still remain in the Thebaid large numbers of its people who present features and bodily conformation precisely similar to those of their remote ancestors, the proto-Egyptians. It was my good fortune to have had the opportunity, in my capacity as professor of anatomy in the Cairo School of Medicine, of studying the structure of these modern people at the same time as I was engaged in dissecting their pre-dynastic ancestors, and it was almost a daily experience during those nine years to find features that served to distinguish modern Egyptians from other peoples repeated in the proto-Egyptian remains, and vice versa." [1]

[1] *The Ancient Egyptians* (2nd edition, London, 1923), pp. 51-2.

INTRODUCTORY—THE RACE PROBLEM

In Crete Mr. H. B. Hawes's anthropometric survey has revealed " a continued thinning of the foreign blood " as " the result of generations of marriages with Cretan natives . . . After nine generations the alien immigrants, vastly inferior in numbers and almost exclusively of the male sex, have bred out." He has found that the old Minoan type still " predominates in the mountain areas ".[1]

Mr. Hawes, dealing with the breeding-out process and the tendency to revert to type, quotes as follows from Dr. Colignon:

" When a race is well seated in a region, fixed to the soil by agriculture, acclimatized by natural selection and sufficiently dense, it opposes, for the most precise observations confirm it, an enormous resistance to absorption by the new comers, whoever they may be."

In Britain, as elsewhere, this " breeding-out " process must have been operating throughout the centuries in consequence of intermarriage between minorities of intruders and the natives, who constituted a vast majority. Proof of the fusion of the early Angles and Saxons with the Britons, whom they overcame, is afforded by the survival of some ancient place-names which had not been translated during bilingual periods. In Northumbria, for instance, the Angles retained the district place-name we know as " Bernicia ". Their rendering, " Bærnicas ", Latinized " Bernicii " in Bede, was, like the Welsh " Brëenych " or " Brenneich ", derived from the old British name of the area occupied by the Celtic " Brigantes " whom the Romans found in possession. " Deira ", the district between the

[1] *Crete the Forerunner of Greece* (2nd edition, 1910), pp. 24-5.

Humber and the Tees, was similarly an Anglian rendering of the Celtic name surviving in Welsh as " Deivr ".[1]

The Anglian and Saxon piratical intruders were mainly of the male sex. It is highly probable that, like the later Vikings, they limited the movements of their women. As the late Professor F. York Powell has shown, the Norse buccaneers did not allow a woman on board a warship or within a fort.[2] Women would have proved a hindrance to piratical operations. There may, withal, have been anthropological reasons for keeping them out of strongholds and war vessels, the magical influence of sex being supposed to operate effectively for good or evil in different spheres of activity.

When evidence is obtainable regarding prominent representatives of intruders in Scotland, it is found that a good deal of race mixing has taken place. The great Earl Thorfinn of Orkney, for instance, had a Scottish mother, the daughter of the eleventh century King Malcolm II; his father, Earl Sigurd, who fell at the battle of Clontarf in Ireland in 1014, had an Irish mother. In the *Orkney Saga*, Thorfinn is referred to as " a man of very large stature, uncomely, sharp-featured, dark-haired, and sallow and swarthy in complexion ". To the native Norsemen he was not only very tall, but " ungainly ". Harold Gilchrist, who became " King Gilli " of Norway, was the son of King Magnus Bareleg and a Hebridean woman.

Scotland had long been famous for its tall and heavy

---

[1] J. Rhys, *Celtic Britain* (London, 1908), pp. 113-4.
[2] *Origines Islandicæ*, Book II, section 2, and *Scandinavian Britain*, p. 35.

INTRODUCTORY—THE RACE PROBLEM

men, in comparison with those of the Irish, Angles, Saxons, Welsh, Norsemen and Danes. Tacitus, the Roman historian, remarks upon the muscular limbs of the inhabitants of Caledonia who opposed Agricola, his father-in-law, in the first century of our era. At a much later date Bishop Ruthal of Durham is found similarly paying tribute to the Scottish physique. In writing of the battle of Flodden (1513) he refers to the Scots as "large, strong and great men", who "would not fall when four or five bills struck on one of them at once". The same writer goes on to say: "Our folk took little regard in taking prisoners, but rid all that came to hand . . . They [the Scots] were no sooner slain but forthwith despoiled of their harness and left lying naked on the field, where men might have seen a marvellous number of goodly men, well fed and fat."

The English likewise noted the remarkable physique of the Scottish dead at the battle of Solway Moss in 1542. "Goodlier men," declares Sir William Musgrave, "I never see of personage for subjects." Similar English evidence with regard to the Scottish physique is on record in connexion with the battle of Pinkie-Cleuch (Musselburgh) in 1547.[1]

There has been, on the part of some writers, too marked a tendency to regard Scotland as a "poor country" in which food has ever been scarce and the conditions of life exceedingly trying. This is due mainly to their concentration upon the evidence with regard to the post-Jacobite period, after military

[1] W. Mackay Mackenzie, *The Secret of Flodden* (Edinburgh, 1931), pp. 87 and 92.

disaster and the sudden introduction of new laws caused confusion, distress and much suffering in large areas in the Highlands.

In the days before rigid game laws obtained, beef, mutton, venison, salmon, trout, birds, &c., were salted or smoked in the autumn and stored for winter food in addition to the harvested cereals. Deer drives were an outstanding feature of Highland life till comparatively recent times. Some outside writers afford us glimpses of the men who took part in these. Two Englishmen, for instance, were guests at a deer drive in Ross and Cromarty in the seventeenth century, and one of them tells that the Mackenzies and Frasers suspended hunting operations for four days to hold competitions in " jumping, arching, shooting, throwing the barr, the stone and all manner of manly exercises ". Food was plentiful, the fare including " beefe, mutton, foule, fishes, fat venison ", and there were " all manners of liquors ". The English recorder declares that he and his friend in all their travels " never had such brave divertisment, and if they should relate it in England it would be concluded meer rants and incredible ".[1] We should not be surprised, therefore, to find that the Flodden warriors, including many Highlanders, were " goodly men, well fed and fat ".

That there has survived throughout Scotland a prominent and distinctive type is made evident by the conclusion of Ripley that it " contains positively the tallest population in Europe and almost in the entire world ". It is likewise supreme in average weight,

[1] W. J. Watson in *The Book of the Red Deer*; D. A. Mackenzie, *Scotland: The Ancient Kingdom*, pp. 212 et seq.

INTRODUCTORY—THE RACE PROBLEM

exceeding the English average by about ten pounds and the Irish by about twenty. The stature average of Scotland was found by Ripley to be about three inches above that of Wales and south-west England, about two inches above that of Norway, and higher than that of Ireland.[1]

Emigration from rural Scotland during the past half century has tended to reduce the average stature. The British Dominions and the United States have proved more attractive for tall, fair Scots than the cities in industrial areas. Dr. Beddoe[2] has stated that in Scottish cities " tall, rapidly developing children, and especially those of fair complexion, have seemed to me less able to thrive without fresh air and abundant food than others ", while the blond adults " being of a more restless and adventurous temperament, are more disposed to wander and to emigrate " than the " stocky " types. He accounts for " the prevalence of the tall, fair types among the colonial born by the sharing of the tall youths in the Australian life of open air and abundant food ".

Dr. Tocher and the late Mr. Gray collected important data regarding Scottish physical characters, during the war, by examining over 5000 recruits. They had previously conducted a survey of the asylums and they have also given us the results of the survey of school children which they organized.

Professor Thomas H. Bryce of the anatomy chair of the University of Glasgow has for many years

---

[1] W. Z. Ripley, *The Races of Europe*, pp. 326, 329, 330, &c.

[2] *The Anthropological History of Europe* (new and revised edition, Paisley, 1912), pp. 24, 33, 34, 181.

made a study of the human remains found in early graves, as well as of the statistics of the living population, and he has collated the evidence from both sides. His conclusion is that the general average of stature is not now exactly known, "but Scotsmen are certainly tall on the average". The mean cephalic index for 6928 men born in all parts of Scotland, for whom records exist, is 78·18. In the north and north-east heads incline to be broader; in the south and east they are longer and narrower. Variations are often slight, but in some instances statistically significant.

The collections of skulls examined by Professor Bryce bring out similar results. The mean is about 76, and there is a larger amount of brachycephals (broad-heads) in the east.

Hair and eye colours in 6937 adult males from all parts of Scotland are shown in the following table:

R = red.   F = fair.   M = medium.   D = dark
J. B. = jet black.   B = blue.   L = light

Eye Colour	Hair Colour					
	R	F	M	D	J. B.	
B	·78	2·93	6·27	4·41	·22	14·61
L	1·33	3·30	6·95	5·33	·23	17·14
M	2·22	4·37	22·60	17·83	1·44	48·46
D	·71	·46	6·18	10·96	1·48	19·79
Totals	5·04	11·06	42·00	38·53	3·37	100·00

The following tables show the hair and eye colours of 182,714 Scottish boys:

HAIR

Red	Fair	Medium	Dark	Jet Black	Frequency
5·477	25·664	42·612	24·932	1·315	182,714

EYES

Blue	Light	Medium	Dark	Frequency
15·476	30·332	32·540	21·652	182,714

Professor Bryce, who prepared these tables for me, says that he eliminated, for obvious reasons, the data for the large towns, taking the figures for the country parishes and the smaller towns in which aliens are rare.

It appears from the available statistics that about a quarter of the inhabitants of Scotland are dark. Nearly half of the population has hair of medium or brown colour and medium eye colour—that is, shades of grey more or less heavily pigmented—the " green eye ", as it is called. The " Irish grey eye " is not common in Scotland, the light eye being often tinted with blue. The pure blue eye averages from 14 to 15 per cent.

The data regarding cranial index indicate that Scotland is, on the whole, mesocephalic. Broad-headedness is commonest in the east from the Lothian area northward. It becomes more pronounced, as Beddoe found, in the Buchan area and along the shores of the Moray Firth to the extreme north of Scotland.[1] The

[1] J. Beddoe, *The Anthropological History of Europe*, pp. 161 *et seq*, quoting Turner, &c.

Nordic long-heads are somewhat rare along the fertile belt. It would appear, therefore, that the majority of the easterners, north-easterners and northerners in Scotland are of the Bronze Age type in skull shapes, but in stature, weight and pigmentation they approximate more closely to the Continental Celts, whom Greek writers referred to as the tallest and fairest people in Europe.[1]

The tall, fair Celts who settled in Scotland appear to have mixed with the Bronze Age peoples with whom they came into contact. Their intrusions were not, however, as were those of the later piratical Angles, Saxons, Norsemen and Danes, mainly of the male sex. Like the Helvetii of Switzerland, with whom Cæsar came into contact in Gaul, the Celts migrated with wives and families and accumulated stores of food.[2] These intruders introduced into Britain their chariots and well-bred horses, some groups crossing the English Channel and others the North Sea. The Pictish migration from western Gaul to the north of Scotland, including Orkney and Shetland, may have introduced a broad-headed element.

In the west the darker Scots have an average in height greater than the average of Ireland. These tall, dark Scotsmen puzzled Ripley, the tallest Scandinavians being blonds.[3]

Pigmentation, however, presents a difficult problem. Interesting evidence regarding it is afforded by St.

---

[1] Ptolemy (lieutenant of Alexander the Great), quoted by Arrian in *Anabasis*, I, iv, § 6; Hieronymus of Cardia, quoted by Pausanias, X, 20; Poseidonius, quoted by Diodorus Siculus, V, 28.

[2] *De Bel. Gall.*, Book I.

[3] *Races of Europe*, pp. 106, 328.

INTRODUCTORY—THE RACE PROBLEM

Kilda. When that island was reached by M. Martin[1] in the seventeenth century, he found, as he records, that the men " have generally very thin beards and those, too, do not appear until the age of thirty, and in some not till after thirty-five; they have all but a few hairs upon the upper lip and point of the chin ". Later writers who visited the island before the desolating smallpox epidemic of about a century ago, which was followed by a Harris intrusion, have stated that the women were invariably much darker than the men.

These original St. Kildans resembled, apart from the pigmentation of the males, the dark proto-Egyptians of the pre-dynastic epoch. Professor G. Elliot Smith,[2] who, as stated, examined and dissected a number of these bodies, informs us that the men had " a very scanty endowment of beard and almost no moustache ". He comments upon the " family likeness " between the proto-Egyptians and the early Neolithic peoples of the British Isles.

It would appear that in an inbred community a radical change in pigmentation, either dark to fair or fair to dark, may result from a very small alien intrusion. Evidence in this regard is afforded by the fisher people of Cromarty, who were formerly blond. The local fishers intermarried mainly with local fishers, and the whole community of a few hundreds was until recently inter-related in varying degrees. About the middle of the nineteenth century a fisherman married a dark gipsy woman. In three or four generations,

---

[1] M. Martin, *A Voyage to St. Kilda*, 1698 (reprint Glasgow, 1818), pp. 6-7.

[2] *The Ancient Egyptians* (2nd edition), pp. 54 *et seq.*

according to the local registrar of births, deaths and marriages, the pigmentation of many families was more or less affected by that gipsy woman. Several individuals were sallow, with dark hair and hazel or blue-grey eyes. Mixed types became common, fair-haired children with white skins having hazel eyes and sallow, dark-haired children blue-grey or green eyes.

Apparently pigmentation has to be referred to with caution when we are dealing with the race question. Robert Burns, the poet, who was born at Ayr, has been, because of his pigmentation, referred to as " Iberian " or " Irish ". He was dark like his father, who hailed, however, from Kincardine on the east coast. His mother, an Ayrshire woman surnamed Brown,[1] was red haired and of fair complexion. In stature Burns was well above the Irish and Welsh averages.

Pigmentation in the east and west Lowlands of Scotland approximates to that of northern England, but the average stature is much higher. Galloway is noted for tallness and weight, its people being as " hefty " as were the Caledonians.

The evidence regarding physical characters emphasizes that the majority of the people of Scotland differ in a marked degree from the Irish, Welsh and Bretons, being taller, fairer and " heftier ".

The division between Scottish Lowlanders and Highlanders, invariably over-emphasized, is the result mainly of the change of language. Although the Highland border on the south and east has been gradually thrust back by eighteenth and nineteenth

---

[1] Brown is from MacBrayne.

century writers, it intruded into the area south of the Clyde at an earlier period. In the fifteenth century the Gaelic-speaking people of Carrick, in Ayrshire, and those of Galloway were regarded as " Erse " (Gaelic) by the eastern Lowlanders, who had themselves become speakers of " Ingliss ". The poet Dunbar refers to Walter Kennedy of Carrick as an " Iersch brybour baird " (a " Gaelic-speaking beggar bard ") and makes fun of the " Heland strynd " (" Highland strain ") in his accent and of the manner in which with his " Carrik lippis " he is accustomed to " blabbar " the " Ingliss " tongue. Kennedy, on the other hand, declares that although Dunbar " lufis (lovest) nane Irische ", it is "the gud (good) language of this land", and he accuses Dunbar's forefather of bringing in, " throu (through) his tresoun (treason) ", the " Inglise rumplis (tail)". Kennedy, who boasts, " I am the Kingis blude (blood) ", goes on to suggest that " Ingland " should be the habitation of Dunbar because his kin did " homage " to " Edward Langschankis (King Edward I) ".[1]

Dunbar shows familiarity with some of the heroes and supernatural beings of Gaelic tradition. But this is not to be wondered at, for there was, as we have seen, a strong Gaelic element in Lothian and the Border counties, King Malcolm II, the victor of Carham, having " planted " Gaelic colonies in these areas. Traces of the linguistic influence of this element are afforded by surviving or recorded place-names. One of very special note is " Balantrodach " (Gaelic, *Baile*

---

[1] " The Flyting of Dunbar and Kennedy " in *The Poems of William Dunbar*, edited by W. Mackay Mackenzie (Edinburgh, 1932), pp. 5 *et seq.*

nan Trodach = " Stead of the Warriors "), now Arnieston, Temple Parish, Lothian. The " warriors " were the Knights Templar, who had a chapel there in the reign of David I (1124–53).[1] Evidently Gaelic was widely spoken in the so-called " Anglo-Saxon " Lowlands before Dunbar's time, not as a result of " cultural contact ", but of the settlement of people from the area now known as the Highlands, who mingled with the old British element and, like them, regarded the English as " the auld enemy ".

The sense of nationality is, of course, as has been emphasized, a stronger operating force than language or race. At the same time, it is evident that in Scotland there is a greater degree of racial unity than many in the past have assumed.

IV. LANGUAGE AND CUSTOMS

<small>Bede as a Pict—Columba used interpreters in Highlands—Pictish and Gaelic languages—No trace of Irish pantheon in Scotland—Culture mixing in Dalriada—Translated place-names—Dual organization in Dalriada, Gaul and Pictland—Pictish law of inheritance—Mother-right and exogamy—Caledonian marriage customs—Roman empress and Caledonian lady discuss customs—" Handfasting " and " bundling "—Twin tribes of Caledonians—Father-son succession introduced in Scotland—Early Celtic settlers in Scotland—The Picts and brochs—No Picts or brochs in Ireland—Irish theories regarding the Picts—Pictish civil king and priest king—Byzantine cultural influences reach Scotland.</small>

Bede,[2] the " father of English historians ", informs us that in his day there were four languages in Britain —" the languages of the Britons, of the Picts, of the Scots and of the Angles ", that is, Old Welsh, Pictish, Gaelic and Northumbrian English. Bede himself

---

[1] W. J. Watson, *History of the Celtic Place-Names of Scotland*, pp. 136 et seq.
[2] *Ecclesiastical History*, III, 6.

INTRODUCTORY—LANGUAGE AND CUSTOMS

may well have been of Pictish descent, for in the *Book of Deer* mention is made of another Bede who was an Aberdeenshire mormaer (" sea-lord ").

When St. Columba in the sixth century sojourned among the Picts of northern Scotland he had to make use of interpreters. In Skye, according to Adamnan (I, xxvii), a decrepit and aged man, the chief of the mysterious " Geona cohort ", was brought to him, and it is stated that " after being instructed in the word of God by the saint *through an interpreter*, the old man believed and was baptized ". When in Lochaber, St. Columba preached to a man and his family " through an interpreter " and all were baptized.[1] There is no mention of interpreters at the Pictish court at Inverness when Columba interviewed King Brude. The explanation may be that the ruler and his senate were bilingual. But evidently the masses of the people who spoke Pictish (a P-Celtic language) could not hold converse with the Gaelic-speaking (Q-Celtic) Irish missionary, Columba.

Thus, although the Picts spoke a Celtic tongue, Irish cultural influence was before the Christian period stemmed back by the language barrier. After the spread of Christianity pagan mythology was an unlikely importation into Scotland from Ireland. It should not surprise us therefore to find that the Danann pantheon of Ireland is absent in Scotland and that there are no references to the association of Danann deities with fairies in Scottish folk-lore, as is the case in Ireland. Even in Dalriada (Argyll), which was occupied by Scots from Ireland, tradition of Danann deities is

[1] Adamnan, *Life of Columba*, Book II, Chapter XXXIII.

awanting. But there was evidently both culture mixing and the mixing of peoples in that area. The Irish intrusion, beginning late in the second century of our era, was a very gradual one. There must have been a good deal of intermarrying and apparently there was a long bilingual period. P-Celtic place-names and surnames were translated into Q-Celtic (Gaelic). Professor W. J. Watson shows that Ptolemy's *Epidion Akron* (Mull of Kintyre), a P-Celtic place-name meaning " horsemen's cape ", was translated into Q-Celtic (Gaelic) as *Ard Echde*. The reference is to the *Epidii*, a clan or occupational name from *epos*, a horse. Kintyre is the home of the MacEacherns, " whose name ", Watson says, " is an Anglicization of *Mac Each-thighearna* (Son of the Horse-lord) ".[1] The Gaelic word for a horse is *each*, Old Irish *ech*.

In the history of Dalriada there are traces of the dual organization of society which appears to be due to Pictish influence. There were two royal families—those of Knapdale and Lorne—and Dalriada was now ruled by a representative of one house and again by that of another.

Pictish dualism is of very special interest, because it appears to throw light upon the neglected problem presented by Julius Cæsar, who wrote regarding the Gauls, or a section of them:

" The most remarkable feature about their political organization is the existence everywhere of two great antagonistic parties. Not merely do these parties divide each independent tribe, but the cleavage extends to every territorial division and

[1] W. J. Watson, *History of the Celtic Place-Names of Scotland* (London, 1926), p. 24.

INTRODUCTORY—LANGUAGE AND CUSTOMS

sub-division, and may almost be said to permeate every individual household."[1]

The Picts were in the north divided into the Orc (boar) and Cat (cat) clans, and Orkney was known to the Irish as *Inse Orcc* ("Isles of the Orcs"), while Shetland was *Inse Catt* ("Isles of the Cats"). There were also "Cats" on the mainland. When the Norsemen imposed their place-names, they called the northeast extremity of Scotland "Katanes" ("Cat Cape"), and the sea between it and the "Isles of the Orcs" the "Pictland Firth" ("*pettaland-fjördhr*"), now the Pentland Firth, obviously being aware that the "Cats" and "Orcs" were Picts. The sea from Orkney to the north of Ireland was in Irish *Muir n-Orc* ("Sea of the Orcs"). A headland on the Pentland Firth is referred to as "Cape Orcas" by Diodorus Siculus, who had it from Pytheas or his contemporary Timaeus (fourth century B.C.). Modern place-names in Sutherland refer to Pictish occupational areas.

The Picts had not only dual organization but descent by the female line. Bede gives an explanation current in his day of this peculiar custom by stating that the Picts were under agreement to take their wives from Ireland. Apparently Pictish dualism and mother-right were accompanied by the custom of exogamy, the prohibition of marriage within blood or clan kinship. In the lists of Pictish kings the names of fathers given include Picts, Irishmen, Britons and one Angle, Anfrid, elder brother of Oswald and Oswy, who reigned in turn over Northumbria. Some modern writers would

---

[1] *Cæsar's Gallic War* (VI, 11), translation by the Rev. F. P. Long (Oxford, 1911), p. 172.

have it that this Pictish law of succession is indicative of a primitive state of society, but a similar system prevailed in ancient Egypt throughout its long history.

The Caledonians appear to have likewise had a system of " mother right " with the custom known in Indo-Aryan literature as " svayamvara "—the selection of husbands by young women. Dio Cassius tells that when the Emperor Severus was in Scotland his wife, Julia Augusta, had a conversation regarding the Caledonian custom with a local lady. He says that at the time adultery was so common in Rome that he, when consul, found a list of no fewer than 3000 cases. Dio writes:

" A very witty remark is reported to have been made by the wife of Argentocoxus, a Caledonian, to Julia Augusta. When the empress was jesting with her, after the treaty, about the free intercourse of her sex with men in Britain, she replied, ' We fulfil the demands of nature in a much better way than do you Roman women; for we consort openly with the best men, whereas you let yourself be debauched in secret by the vilest." [1]

The custom here referred to may be connected with that of " handfasting ", which was formerly common in the Highlands and other parts of Scotland. In Wales, where the custom was also known, it has been recorded of some couples that " they do not engage in marriage until they have previously tried the disposition and particularly the fecundity of the person with whom they are engaged ". Campion [2] states that " they can bee content to marrie for a yeare and a day by probation,

[1] *Dio's Roman History*, Book LXXVII (translation in Loeb Library series by Earnest Cary, Vol. IX, p. 275).
[2] *Historie of Ireland*, p. 23.

and at the yeare's end to return to her home uppon any light quarrels, if the gentlewoman's friendes bee weake and unable to avenge the injurie ".[1] The custom known as " bundling " is another associated custom.

That there was Caledonian as well as Pictish dualism is suggested by references to the " Dicalydones ",[2] the twin tribe of Caledonians. Ultimately the Caledonians were incorporated in the extended Pictish kingdom with other peoples. Bede, as stated, refers to the two sections of the Pictish subjects as the " northern Picts " and the " southern Picts ". To what extent the Pictish law of descent by the female line contributed to the change of dynasty in the ninth century is not certain. It is generally assumed that the succession of King Kenneth mac Alpin, a Galloway Scot, to the throne of the Picts was due to his descent from a royal Pictish heiress. He reigned as " King of the Picts " and not as " King of the Picts and Scots ", as some have assumed. The royal succession of son to father was, according to Fordun, introduced by King Kenneth II (971–95).

The various Celtic settlers in Scotland did not all reach it by the same route—that is, through England. In the Lothian area the Votadini seem to have been an outlying branch of the Brigantes, whose country extended from Hadrian's wall to the midlands of England. In early Welsh Votadini was *Guotodin*, and in Gaelic *Fotudāin*. The Damnonii of Ayr, Renfrew, Lanark and Stirlingshire appear to have migrated by sea from Devon, the country of the Dumnonii, like the

---

[1] Gomme, *Exogamy and Polyandry*, pp. 390 *et seq.*
[2] Ammianus Marcellenus, XXVII, 8; J. Rhys, *Celtic Britain*, pp. 297–8.

Irish Fir-Domnann. But the Caledonian and other peoples north of the Forth and Clyde apparently reached Scotland by sea from the Continent. In his 1934 Munro lectures, Professor V. Gordon Childe connects the Caledonians with the Belgae. They used chariots in war, but no chariots were possessed by the Picts, who, according to Gildas, Bede and Nennius, first settled in the north of Scotland.

The Picts were a seafaring and agricultural people. Their distribution in Scotland coincides with the distribution of those circular stone-built strongholds known as brochs which have so much in common with the *nuraghi* of Sardinia—double walls, spiral staircases always opening on the left, inner courts about thirty feet in diameter, conduits and drains, difficult entrances with " guard chambers ", and defensive outworks. Brochs and *nuraghi* situated in villages were apparently occupied by the ruling caste of a people, who, like the seafaring Greeks, were pirates as well as traders. There are no brochs in Ireland, Wales or England. Those who would have it that the Picts did not erect the brochs have yet to discover the mysterious unnamed people who occupied the Pictish area as late as the Roman period when, as archæological evidence proves, there was contact with Roman civilization.

The still earlier archæological evidence provided by the recently excavated Bronze Age village at Jarlshof in Shetland indicates that the late Bronze Age people in the north were not broch-builders, but that a broch-building people were sudden intruders in the early Iron Age. We know of no other northern intruders of that period except the Picts. In this connexion the place-name " Cape Orcas " of the fourth century B.C. is significant. It testifies to the early arrival of the Picts.

The Pictish question has been greatly confused by those theorists who would have it that the Picts of Scotland were the same people as the " Cruithne " of Ireland. Irish scholars have of late regarded it apparently as almost a national necessity to prove that the Picts were of Irish origin. In doing so they find it necessary to discredit such a reliable authority as Bede and, indeed, to assume that every scrap of evidence which does not accord with their theory must have been " invented ". Even Ptolemy is now spoken of in Ireland as " unreliable " and some actually credit the view that the tribes or nations located by him in Scotland are mere inventions, although the names of most of them have survived in existing place-names. A very notable example, for instance, is " Mertae " in Sutherland. That the true form was " Smertae ", the name of a Gaulish people, is indicated by the surviving hill-name *Carn Smeart*. Other survivals are dealt with by Professor W. J. Watson, who discovered the " Smertae " evidence.[1] If the Ptolemy tribal names have not survived in Ireland, the reason may well be that the change of language in that island was of very much earlier date than in Scotland. The Britons of Ireland ceased to speak their pre-Gaelic language after the overwhelming conquests of the Gaelic people. At a later period the Norse place-names were similarly obliterated, so that only very few now survive.

Both Dr. MacBain and Professor W. J. Watson

[1] *History of the Celtic Place-Names of Scotland*, pp. 10 et seq.

agree that " Picti " cannot be separated etymologically from " Pict-ones ", the name of the people on the Bay of Biscay who provided Julius Cæsar with ships[1] to aid him in the naval war against the Veneti of Brittany, who were apparently their rivals. The Veneti had as allies the English Channel seafaring peoples between modern Brittany and Holland and received aid from the Britons of England.[2] A branch of the Pictones apparently seized the naval bases in Orkney and the north of Scotland for operations, both trading and piratical, in the North Sea and the western sea route. It may be that the Pictones were not long settled in western Gaul when the Picts migrated to northern Scotland.

The Picts[3] were known to the Norse as " Pettr ", and in Old Welsh " Peithwyr " means " Pictmen ". In Old English the rendering is " Peohta " and in Old Scots " Pecht ". Apparently " Pect " is the correct form of the national name. The Pictones of western Gaul are once referred to by Ammianus as " Pectones ". The theory that " Picti " is derived from the Latin " pictus ", " painted " or " stained ", is evidently wrong. A Roman pun on the national name cannot be regarded as evidence that the Picts perpetuated a Roman nickname! The national name was manifestly P-Celtic. There is no primitive " p " in Irish, a Q-Celtic dialect.

The Irish " Cruithne " was the Q-Celtic rendering of the pre-Roman name of the Britons, which was

[1] *De Bel. Gall.*, III, 11.
[2] *Ibid.*, III, 9 and IV, 20.
[3] W. J. Watson, *History of the Celtic Place-Names of Scotland*, pp. 59 et seq.

"Pretani", in Greek "Prettanoi". Among the Britons who settled in Ireland were the Brigantes, the Dumnonii (in Irish " Fir-Domnann ") and the Setantii (Cuchulainn's pre-Irish name " Setanta " indicates that he was one of the Setantii from the neighbourhood of modern Liverpool). The " Cruithne " of Ireland were Britons not Picts. In Irish a P-Celtic name like " Pict " or " Pect " would have been rendered in Q-Celtic as " Cicht " or " Cecht ". There was never a people in Ireland so named. Nor were there Irish peoples known as " Orcs " or " Cats ", the names of the two Pictish clans. The philological evidence, like that regarding physical characters, demonstrates that the Picts were not an Irish people and that there is no trace of genuine Picts in Ireland, except as visitors.

In Irish literature we find that famous heroes like Cuchulainn and Ferdiad received their military training in Skye, Alba (Scotland). Alba was likewise regarded as a place of high culture which gave a student from Ireland a reputation. When Queen Medb visited the prophetess Fedelm and asked, " Whence comest thou?" the answer received was, " From Alba, after learning prophetic skill ".[1]

According to Bede, the southern Picts (the Pictish military aristocrats and their subjects south of the Grampians) were converted to Christianity by St. Ninian, who late in the fourth century or early in the fifth established himself at Whithorn in Galloway and there erected a church which was dedicated to St. Martin of Tours. The northern Picts remained pagan

[1] Joseph Dunn, *The Ancient Irish Epic Tale Táin Bó Cúalnge*, p. 15 and pp. 233, 239, 241-3, 251, 263, 266.

until in the sixth century St. Columba visited King Brude at Inverness and effected his conversion. He was opposed by the Druids, including Broichan, who in Adamnan's *Life of Columba* is referred to as the Pictish king's tutor, pastor or guardian (*nutricius*). It may well be that the Picts, like the Spartans, had two kings—a civil king and a priest king.

Cultural influences " flowed " from the Continent to early Scotland by various routes. Apparently it was across the North Sea that the pre-Christian faith which involved the taboo upon pork as food was carried. By the same sea route must also have come in early Christian times the art motifs of the Pictish sculptured stones of eastern Scotland and the pigments used in illustrating the illuminated Celtic or Gaelic church manuscripts, including lapis-lazuli from Constantinople (Byzantium), the European " clearing house " for that semi-precious Asiatic stone, malachite, &c. The carriers of cultural elements from the Near East may never have been numerous, but evidently they became influential.[1]

[1] See my *Scotland: The Ancient Kingdom* and *Buddhism in Pre-Christian Britain*.

CHAPTER I

Scottish Pork Taboo

Taboo centred in Scotland—Formerly as common in the Lowlands as in the Highlands—Sir Walter Scott's references—Ben Jonson on King James's prejudice—Shakespearean evidence—The " Jewish Scots "—Hanoverian officer on the taboo—Dr. Johnson on Hebridean abhorrence of the pig—Taboo among descendants of Scots in Dalriada and those of Britons of Strathclyde—Galloway pig scares—Dread of swine in Fife—A church " scene "—Fishers' hatred of pig—Miners shared prejudice—Unlucky pig in north-east of England—Pig as the Devil—Reference to pig in Gaelic prayer—" Last year's pig "—Ebbing prejudice—Leverhulme pig scheme in Lewis—Pig despised in Barra—Beginning of Annandale pork trade.

A remarkable and outstanding feature of Scottish folk-lore is the superstitious treatment of the pig, which involves so deep-rooted a prejudice against the use of pork as food as to suggest the existence in ancient times of a definite religious taboo connected with a body of non-Celtic beliefs. There is no trace of a similar prejudice in the folk-lore of Wales or Ireland or in that of any Scandinavian country. In England, where pork has so long been freely eaten, north-eastern fishermen dislike reference being made to the pig in connexion with their work. One wonders if this is a result of a fisher migration from Scotland.

This Scottish taboo is not yet entirely a thing of the past. There are still thousands of Highlanders and groups of Lowlanders who refuse to keep pigs or to

Rump Parliament between the years 1639 and 1661 ".[1]
It contains the verse:

> " The Jewish *Scots* that scorns [*sic*] to eat
> The Flesh of swine, and *Brewers* beat,
> 'Twas the sight of this Hogs-head made 'em retreat,
> *Which nobody can deny.*"

John Graham Dalyell, the Scottish advocate and a pioneer folklorist, refers in his *Darker Superstitions of Scotland*[2] to the query in the *Athenian Mercury*, London, in 1691, " Why do Scotchmen (Scotsmen) hate swine's flesh?", which, he says, was " unsatisfactorily answered, ' They might borrow it of the Jews '."

Dalyell goes on to say:

" The same prejudice, though infinitely abated, still subsists. Yet it is not known that swine have been regarded as mystical animals in Scotland. Early in the seventeenth century the aversion to them by the lower ranks, especially in the north, was so great, and elsewhere, and the flesh was so much undervalued, that, except for those reared at mills, the breed would have been extirpated."

Two eighteenth century English writers, Captain Burt and Dr. Samuel Johnson, during their sojourns in Scotland became interested in the prejudice against the pig. Captain Burt was a Hanoverian officer and was consequently precluded from intercourse with Jacobites. In his sixth letter (1730) he wrote:

" Pork is not very common with us, but what we have is good. I have often heard that the Scots will not eat it. This may be ranked among the rest of the prejudices; for this kind

---

[1] Collected and published in London in 1731, Vol. I, p. 228.
[2] Edinburgh and London, 1834, p. 425.

of food is common in the (eastern) Lowlands, and Aberdeen, in particular, is famous for furnishing families with pickled pork for winter provision as well as their shipping. . . . I own I never saw any swine among the mountains, and there is good reason for it: those people have no offal wherewith to feed them; and were they to give them other food, one single sow would devour all the provisions of a family. It is here a general notion that where the chief declares against pork, his followers affect to show the same dislike; but of this affectation I happened once to see an example. One of the chiefs who brought hither with him a gentleman of his own clan dined with several of us at a public house where the chief refused to eat pork, and the laird did the same; but some days afterwards the latter being invited to our mess and under no restraint, he ate it with as good an appetite as any of us."

Burt also refers to the Scottish prejudice against eating eels and pike.

Jamieson, the annotator of Burt, commenting upon the " taboo ",[1] says:

" The aversion of many of the Scots, both in the Highlands and Lowlands, to eating pork had nothing superstitious connected with it. They could not eat fat of any kind, not having been accustomed to it."

This explanation is far from convincing. Jamieson appears to have been quite ignorant regarding Scottish pig lore.

Dr. Johnson had no theory to urge in making his interesting record. In his *A Journey to the Western Islands of Scotland in 1773* he writes, when dealing with his visit to the island of Raasay:

" The vulgar inhabitants of Skye, I know not whether of

---

[1] Burt's *Letters from the North of Scotland*, 1818 edition.

the other islands, have not only eels but pork and bacon in abhorrence; and accordingly I never saw a hog in the Hebrides, except one at Dunvegan."

Native writers dealing with the prejudice testify as to its widespread character. In Sinclair's *Statistical Account* of Scottish parishes we find a reference to it in the heart of Lorne, for long the territory of the intruding Scots from Ireland. The Rev. Ludovick Grant,[1] says that "the deep-rooted prejudice against swine's flesh is now removed: most of the farmers rear some of that species which, not thirty years ago, they held in the utmost detestation." Another interesting *Statistical Account* record is from the pen of the minister of Lesmahagoe (Lesmahagow), Lanarkshire, in the ancient territory of the Britons of Strathclyde. It is as follows:

"The people of this part of Scotland had formerly a superstitious prejudice against swine; but now there are a number reared and fed in this parish."[2]

The most astonishing evidence comes from Galloway. Mr. Robert Henderson, who during the latter part of the eighteenth and early part of the nineteenth century had been a farmer at Broomhill, near Annan, completed on 13th June, 1811, *A Treatise on the Breeding of Swine*,[3] his aim being to convince Scottish farmers that pigs were profitable and the prejudice against them absurd. He gives an astounding and entertaining

[1] *The Statistical Account of Scotland*, Vol. VI, p. 177; edited by Sir John Sinclair (Edinburgh, 1793).
[2] *Ibid.*, Vol. VII.
[3] This very rare book was picked from a barrow of an itinerant second-hand bookseller by the late Dr. George Neilson, Glasgow, the Scottish historian, who sent it to me.

account of the appearance of the first swine in Dumfriesshire about 1724:

"Within the last century (probably about ninety years ago) a person in the parish of Ruthwell, in Dumfriesshire, called 'Gudeman o' the Brow', received a young swine as a present from some distant part; which, from all the information I could get, seems to have been the first seen in that part of the country. This pig having strayed across the Lochar into the adjoining parish of Carlavroc, a woman who was herding cattle on the marsh, by the seaside, was very much alarmed at the sight of a living creature, that she had never seen nor heard of before, approaching her straight from the shore as if it had come out of the sea, and ran home to the village of Blackshaws screaming. As she ran, it ran snorking and grunting after her, seeming glad it had met with a companion. She arrived at the village so exhausted and terrified that before she could get her story told she fainted away.

"By the time she came to herself a crowd of people had collected to see what was the matter, when she told them that there was a diel (devil) came out of the sea with two horns in his head (most likely the swine had pricked ears) and chased her, roaring and gaping all the way at her heels, and she was sure it was not far off.

"A man called Will's Tom, an old schoolmaster, said if he could see it he would 'cunger the diel,' and got a Bible and an old sword. It immediately started up at his back and gave a loud grumph, which put him into such a fright that his hair stood upright in his head, and he was obliged to be carried from the field half dead.

"The whole crowd ran some one way and some another; some reached the house tops, and others shut themselves in barns and byres. At last one on the housetop called out it was 'the Gudeman o' the Brow's grumphy,' he having seen it before. The affray was settled, and people mostly reconciled, although some still entertained frightful thoughts about it, and durst not go over the door to a neighbour's house after dark without one to set or cry them. One of the crowd, who had some compassion on the creature, called out, ' give it a tork of straw to eat, it will be hungry.'

"Next day it was conveyed over the Lochar, and it seemed to find its way home. It being near the dusk of evening, it came grunting up to two men pulling thistles on the farm of Cockpool. They were much alarmed at the sight, and mounted two old horses they had tethered beside them, intending to make their way home. In the meantime the pig got between them and the horses, which caused them to scamper out of the way and land in Lochar moss, where one of their horses was drowned, and the other with difficulty relieved. The night being dark, they durst not part one from the other to call for assistance, lest the monster should find them out and attack them singly; nor durst they speak above their breath for fear of being devoured. At daybreak next morning they took a different course, came by Cumlongon castle and made their way home, where they found their families much alarmed on account of their absence. They said that they had seen a creature about the size of a dog, with two horns in his head, and cloven feet, roaring out like a lion, and if they had not galloped away, it would have torn them to pieces. One of their wives said, ' Hout man, it has been the Gudeman o' the Brow's grumphy; it frightened them a' at the Blackshaws yesterday, and poor Meggie Anderson maist lost her wits, and is ay out o' ae fit into anither sin-syne.'

"The pig happened to lie all night among the corn where the men were pulling thistles, and about daybreak set forward on its journey for the Brow. One Gabriel Gunion, mounted on a long-tailed grey colt, with a load of white fish in a pair of creels swung over the beast, encountered the pig, which went nigh among the horse's feet and gave a snork. The colt, being as much frightened as Gabriel, wheeled about and scampered off sneering, with his tail on his riggin, at full gallop. Gabriel cut the slings and dropt the creels, the colt dismounted his rider, and, going like the wind, with his tail up, never stopped till he came to Barnkirk point, where he took the Solway Firth and landed at Bowness, on the Cumberland side. As to Gabriel, by the time he got himself gathered up, the pig was within sight, he took to his heels, as the colt was quite gone, and reached Cumlongon wood in time to hide himself, where he stayed all that day and night, and next morning got home almost exhausted. He told a dreadful story. The fright caused him to imagine the pig as big as a calf, having long horns, eyes like trenchers, and a back like a hedge-hog. He lost his fish, the colt was got back, but never did more good, and as to Gabriel, he soon after fell into a consumption, and departed this life about a year after.

"About this time also a vessel came to Glencaple quay, a little below Dumfries, that had some swine on board, most likely for the ship's use; one of them having got out of the vessel in the night, was seen on the farm of Newmains next morning. The alarm was spread, and a number of people collected. The animal got many different names, and at last it was concluded to be a brock (badger). Some got pitchforks, some clubs, and others old swords, and a hot pursuit ensued; the chase lasted a considerable time, owing to the pursuers losing heart when near their prey and retreating. Rob's Geordy, having a little more courage than the rest, ran ' neck or nothing ', forcibly upon the animal, and run it through with a pitchfork, for which he got the name of ' stout-hearted Geordy ' all his life after. There is an old man, nearly a hundred years of age, still alive in the neighbourhood where this happened, who declares he remembers of the Gudeman o' the Brow's pig, and the circumstances mentioned; and he says it was the first swine ever seen in that country."

Dean Ramsay [1] (1793–1872) has an equally amazing story to tell regarding a church scene in Fife.

A clergyman of a fishing village on the east coast had informed a visiting clergyman regarding the local superstitions regarding swine, and finding him incredulous, asked him to conduct a Sunday service.

"It was arranged that his friend was to read the chapter relating to the herd of swine into which the evil spirits were cast. Accordingly, when the first verse was read in which the unclean beast was mentioned, a slight commotion was observable among the audience, each one of them putting his or her hand on any piece of iron—a nail on the seat or bookboard, or to the nails on their shoes. At the repetition of the word again and again, more commotion was visible, and the words ' cauld airn ' (cold iron), the antidote to this baneful spell, were heard issuing from various corners of the church. And finally, on his coming over the hated word again, when the whole herd ran violently down the bank into the sea, the alarmed parishioners, irritated beyond bounds, rose and all left the church in bodies."

Dean Ramsay tells that " the lower orders " in Fife retained " till very recently " a " great horror of swine " and even mention of them. " I can observe," he says, " a great change to have taken place amongst Scotch people generally on this subject. The old aversion to the ' unclean animal ' still lingers in the Highlands, but seems in the Lowland districts to have yielded to a sense of its thrift and usefulness . . . I recollect an old Scottish gentleman, who shared this horror, asking very gravely, ' Were not swine forbidden under the law and cursed under the gospel?' "

[1] *Reminiscences of Scottish Life and Character*, Chapter II.

SCOTTISH PORK TABOO

Mr. J. M. M'Bain[1] testifies as to the prejudice among the fisher people of Arbroath and Auchmithie:

"They had a great aversion to the flesh of the pig coming into contact with their boats. If any evil-disposed person had managed surreptitiously to place a piece of pork on board a boat before its leaving the harbour on a fishing expedition, although its presence had not been discovered till the boat had reached the fishing ground, those on board would return to the land without shooting their nets rather than proceed with their fishing with the hated junk aboard."

Dean Ramsay tells that if a pig crossed the path of fishermen " when about to set out on a sea voyage, they considered it so unlucky an omen that they would not venture off ". In the writer's boyhood a similar superstition prevailed around the shores of the Moray Firth. Caithness fishermen when at sea considered it unlucky to refer by name to a pig or a clergyman. One had to be designated the " could-iron beastie " and the other the " could-iron gentleman ". The pig was similarly a beast of ill-omen south of the Forth. Within living memory the fishermen of Newhaven (near Edinburgh) were greatly enraged when mischief-making Leith youngsters shouted to them as they put to sea, " There's a soo at the boo!"—meaning " There's a sow at the bow of the boat." The Rev. Walter Gregor says that " among some of the fishing population it was accounted very unlucky for a marriage party to meet a pig ".[2] The miners of Prestonpans, East Lothian, shared the fishermen's prejudice against swine, and refused to descend a coal pit if on going

[1] *Arbroath: Past and Present* (Arbroath, 1887), pp. 75–6.
[2] *Folklore of the North-east of Scotland*, p. 129.

towards it they met a pig. Traces of the lingering abhorrence of the pig extended along the north-east of England as far south as the fishing centres of Yorkshire. Mr. R. Blakeborough [1] has recorded:

"If whilst a fisherman was baiting his nets anyone mentioned anything in connexion with a pig, or *dakky*, as it was called, the worst of luck would be looked for."

The Rev. Walter Gregor refers to the superstition that " pigs have from three to five round marks ranged in the shape of a crescent on the foreleg above the ankle " and says that these " go by the name of the ' Devil's mark '. The men of several villages would not pronounce the word ' swine ' when they were at sea. It was a word of ill-omen. The bite of a pig was regarded with horror. It was deemed impossible or next to impossible to cure and was supposed to produce cancer." [2]

In the Highlands the devil had a swine form and was referred to as " The Big Black Pig " (*Muc Mhór Dhubh*). When he appeared in human form he had " usually ", writes the Rev. John Gregorson Campbell,[3] Tiree, " a horse's hoof, but also sometimes a pig's foot ". He was in the habit of visiting young people who played cards.

" Cards are notoriously known as the devil's books. When boys play them the fiend has been known to come down the chimney feet foremost, the horse's or pig's foot appearing first. When going away he disappears in smoke and neighs horribly in the chimney.

---

[1] *Wit, Character, Folklore and Customs of the North Riding of Yorkshire*, p. 141.
[2] *Folklore of the North-east of Scotland*, p. 129.
[3] *Superstitions of the Scottish Highlands* (Glasgow, 1900), pp. 290-2.

The belief was, until recently, widespread that if one ate pork one would contract some horrible disease like leprosy.

Highlanders who have acquired the habit of eating pork usually make fun of those who perpetuate the immemorial superstition. The Rev. Alexander MacGregor, an Inverness clergyman, was one of these " pioneers " and tells [1] of a Skye man, named Farquhar, who had dinner at his manse each Sunday.

" It frequently happened that the servants' dinner consisted of pork or bacon, the look of which Farquhar could not bear, and yet he often dined on it. The servants, knowing his prejudices, had beforehand prepared a quantity of the lean parts of the meat for the old man, which they passed off as mutton and which he never suspected. When partaking of it, however, he frequently said, to the no small amusement and tittering of the domestics: ' *Bu tu féin an fheoil mhaith, cheart, agus cha b'i a' mhuc ghrannda shalach.*' (' Thou art the good right meat, and not the filthy unclean pig ')."

A humorous Gaelic folk-story tells of a Jock Mackay employed by a Lowland farmer who had settled in the county of Sutherland. For some years the farmer imported from Leith for the festive season a large box of foodstuffs, including a smoked ham. On New Year's Day morning Mackay had for breakfast, instead of the customary porridge and milk, a dish of ham and eggs.

The farmer began to keep pigs, much to the disgust of Jock, who had to feed them. When the next festive season was at hand, a pig was killed, and on the New Year morning Jock was given a dish of fried pork and

[1] *Highland Superstitions* (Stirling, 1901), p. 17.

eggs. He expressed disgust at the idea of his partaking of pork. "But," the farmer's wife reminded him, "you used to be fond of ham." "Is ham pig?" asked Jock, turning pale. He was assured it was, and he immediately fled from the kitchen and vomited outside. Hence the proverbial saying in Gaelic when an individual recalls something unpleasant to his hearers, "You are like Jock Mackay, vomiting last year's pig!"

Members of the Campbell clan used to be greatly offended when a non-Campbell referred to a pig as "Sandy Campbell".

The writer must confess to being one of those Highlanders who prefer not to eat pork in any form, but for no other reason than an inherited prejudice such as Englishmen, as well as Scotsmen, entertain towards a diet of horse flesh. During his lifetime the prejudice has been " ebbing " in the Highlands, especially since the experience of food shortage during the war. The rising generation eat ham or bacon, but fresh pork is not very popular. When the late Lord Leverhulme thought he could develop Lewis, one of his schemes, which certainly did not meet with success, was that the crofters should keep pigs. In 1920 there were eight pigs in Lewis, which had then a population of 24,299, but in 1921 there were only two. A native of Barra informed me that in his boyhood he used to hear that only two pigs were ever seen in his native township. They had been washed ashore from a wreck and were promptly committed to the deep again.

The rapidity with which, in some parts of Scotland, the prejudice against pigs and pork has declined is illustrated by the Dumfriesshire evidence. Mr.

Robert Henderson[1] tells that about 1760 there were only about twenty swine in the parish. Ten years later they became more plentiful " and every farmer kept one or two ". The curing of pork began with a young woman named Betty Liddle, a farmer's daughter in the parish of Middlebie. " A number of the old people thought it was witchcraft, for they could not understand how she could cure them with the bone in." The trade in cured hams and flitches increased quickly and in 1790 was a general business. The pioneer of the Annandale trade, which was to become so considerable, was one Simeon Johnston. In a generation the Lockerbie market trade rose to the value of about £9000 annually.

---

[1] *Op. cit.*, pp. 19 *et seq.*

CHAPTER II

Swine Cults: Sanctity and Abhorrence of Pig

Scottish pork taboo not of biblical origin—Monks and Norman barons kept pigs—Taboo acquired by descendants of intruders—Cult of sacred pig in Scotland—The " Happy Boar "—Sacred white boar in St. Kentigern legend—Black pig in divination ceremony—Inverness and Argyll boar figures—Picts and boar-god—Annual sow sacrifice in Orkney—Raasay sacrifice—Irish pig sacrifice—Pork eaten by Picts—Hebridean " sow-mother "—St. Anthony and the pig—" Lucky boar " of Celts—Celtic Diana rides on boar—Celts as pork merchants—Pigs' bones in Celtic graves—Pigs in Bronze Age graves—Why Celtic Galatians tabooed pork—Anatolian influences reach the West—Attis myth in Gaelic—Sanctity and abhorrence of pig in the Near East—Anatolian evidence—Scottish pork taboo due to an imported faith—Swine devouring dead—Mixing of pig lore—Pig medicines—Irish and Welsh pig lore—Arcadian pork taboo—Egyptian treatments of the pig.

Some recent writers have suggested, as did the editor of the *Athenian Mercury*, London, in 1691, that the Scottish hatred of the pig and the abhorrence of pork " was borrowed from the Jews "—that, in other words, the taboo had origin in early Christian times. References are made in this connexion to Christ causing demons to enter the bodies of the Gadarean swine and to the Old Testament taboos:

" And the hare, because he cheweth the cud, but divideth not the hoof; he is unclean to you. And the swine, though he divideth the hoof and be cloven-footed, yet he cheweth not the cud; he is unclean to you."[1]

[1] *Leviticus*, xi, 6-7.

SWINE CULTS

There is no evidence, however, that the early Christian missionaries in Scotland tabooed pork. The earliest of these of whom we have definite knowledge was St. Ninian, who died about A.D. 432. He was connected with the Welsh church and there is no trace of the taboo in Wales. St. Columba migrated from Ireland to Iona in the sixth century, and as pork was eaten freely in Ireland long before he was born, and continued to be eaten there during and after his lifetime, we are not justified in assuming he tabooed pork. The only reference in his *Life* by Adamnan to a food taboo concerns horse flesh.[1]

We find that pigs were kept later at Scottish monasteries and their flesh eaten by the clergy. In the reign of David I (1124–53) a royal grant permitted the monks of Holyrood to cut wood in the royal forests of Stirling and Clackmannan and to pasture swine in them. Scottish barons had " huge herds of swine " and ate pork freely.[2]

Dalyell points out that " the duty, rent or tribute, called *pannagium*, which is generally interpreted as due for feeding swine on acorns, is named in ancient writings, such as a grant in the year 1203 ".[3]

If we are to assume that the Scottish prejudice was of biblical origin, we have not only to explain why the monks ignored it, but why it did not obtain among the early Christians of England, Wales or Ireland. This theory of biblical origin really credits the people of Scotland with a more intimate knowledge of the

[1] Book I, Chapter XV.
[2] P. Fraser Tytler, *The History of Scotland* (1864 edition), Vol. I, pp. 233–6.
[3] *The Darker Superstitions of Scotland* (1834), pp. 425–6, and *Analysis of the Records of the Bishopric of Moray*, p. 69.

Old and New Testaments than was possible before these sacred books were translated into the local languages and the masses of the people learned to read and write. Long before a Gaelic translation of the Bible was available the pork taboo prevailed. Bishop Leslie in his history [1] (1578) states casually that in Scotland the flesh of fat oxen is salted "as swyne fleshe is uset in uthir cuntries, of quhilke our cuntrie peple hes lytle plesure ".

The taboo must have been established before the introduction of Christianity, and unless it had been connected with a body of pagan religious beliefs, it could not have survived, as it did, the influence exercised by intruding pork-eating peoples and especially the Christian clergy. Ultimately, as we have seen, the Scottish king and certain of the descendants of Norman or Normanized barons became infected by the local prejudice, as did also the descendants of the Irish Scots who settled in Dalriada (Argyll) and of those of the Norsemen who elected to remain in the Hebrides after the Treaty of Perth in 1266.

An important fact which emerges when we investigate the swine lore of Scotland is that there were two quite different attitudes towards the pig in early times. One cult appears, as has been shown in the previous chapter, to have regarded the animal with abhorrence; another cult regarded the pig as a sacred animal in association with the worship of the mother goddess.

Evidence of the sanctity of the pig is afforded by its Hebridean reputation as a bringer of increase and

[1] Scottish Texts Society edition, London and Edinburgh, 1885, Vol. I, p. 32.

luck in agricultural operations. The Rev. J. Gregorson Campbell [1] provides evidence in this connexion when giving examples of " fairy assistance ". It is evident that a pig deity had been invoked by a sower of seed, and that the spell operated successfully until that sower had been interrupted by one who gave expression to a counter spell. Campbell writes:

" A man in the Ross of Mull, about to sow his land, filled a sheet with seed oats, and commenced. He went on sowing, but the sheet remained full. At last a neighbour took notice of the strange phenomenon and said, ' The face of your evil and iniquity be upon you, is the sheet never to be empty?'

" When this was said a little brown bird leapt out of the sheet, and the supply of corn ceased. The bird was called *Torc Sona*, i.e. *Happy Hog* (more correctly *Happy Boar*), and when any of the man's descendants fall in with any luck they are asked if the *Torc Sona* still follows the family."

Here the pig is a shape-changing deity or demon.

The Lucky, or Sacred, White Boar figures in one of the legends associated with Glasgow's patron saint, St. Kentigern (St. Mungo). Joceline, a monk of Furness, relates that when " the most holy St. Kentigern " was in Wales he " found a place fit for building a tabernacle (monastery) to the Lord, the God of Jacob " by following a wild boar. The saint, accompanied by a crowd of disciples, was wandering over hills and through valleys and forests when

"a single wild boar from the wood, entirely white, met them, and approaching the feet of the saint, moving his head, sometimes advancing a little and then returning and looking backwards, motioned to the saint and to his companions with such

[1] *Superstitions of the Scottish Highlands* (Glasgow, 1900), p. 99.

gesture as he could to follow him. On seeing this they wondered and glorified God, who worked marvellous things, and things past finding out in His creatures. Then step by step they followed their leader, the boar, which preceded them.

"When they came to the place which the Lord had predestinated for them, the boar halted, and frequently striking the ground with his foot, and making the gesture of tearing up the soil of the little hill that was there with his long tusk, shaking his head repeatedly and grunting, he clearly showed to all that that was the place designed and prepared by God."[1]

A black pig plays a similar part in a search for the hidden corpse of a murdered man in a Gaelic folk-story entitled "The Tale of the Shifty Lad", from Arrochar, Loch Lomond.[2]

"They got the black pig and they were going from farm to farm with her, trying if they could find out where the body was buried."

The pig "hit upon the body in a garden" while those men who had accompanied it were being supplied with food in the adjoining house. The watchful villain stole out and slew and buried the animal. He afterwards pretended that the pig had gone away and the men departed in the direction he indicated, believing they were following it.

A wild boar is a striking figure on the "boar-stone" situated at the margin of a field on the farm of Knocknagael (*Cnoc nan Giall*, "Hill of Hostages"), about three miles distant from the town of Inverness. It is incised on the flat surface of an upright boulder and above the head is a double-ring symbol, apparently

---

[1] *Lives of St. Ninian and St. Kentigern* (Edinburgh, 1874), pp. 75–6.
[2] J. F. Campbell, *Popular Tales of the West Highlands*, Vol. I, No. XVII *d*.

representing the sun and suggesting that this was a " solar boar ", or a " boar of heaven ".

On a flat rock surface at Dunadd in Argyll are three rock carvings, consisting of a stone basin, the imprint of a human foot and the incised figure of a wild boar, a long-snouted " rooter ", like the Inverness boar and similarly of excellent draughtsmanship.[1]

Dunadd is an ancient fort on the summit of a rocky hill and occupies a strategic position in the strath between the head of Loch Gilp and Crinan Bay. Through the valley runs the modern Crinan Canal. Near Dunadd are monuments of the Bronze Age. From the beginning of the sixth century till the eighth, or perhaps the ninth, century Dunadd was a stronghold of importance. Withal, there is "an earlier legendary history extending to the beginning of the Christian era ".

It may be that the Inverness boar-stone was connected with the Orc (boar) clan of the Picts. When in the sixth century St. Columba visited King Brude I he found that his headquarters were in the vicinity of Inverness. Brude had previously subdued Dalriada and the boar at Dunadd fort had perhaps a connexion with the recognition of his sovereignty. The carved footprint is of interest in this connexion, because, as will be shown, the custom survived among the MacDonalds of investing a new Lord of the Isles with authority while he stood upon a stone on which footprints had been carved. The basin-like hollow beside the pig was probably used for libations.

[1] *Proceedings of the Society of Antiquaries of Scotland*, Vol. LXIV, sixth series, Vol. IV, Edinburgh, 1930, p. 112.

The figures of the boars at Inverness and Dunadd are evidently those of holy animals and suggest that, as in Greece and part of Anatolia, there were purificatory sacrifices of swine. No horror of the pig could have existed among a people who had boars carved on rock or on standing stones. Other animals incised on Scottish pagan standing stones include the horse, the stag, the bull, the wolf and the so-called eagle or raven on the Strathpeffer stone, which may have really been intended for a falcon hawk.

Orkney (*Inse Orcc*, " Islands of the Boars ") was for long occupied by the Picts, and a curious custom which survived till the eighteenth century in one of its parishes suggests an original pig sacrifice. It is referred to in Sinclair's *Statistical Account of Scotland* (1793) as follows:

" In a part of the parish of Sandwick, every family that has a herd of swine kills a sow on the 17th of December, and thence it is called ' Sow Day '. There is no tradition as to the origin of this practice."

James Boswell in his *The Journal of a Tour to the Hebrides with Samuel Johnson, LL.D.*, refers to what appears to be a tradition of a pig sacrifice in connexion with a loch in the island of Raasay:

" There was once a wild beast in it (the loch), a sea-horse, which came and devoured a man's daughter, upon which the man lighted a great fire and had a sow roasted in it, the smell of which attracted the monster. In the fire was put a spit. The man lay concealed behind a low wall of loose stones. The monster came, and the man with the red-hot spit destroyed it."

Pigs appear to have been sacrificed in parts of

ancient Ireland. In the *Three Irish Glossaries*[1] the names of different varieties of pigs are given. One is *lupait*, and it is explained as " the name of the pig that is killed on Martin's festival "; the commentator adds, " and it seems to me that it is to the Lord it was offered ".

Dr. George Henderson[2] draws attention to the obsolete phrase *an t-sreath chuileanach*, left untranslated in Campbell's *Popular Tales of the West Highlands*, and says it should read *an treith chuileanach 's a dà chuilean deug* (" the mother sow with her litter of twelve "). He refers to *Orc treth* in Cormac's *Glossary* and connects *treth* with *triath*, meaning " lord, chief ", from *treitos*, which Stokes compared with the Latin *tritavos*, an ancestor in the sixth degree.

Those who would here suggest that the Pictish " Orcs " had a belief in a boar ancestor and therefore carved boars on standing stones and rock must find a solution of the problem presented by the fact that no cat images were carved by the Pictish " Cat " clan. The available evidence is against the theory of a Pictish totemic origin of the pork taboo in Scotland. In the prehistoric Pictish Orkney village of Skara Brae pork appears to have been eaten.[3]

Dr. George Henderson found a Hebridean reference to the " mother sow " which suggests an original connexion between the pig and mother goddess:

" I noted a children's game in Eriskay (island) called *Mathair*

---

[1] London, 1862, edited by Whitley Stokes; preface, p. l.

[2] *Survivals in Belief Among the Celts* (Glasgow, 1911), p. 175.

[3] *Skara Brae: A Pictish Village in Orkney*, by V. Gordon Childe (London, 1931), pp. 96, 149, 203.

Mhòr, ' Big Mother ',[1] where the mother was feigned to be a pig! It is possibly a relic of early ritual."[2]

While in Scotland the pig was in an evil sense a symbol of the devil, it was in a good sense, as elsewhere, a symbol of St. Anthony. The preceptory of St. Anthony was founded in Leith about 1430 and it was the only one of its kind in Scotland. On its seal, preserved in the National Library of Scotland, Edinburgh, St. Anthony wears a hermit's mantle and at his feet is a sow with a bell suspended from her neck. The poet Lindsay in his *Pardouner* refers to

" The gruntil of Saint Anthony's sow quilk bare his haly bell ".

St. Anthony was reputed to protect mariners and the canons visited ships. The chapel of St. Anthony on Arthur's Seat, Edinburgh, commanding a fine view of the Forth, appears to have been associated with the Leith preceptory. There are no Scottish Celtic place-names connected with St. Anthony, who does not appear to have any particular connexion with a pork taboo. He was himself in his youth a swineherd.

The " lucky boar " is referred to in the *Germania* of Tacitus (Chapter XLV). He informs us that the Æstyi, a people of Celtic speech, who engaged in the amber trade, " worship the mother of the gods and wear figures of wild boars as an emblem of their superstition ". These emblems were reputed to protect warriors in battle. That they were worn by Celts who reached south-eastern England is demonstrated by the bronze boar amulets from Hounslow, Middlesex, and

[1] Or " Great Mother ".
[2] G. Henderson, *op. cit.*, p. 24, note 1.

the Witham shield boar in the British Museum. The Gauls had a pig-god called Succellos and another named Moccus. Anwyl[1] reminds us that the wild boar " was a favourite emblem in Gaul " and that " there is extant a bronze figure of a Celtic Diana riding on a boar's back ". But there is no surviving trace in Gaul of the pork taboo which prevailed in Scotland. Nor is that surprising. The Continental Celts were, as a matter of fact, breeders of swine and curers of pork, which they ate freely. They exported large quantities of salted pork, smoke-cured hams and flitches and " black puddings ", made of the blood of pigs, to Rome and all parts of Italy. The ancient Irish were similarly pork-eaters. Varro refers to the Celtic hams as *taniaccae* or *tanacae,* and Dr. Sullivan points out that the Gallo-Roman word is almost identical to the old Irish *tineiccas,* the name for smoke-cured hams and flitches.[2] The La Tène settlements of the early Celts on the Continent are usually found to be associated with salt mines. When in the early Iron Age the Celts began to settle in Britain they continued to eat pork. Professor T. H. Bryce of the University of Glasgow in his Rhind lectures in the University of Edinburgh in 1924 referred to five southern Scottish graves dating back till the first century B.C. Near the head of one human skeleton were the jaws and other bones of a young pig. In graves of the same period in the East Riding of Yorkshire the bones of pigs have been found. These and

[1] *Celtic Religion* (London, 1906), p. 30.
[2] Strabo, IV, Chapter 4, § 3, and Sullivan's " Introduction " to O'Curry's *Manners and Customs of the Ancient Irish,* 1873, pp. ccclxix *et seq.*

the Scottish graves link with Gaulish graves in the Department of Marne, France, which have similarly been found to contain pigs' bones and in some cases entire skeletons of boars.

J. F. Campbell in his " Introduction " to his *Popular Tales of the West Highlands* refers to the strong Highland prejudice against pork, but tells, however, that he " once found a boar's tusk in a grave accidentally discovered close to the bridge of Poolewe (Gairloch, Ross and Cromarty) ".

The Scottish pork taboo does not appear to be of early Celtic origin. Nor can it be held to be a survival from the Bronze Age. Professor R. W. Reid of the University of Aberdeen, in an article on the Bronze Age relics of Buchan, Aberdeenshire, referring to the contents of graves, says that " the presence of the bones of a pig in one of the cists shows that this animal . . . may have formed one of their sources of food supply ".[1]

The first instance on record of Celts becoming haters of pork is afforded by Pausanias (VII, 17), who, apparently drawing upon Hieronymus of Cardia (fourth century B.C.), states that the Celtic Galatae, who intruded in Anatolia, ceased, after occupying Pessinus, to eat pork because Attis had been slain by a boar. In other words, they became converts to the cult of Attis and the Great Mother, and adopted its food taboos. The Galatians' acquired prejudice against the pig had an undoubted religious significance.

Now, these Anatolian Celts were much employed as military mercenaries by various kings in the Near

[1] *The Book of Buchan* (Peterhead, 1910), p. 72.

East.¹ The Galatians must have drawn recruits from the western Celtic area, and in this connexion it is interesting to find St. Jerome stating that after a period of about seven centuries the Galatians were able to hold converse with the Gauls. When Alexander the Great was planning a campaign in central and western Europe the envoys who visited him in Babylon included Celts and Iberians, a sure indication that the eastern and western Celts co-operated in various wars as allies and mercenaries. Xenophon refers to Celts being employed by Dionysius of Sicily to assist his Lacedæmonian allies in the Peloponnesian war. Twenty triremes carried Celtic and Iberian mercenaries to Greece.² Pyrrhus and Antigonus, son of Demetrius, both employed Celts in their struggle for supremacy, as Plutarch states in his account of Pyrrhus.

As the Roman soldiers introduced from the Near East the cult of the Persian god Mithra into Italy, central Europe and Britain, so may Celtic warriors, returning to their western homes, have introduced from Galatia the religion of Attis and the Great Mother. Interesting evidence is afforded in this connexion by the silver Gundestrup cauldron found in the dried peat moss of Raevmose in the district of Aalborg, Jutland.³ Figures in repoussé work adorn the various plaques and include not only European but Asiatic flora and fauna. A young god wearing a La Tène helmet may represent a Celticized Attis; the Great

[1] *Justin*, XXV, 2.
[2] *Hellenica*, VII, 1, § 20.
[3] My *Buddhism in Pre-Christian Britain*.

Mother is shown in characteristic pose, but flanked by Indian elephants; and the horned god Cernunnos is associated with the stag and the hyæna. This hyæna was evidently identified with the European wolf, as is suggested by later evidence.

We find traces of the influence of the Cernunnos cult in the *Life of St. Kentigern*. The saint renders fertile a stretch of barren soil in Glasgow by yoking to his plough a stag and a wolf.

The myth of Attis, who was slain by the boar, appears to survive in the Gaelic story of Diarmaid, who met his death in a wild-boar hunt, a bristle having pierced the vulnerable spot upon his heel which he shared with the eastern Achilles. Diarmaid, like other heroes, had evidently a share of floating or imported lore attached to his memory. Probably the elements of the Attis cult, including the pork taboo, were carried to Scotland across the North Sea by Celtic intruders from the Continent.

We find in the Near East, as in Scotland, that there were two very different treatments of the pig. Lucian in his *De Dea Syria* says of the Galli:

"They sacrifice bulls and cows alike and goats and sheep; pigs alone, which they abominate, are neither sacrificed nor eaten. Others look on swine without disgust, but as holy animals."[1]

Sir William M. Ramsay,[2] who reminds us that "history shows a continuous process of religious influence from East to West", has found that in Anatolia the horror of the pig prevails to the east of the river

---

[1] H. A Strong and John Garstang, *The Syrian Goddess* (London, 1913), p. 85.
[2] *Historical Geography of Asia Minor* (London, 1890), pp. 31 *et seq.*

SWINE CULTS

Halys, but not to the west. He considers the sacredness of the pig, as a purificatory sacrifice in the religion of Greece, to be an import from Lydia. In Lycia " we see a pig under the seat of the deified dead on the Harpy Tomb. . . . In Phrygia the custom of sacrificing the pig is proved to have existed by the curious story which Strabo tells of Cleon, the Phrygian robber chief, who was raised by Augustus to the high priesthood of Komana Pontica and who shocked the priests there by sacrificing pigs; it is clear that he was simply carrying out his national habit of sacrifice."

Sir William suggests that the horror of the pig to the east of the Halys was due to the conquest of that part of Asia Minor by the Assyrians, who never actually penetrated west of the Halys. He goes on to say:

"The boundary between the pig-eaters and the pig-haters was not exactly at Halys. In Pessinus, according to Pausanias (VII, 17, 10) the rule of abstinence from the flesh of the pig existed and this abstinence may be taken to imply general horror of the animal and the belief that it caused impurity to every thing and person that touched it. . . .

"Whatever be its origin, the difference between Western Asia Minor and Greece, on the one hand, and Eastern Asia Minor, beginning from Pessinus, on the other, is most striking. In the west the pig is used in the holiest ceremonies; its image accompanies the dead to the graves to purify them and the living wash with their own hands (in Greece at least) the pig which is to be their sacrifice. In the east the very presence of the pig in the holy city is a profanation and an impurity."

Sir William's theory of explanation is that " the religion which prevailed throughout Asia Minor in early time was the religion of the northern race, which had no horror of the pig, and that Semitic influence subsequently introduced that horror into the eastern parts of the country ". He considers that " the detestation of the pig is natural to the hotter countries of the south, where its flesh is unhealthy and hardly eatable food. A northern race does not naturally share this horror."

The existence of the pig taboo in Scotland, therefore, must be due to the influence of an imported faith in early times. The Scottish taboo could scarcely be of independent origin.

The Rev. Walter Gregor records a superstition which may have been originally an imported tradition:

" A mysterious dreaded sort of animal, called ' the yird (earth) swine ', was believed to live in graveyards, burrowing among the dead bodies and devouring them."[1]

In the " hotter countries " referred to by Sir William Ramsay, the pigs were no doubt in the habit of raiding the sandy cemeteries and devouring corpses. This fact may lie at the root of the abhorrence of swine. The Egyptian myth of Set, who had himself a boar form, hunting a boar in the delta area in moonlight and finding and rending into fourteen parts the body of Osiris,[2] may well have been a memory of the swine raids upon graves. Attis and Adonis, who had links with Osiris, were, as stated, slain by boars, and the Gaelic Diarmaid met his death after killing a boar, being wounded by a poisonous bristle while measuring it. In Skye the writer was informed that a fresh wave of prejudice against swine was raised

---

[1] *Folklore of the North-east of Scotland*, p. 130.
[2] Plutarch, *Isis et Osiris*, 8, 18.

by a horrible happening. A pig wandered into a house and killed and partly devoured a baby lying in a cradle. Whether this incident happened or not is uncertain. The story has, however, served to keep alive the tradition of the tendency of the pig to devour human flesh.[1] Much care must have been taken to protect graves in ancient Egypt against the burrowing animal. The custom of building brick and stone tombs may well have originated in the need for preventing cemetery raids by the pig and the hyæna.

There is evidence in Scottish folk-lore of the mixing of traditions regarding the sacred pig and the devil pig.

" The pig," writes the Rev. Walter Gregor, " was regarded as a kind of unclean animal, although its flesh is used . . . Soup made of fresh pork, or ' pork bree ', was looked upon as a sovereign remedy for many diseases—dyspepsia, consumption, &c. . . . It is a very common notion that the pig sees the wind " (suggesting a connexion with the sacred sky-boar which controlled the elements). At the same time the sinister reputation of the pig as an unlucky animal was perpetuated in proverbial sayings. " To signify that an undertaking had failed, there was used," writes Gregor, the proverb, " The swine hiz (has) gane throu it (through it) ", or " The swine has gane throu the kail ".[2]

In the Highlands " swine's blood is held to be a

---

[1] The Rev. Alexander MacGregor (*Highland Superstitions* (Stirling, 1901), pp. 28–9) tells that the pig devoured the baby's arms and face and that the incident took place in the village of Earlish, parish of Snizort, Skye. In Malaya and elsewhere in the East men have been killed and partly devoured by wild pigs.

[2] *Folklore of the North-east of Scotland*, pp. 129, 130.

sovereign cure for warts ",[1] a belief which was probably connected originally with the sacred pig. Another Scottish cure was effected by " south-running water and an unction of hog's lard ".[2]

Irish pig lore accords with the view that the pig was a sacrificial animal and not abhorred. " Magical swine " issued from the cave of Cruachan.[3] In Greece the pig was " specially consecrated to the powers of the lower world " and was " used for the purification of the ploughed field ". The Irish " magical swine " similarly exercised an influence upon crops. At Potinae in Bœotia " . . . a sucking pig was thrown into an underground megaron as an offering to Demeter and Kore ". In Attic Theomorphia women descended to a secret chamber to bring up the decaying remnants of sacrificed pigs and they placed them on altars " mixed with grain " to ensure an " abundant harvest ".[4]

Miss Eleanor Hull,[5] in her article on " The Black Pig of Kiltrustan ", has brought together a great deal of material regarding the pig lore of Ireland and shows that there is evidence to suggest that the pig was anciently " a sacrificial beast ". The Irish " enchanted swine " were invariably " transformed human beings " and their connexion is mainly with " the earliest race of deified beings, Manannan, Lugh, Ler and Angus "; they were " usually slain in Connaught ". There were pigs in the Irish Elysium of Manannan

[1] George Henderson, *Survivals in Belief among the Celts*, p. 175; MacGregor's *Highland Superstitions*, p. 37.
[2] Dalyell's *Darker Superstitions of Scotland*, p. 84.
[3] *Revue Celtique*, Vol. XIII, pp. 426 *et seq.*
[4] Farnell, *Cults of the Greek States*, Vol. III, pp. 32, 45, 64, 66, 90, 221.
[5] *Folklore.*

which " preserved those who partook of them from decay or death ". The " Pig of Truth " could not be cooked " if any falsehood were uttered while it was in the pot ". In Wales the story of the hunt of the enchanted boar *Twrch Trwyth* closely resembles the tales of the Irish hunts of magical swine.[1] An Anatolian hunt of like character is given by Herodotus (I, 35 *et seq.*).

Apart from Scotland the only other European area in which the horror of the pig has survived is northern Arcadia in Greece. There, according to Dr. J. G. Lawson,[2] " the flesh of the pig . . . is taboo, and the result of eating it is believed to be leprosy ", a belief which, as we have seen, obtained in Scotland. Lawson suggests that the Arcadian taboo, the only pork taboo in modern Greece, may be a survival from an ancient cult and he suggests ancient Egyptian influence in this connexion. Herodotus (II, 47, 48) states that the Egyptians regarded the pig as an unclean animal. If a man touched one accidentally he plunged into the Nile to purify himself. Swineherds were forbidden to enter temples. Once a year the pig was sacrificed to Osiris and the moon. In Scotland, as in eastern Anatolia, however, the taboo was not accompanied by an annual sacrifice. But even in Egypt the treatment of the pig was not always uniform. In the " Carnarvon Tablet ", for instance, which deals with the expulsion of the Hyksos by Kamōse, occurs the passage:

" We are at ease holding our (part of) Egypt. . . . Men till

---

[1] A famous Irish pig hunt is given by O'Grady in *Silva Gadelica*, pp. 512–3.
[2] *Modern Greek Folklore and Ancient Greek Religion* (Cambridge, 1910), pp. 87 *et seq.*

for us the finest of their land; our cattle are in the papyrus marshes. Spelt is trodden out (?) for (?) our swine. Our cattle are not taken away." [1]

The Egyptians who believed that the souls rejected by Osiris became pigs, or that evil men returned to earth as pigs, could not have been adherents to the same cult as those which permitted of the domestication of swine and apparently the eating of their flesh. The fusion of cults and the identification of Set with the pig may have ultimately made all the Egyptians sharers in the pork taboo.

[1] *Journal of Egyptian Archæology*, Vol. V, p. 46.

CHAPTER III

Scottish Mouse Feast and More Taboos

Mouse Apollo—Ceremonial mouse feast in Scotland—Mouse brothers and blood covenant—Mouse feasts in Near East—Hebrew mouse and pork feasts—Origin of mouse lore—Mouse and the gods Horus and Apollo—Mouse medicine in pre-dynastic Egypt—Mouse medicine in Scotland and England—Mouse cure for smallpox, whooping cough, chilblains, &c.—Mouse fertilizes apple tree—Mouse stone in Perthshire—Highland fish and fowl taboos—Scottish prejudice against eel—Ancient Britons tabooed hare and goose—Scottish fishers' dread of hare—Witches as hares—Harvest hare in Galloway and Ayrshire—Continental harvest hare—Treatment of hare in England, Ireland, Brittany and Wales.

The pork taboo is not the only relic of a Near East cultural connexion with Scotland. There is evidence of the importation of the cult of the god Apollo Smintheus ("Mouse Apollo"), or "Apollo, Lord of Mice", as Andrew Lang puts it.[1]

In the Irish *Book of Leinster* there is a remarkable account of a ceremonial mouse feast in Alba (Scotland) in connexion with the events which led to the battle of Mag Mucrime.

A Munster ruler named Lugaid Mac-con had been defeated in battle and took flight to Scotland. Lugaid concealed his identity from the king of Alba, to whom he and his band of warriors gave military service,

[1] *Custom and Myth*, p. 103.

which was greatly appreciated. Lugaid feared that Art, High King of Ireland, might ask the Scottish king to put him to death. He therefore forbade his men to mention his name or treat him as their ruler, and the whole band therefore behaved " as if every man of them was a king to the other ".

The king of Scotland came to hear of Lugaid's flight from Munster and strongly suspected the identity of his ally. He wished to help Lugaid, and therefore ordered that a number of mice should be killed and supplied to the Irishmen as food! The *Book of Leinster* story proceeds:

" Then he (the king) puts on the portion of each man of them a mouse, and it red raw, with its hair on. And then their portions are set before them, and they are told that they would be killed unless they ate the mice. . . . Therefore they became very pale. Never had a more grievous annoyance been brought to them."

The king instructed his major-domo to inform the Irishmen that they would be killed unless they ate the mice. The guests were consequently in great distress.

" ' No luck be to him by whom (this) was commanded!' said Lugaid, putting the mouse into his mouth, while the king observed him.

" Thereat all the men put them (into their mouths). There was one unhappy man of them who would vomit when putting the tail of the mouse to his lips.

" ' A sword across thy throat,' said Lugaid. ' The eating of a mouse includes its tail.'

" Then the man swallows the mouse.

"' They[1] do something for thee,' says the king from the door.

"' So do I for them,' says Lugaid.

"' Art thou Lugaid?' asks the king.

"' That is my name,' said Lugaid.

"' Welcome to thee in sooth!' says the king. 'Why hast thou hidden thyself from me?'

"' For fear of thee,' says Lugaid.

"' I would avenge thy sighing up to this day had I known thee.'"

The king of Alba was as good as his word. He raised a strong army and, invading Ireland, won a great victory which brought the overlordship of the whole island to Lugaid.

In this narrative[2] a mouse feast takes the place of the blood covenant which obtained in Ireland, the blood of the parties concerned being dropped into a vat, mixed with new milk and wine and then drunk by the contracting parties.[3] Lugaid and his men became " mouse brothers " to the king of Alba and his subjects.

There is no record of an ancient mouse ceremony of this kind in England or Wales or, indeed, in western Europe. One must, as in dealing with the pork taboo, seek for the source of origin in the Near East, where Apollo Smintheus was adored. Andrew Lang in his *Custom and Myth*[4] would have it that the connexion of the mouse with Apollo, the mouse place-names, the mouse names of individuals and the mouse feasts at

---

[1] The mice.
[2] *Revue Celtique*, Vol. XIII, pp. 426 *et seq*, translation by Whitley Stokes.
[3] *Revue Celtique*, Vol. XIII, p. 75.
[4] Pp. 103-20.

Rhodes, Gela, Lesbos and Crete provide evidence of totemism. He refers to the mouse feast mentioned in *Isaiah* (lxvi, 17):

"They that sanctify themselves and purify themselves in the gardens behind one tree in the midst, eating swine's flesh, and the abomination and the mouse, shall be consumed together saith the Lord."

It will be noted that the pig and mouse are associated in this passage.

The curious lore associated with the mouse and the reputation of that animal as a "life giver" appear to have had origin in ancient Egypt. When in the Nile valley, during the inundation, mice were seen emerging from cracks in the soil, their hind parts covered with mud, it was thought the animals had been created from earth by the combined generative influence of the "new water" and the sun. This belief is referred to by Pliny[1] and Diodorus Siculus (I, 10), the latter remarking that nowhere else in the world can such a wonder be witnessed. There is evidence that the mouse was sacred to the Letopolite Horus, to whom figures of mice were dedicated. This god was usually referred to by the Greeks as Apollo. It may be that the influence of Egypt is to be traced in the mouse lore connected with Apollo Smintheus in Anatolia.

The earliest instances of devouring mice as medicine have been obtained from Egypt. In the pre-dynastic cemetery at Naga ed Dêr in upper Egypt were found many bodies which had been naturally preserved in the

---

[1] *Natural History*, IX, 84.

hot, dry sand. Professor G. Elliot Smith, who dissected a number of them, found " the remains of mice in the alimentary canals of children under circumstances which prove that the small rodent had been eaten after being skinned ". Dr. Netolitzky informed him that the body of a mouse was the last resort of medical practitioners in the East several millennia later as a remedy for children *in extremis*, as it still is in Europe.[1] The writer in his boyhood once saw an elderly Highland woman taking the liver from a newly caught mouse to be given to a child who was supposed to be dying. The cure proved satisfactory, for the child revived and ultimately recovered. Roasted mouse was reputed in Scotland to be a cure for whooping-cough and smallpox.[2] It was also a cure for jaundice. The field-mouse, called " the thraw mouse ", running over the foot of a person, was supposed to produce paralysis of the foot.[3] The writer has heard it stated that if a mouse runs over a sleeping person or domestic animal, the parts traversed become paralysed. " Mouse medicine " is still regarded as a cure for whooping-cough in Gloucestershire, Leicestershire, Norfolk and Suffolk.[4] Mr. Warren R. Dawson gives many instances of the use of mice as medicine in ancient and modern times.[5] In the Beaumont and Fletcher play " The Knight of the Burning Pestle " the wife of the Bell Inn, hearing

[1] G. Elliot Smith, *The Ancient Egyptians* (London, 1923, 2nd edition), p. 50.
[2] A. MacGregor, *Highland Superstitions* (Stirling, 1901), pp. 37-9.
[3] Rev. Walter Gregor, *Folklore of the North-east of Scotland* (London, 1881) p. 127.
[4] E. S. Hartland, *County Folklore—Gloucestershire* (London, 1892), p. 51; C. J. Billson, *County Folklore—Leicestershire and Rutland* (London, 1895), p. 55.
[5] *The Bridle of Pegasus* (London, 1930), pp. 101 *et seq.*

that young Michael is suffering from chilblains, advises Mrs. Merrythought, his mother, to have his feet rubbed with the skin of a newly caught mouse. Mrs. E. Tawse Jollie, Hervetia, S. Melsetter, South Rhodesia, in a letter to the writer tells that Boer women give roasted mouse to children as " a cure for weakness of the bowel ".

In the north of Scotland the writer used to hear old gardeners declare that a mouse should be buried under an apple tree and a cat under a pear tree to ensure good crops of fruit. Professor W. J. Watson informs me that at Fortingal in Perthshire a standing stone is known in Gaelic as that of " my little (or sacred) mouse ". Evidently the Near Eastern mouse cult reached Scotland as well as England, but it is only in Scotland that the ceremonial mouse feast can be traced. In Ireland there are ancient manuscript references to " mouse lords " which were demons.

Other Scottish taboos are those involving fowls and fish. Highlanders were wont to refrain from eating " white flesh " and " feathered flesh ". The Sassenach (Saxon) was despised as an eater of white fish. Elton refers to the view that this prejudice was originally " derived from some ancient colonists from Asia ".[1] Salmon and trout were, however, freely eaten.

During the Great War (1918) the Scottish Freshwater Committee issued a pamphlet entitled " The Common Eel and its Capture; with Suggestions applicable to Scotland ", in which it was set forth that " the prejudice which exists against the eel in Scotland is most unfortunate, since it prevents Scotsmen taking

[1] *Origins of English History* (1882), p. 170.

advantage of a most nutritious fish ". It is mentioned that in the Highlands the mackerel is not eaten, and that on the Solway, until recently, skate was despised as food.

Julius Cæsar found that the ancient Britons tabooed the hare, the domestic fowl and the goose. The hare is still taboo to many Scots.

Mr. J. M. M'Bain testifies as to the prejudice against the hare in parts of Angus. In Arbroath and Auchmithie,

"Nothing would arouse the indignation of a fisher wife more readily than to shout after her, 'there's a hare foot i' yer creel'."

The same writer tells of a sensation aroused among the fisher people by a practical joker who placed a stuffed hare on the bow of a boat drawn up on the beach. It was believed that the demon had sprung out of the earth to fix itself on the bow of the boat and work an evil spell.[1] Farther north a similar prejudice against the hare was shown not only by fishers but by agriculturists. The Rev. Walter Gregor[2] has written in this connexion:

"To say to a fisherwoman that there was a hare's foot in her creel, or to say to a fisherman that there was a hare in his boat, aroused great ire, and called forth strong words. The word 'hare' was not pronounced at sea.

"To have thrown a hare, or any part of a hare, into a boat would have stopped many a fisherman in bygone days from going to sea; and if any misfortune had happened, however long afterwards, it was traced to the hare.

---

[1] J. M. M'Bain, *Arbroath Past and Present* (Arbroath, 1887).
[2] *Folklore of the North-east of Scotland* (London, 1881), pp. 128-9.

"A hare crossing the path portended mishap on the journey. To counteract the evil effects of this untoward event, a cross had to be made upon the path and spat upon.

"Hare lip was produced by a woman *enceinte* putting her foot into a hare's lair. If the woman noticed she had done so, she immediately took two stones and put them into the lair. The evil effects were averted.

"It was accounted very lucky if a hare started from amongst the last cut piece of grain."

Witches were reputed to assume the form of a hare. They also appeared as rats, cats, sheep, whales, cormorants and gulls.[1]

The Rev. Walter Gregor records the widespread belief that in her hare form a witch steals milk from cows. She could not be shot by using a leaden bullet. A "crooked sixpence" had to be used instead. If such a hare crossed a sportsman's path, all his skill was baffled in pursuit of her, and the swiftest dogs were soon left far behind. The hare had the power of rendering herself invisible for a time. If it was shot by a silver missile, the old woman would subsequently be found in bed "panting and bleeding".[2]

In Galloway the last portion of a field of grain was at harvest time referred to as the "hare", and the cutting of it as "cutting the hare". The reapers carried home the pleated stalks called the "hare", which they presented to a maidservant in the farmhouse kitchen, and she fixed it on the inside of the door, where it usually remained until the next harvest.

[1] J. G. Campbell, *Witchcraft and Second Sight* (Glasgow, 1902), pp. 10, 18, 23, 33, 42–4.

[2] Rev. Walter Gregor, *op. cit.*, pp. 128–9; Henderson, *Folklore of the Northern Counties*, pp. 201–4.

The bachelors ran from the field to the farm-house after the " hare " was cut in the parish of Minnigaff, and it was believed that the winner of the race would be the first to get married.[1]

In southern Ayrshire a similar harvest ceremony was formerly observed.[2] The hare was associated with the final harvest operations in various parts of Germany, in Transylvania, Norway, Sweden, Holland, France and Italy.[3]

Dio Cassius (lxii, 3) tells that the British queen Boadicea (Boudicca) before her final battle against the Romans " loosed a hare from her robe, observing its movements as a kind of omen ". When the animal " turned propitiously the whole multitude rejoiced and shouted ".

In Ireland the hare was eaten in ancient times. The kings of Tara claimed the right to be fed on " the hares of Naas ".[4]

The bones of hares have been found associated with relics of the Neolithic industry in England, indicating that the hare was eaten in pre-Celtic times.[5] In western Brittany, on the other hand, the peasants not only tabooed the hare as food, but could not bear to hear mention of the animal.[6]

The Welsh had curious lore regarding the hare. Pennant, in his *Tour through Montgomery*, tells that the

[1] W. Gregor, "Preliminary Report on the Folklore of Galloway, Scotland," in *Report of the British Association* for 1896, p. 623; and Sir J. G. Frazer, *Spirits of the Corn and of the Wild*, Vol. I, p. 279.
[2] *Folklore Journal*, VII (1889), pp. 47 *et seq.*
[3] Sir J. G. Frazer, *op. cit.*, pp. 279–80.
[4] O'Curry, *Manuscript Materials*, Vol. II, p. 141.
[5] Sir William Boyd Dawkins, *Cave Hunting*, p. 217.
[6] *Revue Celtique*, IV, p. 195.

natives refrained from killing hares and referred to them as "St. Monacella's lambs". If a hare was pursued by dogs it was believed that it would escape if anyone cried out "God and St. Monacella be with thee!"

Evidently the taboos referred to by Julius Cæsar have had tardy survival.

CHAPTER IV
The Blue Men of the Minch

The sacred isles—Origin of name—The "annat"—Seal-folk beliefs—Clan Codrum—Seal-folk as "fallen angels"—Hebridean groups of "fallen angels"—Blue Men as weather controllers—Seafarers' beliefs—The "Current of Destruction"—Blue Men as wreckers—How they were thwarted—Sleeping Blue Men—The "beast" or goddess of Loch Etive—Song of the Blue Men—Hebridean grouping of supernatural beings—Blue Men of history—Viking story from Irish annals—Blue Men imported from Morocco—The Blue Sultan and his people—Skin-staining custom—Blue Men marooned in Shiant Isles—Theory of independent origin—Its history—A test of value of tradition—Process of culture blending—Shiants and Iona.

Scottish folklore affords us not only interesting proofs of the reality of the diffusion of myths and legends and of religious practices, but at least one notable instance of the independent origin of a particular group of supernatural beings known as "the Blue Men" (*na Fir Ghorm*). These Blue Men have long been reputed to haunt the Minch and especially the strait between the Long Island and the Shiant (or Shant) Islands (*na h-Eileanan Sianta*), still known to Gaelic speakers as the "Stream of the Blue Men" (*sruth nam Fear Gorm*). The Shiant Isles are "hallowed", "sacred" or "charmed" islands, *seun*, or *sian*, meaning "holy", "charm" or "good luck". In Old Irish the form is *sén*, signifying "blessing", "charm" or "sign"; in Welsh it is *swyn*, "charm", "magic", "preservative". Philologists connect the word with the Latin *signum*, "a sign, especially the sign of the cross".

Professor W. J. Watson says that from *sén* " comes the verb *sénaim*, ' I consecrate, hallow ', with the passive participle *sénta*, now *séanta*, ' consecrated ', ' hallowed ', ' charmed ', often in Scottish Gaelic *sianta*. Examples are *a' Bheinn Sheunta*, ' the sacred peak ', in Jura and in Ardnamurchan; *an Loch Seunta*, ' Holy Loch ', in Cowal; *na h-Eileanan Sianta*, ' the Shiant Isles ', ' the hallowed isles '; *an Uaimh Shianta*, ' the hallowed or sacred cave ', in Applecross. Martin gives a most interesting account of ' Loch Siant Well ', in Skye, the water of which was believed to cure diseases ".[1]

One of the Shiant islands has an " annat " (Gaelic, *annaid*), a name applied to a religious settlement. In Ireland it signified a church of a patron saint or one containing relics of the founder. Professor W. J. Watson [2] is uncertain how far this held with regard to the numerous Scottish " annats " and writes regarding them:

" As a rule they appear to have been places of no particular importance. They are often in places that are now, and must always have been, rather remote and out of the way. It is very rarely indeed that an ' annat ' can be associated with any particular saint, nor have I met any traditions connected with them. But wherever there is an ' annat ' there are traces of an ancient chapel or cemetery, or both; very often, too, the ' annat ' adjoins a fine well or clear stream."

The Shiant Isles would appear to have originally derived their sanctity as " deserts " in which early

---

[1] W. J. Watson, *History of the Celtic Place-Names of Scotland* (1926), pp. 268–9; Alexander Macbain, *An Etymological Dictionary of the Gaelic Language*, pp. 309, 321.

[2] *Op. cit.*, pp. 250 *et seq.*

Christian ascetics lived in solitude. A landing can be effected on the difficult rocky beaches only in certain states of wind and tide. In winter, and even in summer, they are but rarely approachable.

Seals haunt the islands and there are vague Gaelic references to a gigantic seal, " the father of all the seals ", being located there. The " seal-folk " have long been reputed to be human beings under spells, who occasionally appear as men and women divested of their " seal coverings ". They link with the mermaids and even the " swan maidens ". The Mac Codrums of the Outer Hebrides are reputed to be descended from a seal-woman whose " skin covering " had been taken away by an islander. She had to follow this man and he made her his wife. After she had borne children to him, she recovered her " seal covering " and returned to her people in the sea. In Gaelic her descendants are known as *Clann 'ic Codrum nan ròn* (" Clan Codrum of the Seals "). In the north of Scotland the " seal-folk " are in folk-tales reputed to be a section of the " fallen angels ".[1]

The " Blue Men of the Minch " have similarly been included among the fallen angels, but before they were thus accounted for by the early theologians of the Highlands and Islands they had acquired some of the attributes of the " seal-folk ".

These Blue Men were, as sea beings, formerly credited with keeping restless the waters in the immediate vicinity of the Shiants even on peaceful days,

[1] J. Gregorson Campbell, *Superstitions of the Highlands and Islands of Scotland*, p. 284. The belief in seal-folk is more widespread in the north and north-east of Scotland than Mr. Campbell appears to have been aware.

no account being taken of the shallows over banks and the influences of wind and tide. It was only when the Blue Men were asleep in their subaqueous caves, or as they floated on the surface of the sea, that their strait remained calm. Fishermen regarded them as weather controllers. According to folk-beliefs formerly prevalent in north-western Skye, a wild storm was in prospect if they were seen disporting in the sea off the headland of Rudha Hunish. Lewis, Harris and Skye fishermen believed that they followed their boats when, owing to their influence, the weather grew suddenly rough, seizing hold of the helm or keel and smiting the planks in their endeavour to swamp them. They objected particularly to any large vessel passing through their strait and were credited with causing numerous wrecks. The " Blue Men's Stream " was consequently known also as " The Current of Destruction ". In folk-stories it is told that Blue Men sentinels always kept watch for ships, and sailors were so afraid of their fierce enemies of the sea that they preferred, when sailing northward, to pass round the Shiant Isles rather than take the " shorter cut " through the strait.

When the sentinels caught sight of a vessel making for their strait, they informed the chief of the Blue Men, who immediately summoned his followers resting in their caves at the bottom of the sea and around the Shiant Isles. A great horde then assembled to attack the ship. First of all the chief of the Blue Men shouted a challenge in two lines of Gaelic verse. If the skipper could not reply in a pointed couplet, his vessel was seized and wrecked.

" True, indeed," runs one folk-tale, " is the saying, ' There comes with time what comes not with weather '." One day, when the wind was high and the sea somewhat rough, a big and stately ship with white sails came briskly towards the southern entrance of the strait. Royally she ploughed her way through the billows. The Blue Men sentinels gave warning to their chief, and soon his followers rose from the depths, but they wondered greatly that the ship was so swift and strong. Many of them grasped the keel, but marvelled to find it steady and heavy as it sped on swiftly like a spear in flight. In vain they smote the sides of the vessel; the thick, smooth planks resisted their attacks.

The chief of the Blue Men reared himself waist high among the billows and shouted couplets to the skipper, who was, however, skilled in verse and made quick and apt responses. The following are free renderings from Gaelic of this poetic competition:

Blue Chief. Man of the black cap, what do you say
　　　　　　As your proud ship cleaves the brine?
Skipper. My speedy ship takes the shortest way
　　　　　　And I'll follow you line by line.
Blue Chief. My men are eager, my men are ready
　　　　　　To drag you below the waves.
Skipper. My ship is speedy, my ship is steady.
　　　　　　If it sank it would wreck your caves.

Outwitted and defied, the chief of the Blue Men sank below the waves. Never before had he been answered so promptly and so well. He could not cast a spell over the ship and his men were unable to injure it or divert it from its course. The Blue Men all retreated to their caves and the big ship passed proudly through the strait, its snow-white sails swallowing the wind.

A folk-tale summarized by the Rev. John Gregorson Campbell, Tiree, tells that a ship passing through the strait came upon one of the Blue Men sleeping on the surface of the sea.

" He was taken on board and, being thought of mortal race, strong twine was coiled round and round him from his feet to his shoulders, till it seemed impossible for him to struggle, or move foot or arm. The ship had not gone far when two men (Blue Men) were observed coming after it on the waters. One of them was heard to say, ' Duncan will be one man,' to which the other replied, ' Farquhar will be two.' On hearing this, the man who had been so securely tied sprang to his feet, broke his bonds like spider threads, jumped overboard and made off with the two friends who had been coming to his rescue." [1]

The writer first heard of the Blue Men of the Minch from an old Hebridean sailor when crossing Connel Ferry, Loch Etive, some years before the railway bridge was erected. The Falls of Lora were beginning to roar and the swift tide, which taxed the skill of the ferryman, was credited by him to the influence of the " beast " of Loch Etive.[2] The sailor then told about the Blue Men and the writer subsequently rendered in the following verses the folk-beliefs regarding them:

[1] J. G. Campbell, *Superstitions of the Scottish Highlands*, p. 200.

[2] Professor W. J. Watson shows in his *History of the Celtic Place-Names of Scotland*, p. 46, that Etive is a rendering of a feminine proper name meaning " foul one ". She was " the goddess of the loch and river ", and is also referred to as *Éiteag*, " the little horrid one ".

When the tide is at the turning and the wind is fast asleep,
And not a wave is curling on the wide, blue deep,
Oh, the waters will be churning in the stream that never smiles,
Where the Blue Men are splashing round the Shiant [1] Isles!

As the summer wind goes droning o'er the sun-bright seas,
And the Minch is all a-dazzle to the Hebrides,
They will skim along like salmon—you can see their shoulders gleam,
And the flashing of their fingers in the Blue Men's stream.

But when the blast is raving and the wild tide races,
The Blue Men are breast-high with foam-grey faces;
They'll plunge along with fury while they sweep the spray behind,
Oh, they'll bellow o'er the billows and wail upon the wind!

And if my boat be storm-tossed and beating for the bay,
They'll be howling and be growling as they drench it with their spray;—
For they'd like to heel it over to their laughter when it lists,
Or crack the keel between them, or stave it with their fists.

Oh, weary on the Blue Men, their anger and their wiles!
The whole day long, the whole night long, they're splashing round the isles;
They'll follow every fisher—ah! they'll haunt the fisher's dream—
When billows toss, oh! who would cross the Blue Men's stream?

The Blue Men of folk-lore were, by theorizing Gaelic theologians who believed in their existence, included, as stated, in the group of fallen angels driven

[1] Pronounced shee′ănt.

out of Paradise. Another division was formed by the fairies and a third by the Aurora Borealis, or "Merry Dancers", known in Gaelic as *na fir chlis* ("quick, active" or "nimble men"). The Rev. J. Gregorson Campbell says that "this explanation belongs to the north Hebrides" and was heard by him in Skye. "In Argyllshire," he adds, "the Blue Men are unknown and there is no mention of the 'Merry Dancers' being congeners of the Fairies."

The Blue Men and associated beliefs are confined to a limited area in the Minch. They are not found elsewhere in Scotland, or, indeed, in any other part of the world. We must therefore, as indicated, regard them as being of independent origin. It does not follow, however, that they were of spontaneous creation and devoid of a history—mere products of "folk imagination". I have found it possible to provide proof that there is a historical basis for the Blue Men beliefs, and to show that these are of much interest in connexion with the study of tradition.

In the *Annals of Ireland*, by Duald mac Firbis, there is an account of a Viking expedition and the importation of Blue Men into Ireland as prisoners of war. These *Annals*, it may be explained, date from the sixth till the early part of the tenth century. Some fragments were copied from writings that no longer exist; others were apparently drawn from oral tradition, like the Icelandic sagas. An interesting fact is that the word "blue" is applied to the Moors in Norse as well as in the Gaelic narrative by Duald mac Firbis.

The *Annals of Ireland*, by Duald mac Firbis (Dubhaltach mac Firbisigh), were edited and translated by

J. O'Donovan in the *Proceedings* of the Archæological and Celtic Society (Dublin, 1860), the corrected dates being taken from the *Annals of Ulster*, the most reliable of the ancient Irish chronicles. There are extracts in Skene's *Picts and Scots* (pp. 401–7) and in A. O. Anderson's *Early Sources of Scottish History*, A.D. *500 to 1286* (Edinburgh, 1922), Vol. I, pp. 293–4.

Dr. Anderson dates the Blue Men narrative of mac Firbis about the year 864, accepting the usual Norse chronology, which begins the reign of Harold Fairhair between 860 and 864. A new chronology, however, brings the dating down to 875–80. Harold appears to have been selected as king when a boy of about only ten by the Norse nobles, who were pursuing the policy of suppressing rival chiefs in Norway and resisting the encroachments of Sweden.

When Harold began to reign " Swedish merchant princes ", as Mr. Kendrick relates, " were established along the waterways leading to the Arabic East and to Constantinople ". Norway was involved in " the bitter piratical warfare waged by neighbour upon neighbour ".[1]

Duald mac Firbis tells that when there was " all manner of war and strife " in Lochlann (here Norway), Ronald, eldest son of Halfdan, had been expelled by two young brothers [2] " for fear lest he should take the kingdom of Lochlann after their father ". Ronald fled to Orkney with his three sons, and the two elder sons collected a great host " from every quarter " and set out on a Viking expedition against the French and

[1] T. D. Kendrick, *A History of the Vikings* (1930), pp. 108–10.
[2] Half brothers.

Saxons. They assumed that their father would return to Lochlann.

The brothers eventually reached Spain, and while plundering in that country " did many evils ". They ultimately reached the Gaditanean Strait (Gibraltar) and crossed to the African coast. There they gave battle to the Moors and made a " great slaughter ". One of Ronald's sons remarked to his brother that it seemed foolish and reckless to be waging war " throughout the world " instead of doing their father's will by winning their own ancestral land in Lochlann. He had dreamed that his younger brother fell in a battle from which his father escaped with difficulty—which the annalist tells was in fact fulfilled.

This son reached the king of the Moors in the battle and cut off one of his hands. Both sides fought hard, but neither achieved victory.

Next day the Scandinavians advanced to renew the struggle, but the Moors, discovering that their king had deserted them during the night, broke in flight " after great slaughter had been made of them ".

The narrative concludes:

" After that the Scandinavians went through the country and ravaged it; and they burned the whole land; and they brought a great host of [the Moors] in captivity with them to Ireland. These were the ' blue men ' [*fir gorma*], because Moors are the same as negroes; Mauritania is the same as negro-land [literally, ' the same as blackness ']. Scarcely did every third man of the Scandinavians escape, what with those that were killed and those of them that were drowned in the Gaditanean Straits.

" Long were these Blue Men in Ireland." [1]

---

[1] Dr. Anderson's translation.

The Blue Men are still represented to the south of Morocco and are ruled over by a despot known as the "Blue Sultan". French airmen who have had the misfortune to effect forced landings in their country tell of the Blue Men's antipathy to Europeans, whom they treat as slaves and spare only to secure ransoms. The habit still prevails among them of staining their skins blue, and, according to the Frenchmen and Spaniards who have come into contact with them, a woman will not marry a man until he is coloured to the finger tips. They are quite distinct from the "veiled Tuaregs" of the Sahara, but, like them, perpetuate immemorial habits of life and thought. In the Viking Age they overran a great part of Morocco and even invaded Spain.[1] It was apparently with these Blue Men that the Viking brothers referred to by Duald mac Firbis were in conflict.

The aliens appear to have been utilized by the pirates of the Viking Age, and their association with the Shiant Isles suggests that some of them were wintered there. In the lore regarding Blue Men swimming out from the islands and attempting to capture sailing vessels, we appear to have memories of the marooned foreign slaves who must have inspired general alarm. Their association with the strait which still bears their name is an interesting example of the persistence of tradition, although it is the only record of their transference to the Minch area.

As supernatural beings the Hebridean Blue Men afford, as has been indicated, an interesting instance

---

[1] D. B. Wyndham Lewis in the *New York Herald Tribune Magazine*, January, 17th, 1932, deals at length with the Blue Sultan and his blue-stained subjects.

of the independent origin of distinctive beliefs in a circumscribed area. It is of interest, therefore, to consider them from this particular viewpoint.

The theory of independent origin was first urged in connexion with the study of Scottish folk-lore by Hugh Miller, the geologist and anthropologist. He applied it when dealing with the myths, traditions and legends of Cromarty and district, and after a cursory and inexpert examination of flints and stone axes in a museum in Inverness, writing:

"The most practised eye can hardly distinguish between the weapons of the old Scot and the New Zealander.... Man in the savage state is the same animal everywhere, and his constructive powers, whether employed in the formation of a legendary story or of a battleaxe, seem to expatiate everywhere in the same rugged track of invention. For even the traditions of this first stage may be identified, like its weapons of war, all the world over."

So theorized the Cromarty scientist[1] a century ago as a disciple of Dr. William Robertson (1721–93), principal of the University of Edinburgh, who in his *The History of America* [2] wrote:

"Were we to trace back the ideas of other nations to that rude state in which history first presents them to our view, we should discover a surprising resemblance in their tenets and practices; and should be convinced that, in similar circumstances, the faculties of the human mind hold nearly the same course in their progress and arrive at almost the same conclusions."

[1] *Scenes and Legends* (1st edition, 1835), pp. 31–2; my *Ancient Man in Britain* (1922), pp. 11–2; and my *Myths of Pre-Columbian America* (1923), pp. 39–43. Professor G. Elliot Smith, *The Diffusion of Culture* (1933), discusses the matter at fuller length.
[2] Book IV, § 7.

E. B. Tylor and Andrew Lang so popularized this doctrine that in *The Golden Bough* Sir James G. Frazer contended that " recent researches into the early history of man have revealed the essential similarity with which, under many superficial differences, the human mind has elaborated its first crude philosophy of life ".[1]

According to the doctrine of independent origin, or spontaneous generation, the Blue Men beliefs should have become manifest in all areas in which the mind of man had reached a similar stage of development. There should be groups of supernatural Blue Men in various coastland areas of Scotland, Wales, Ireland, Brittany and other parts of Europe, Asia, &c. What we really do find is that the independent origin of the Blue Men as supernatural beings has been confined to a very restricted area in the Outer Hebrides. The mind of man elsewhere failed to follow " the same rugged track of invention " and to invent Blue Men!

Another phase of the problem is presented by the fact that the Hebridean Blue Men had human prototypes. It would be rash to assume in this connexion, however, that all other supernatural beings, including the fairies and the giants, have had a similar family history.

We cannot help citing the Blue Men evidence as proof of the reality of the persistence in tradition of certain historical elements. But here again caution is necessary and it must not be assumed that the case for tradition is proved. In the absence of the evidence afforded by Duald mac Firbis, it would be impossible

[1] *The Golden Bough* (*The Magic Art*), Vol. I, p. 10 (3rd edition).

to account for the Blue Men of the Minch. The mystery of their origin would have remained and no light could have been thrown upon the process by which in this particular case, and in it alone, human beings became transformed into supernatural beings and made partakers of the attributes of the seal-folk, so that they were ultimately grouped with the fairies and the spirits of the Aurora Borealis and regarded as " fallen angels ". The process appears to have been one of culture blending. Pagan supernatural seal-folk were confused with human beings, and ultimately the superstitions were tinged with Christianity.

It was not because of their connexion with the Blue Men that the Shiant Isles were regarded as " sacred ", " holy " or " charmed ". That reputation came from their association with Christian hermits, as has been indicated. At the same time, it may be that before the islands were occupied by these devout men there was a connexion with pagan practices. Iona, which St. Columba selected for his monastery, had previously been the centre of a Yew cult, and its name appears to have been derived from *Ivova*, " Yew-place ", the place of a Yew divinity.[1]

There are classical references to desolate islands being regarded by Celtic peoples as habitations of demons or deities and their priestesses and of sacrifices being offered in them.[2]

---

[1] W. J. Watson, *History of the Celtic Place-Names of Scotland*, pp. 87 *et seq.*

[2] Mela, *Chorogr.*, III, 6, 48; Strabo, IV, 4, 6; Plutarch, *Moralia: De defectu oraculorum*, XVIII.

CHAPTER V

Giant Lore of Scotland

Fomorian giants on hills—Fomorians of sea and islands—Everlasting combats of giants—Boulders and other missiles—Story of female Fomorian—Gargantuan jesting—Stories connected with boulders—Ben Ledi giant renamed Samson—Fife giant as Devil—Devil's stone at Dundee—Giants called after famous heroes—Giant of Arthur's Seat, Edinburgh—Arthurian giants in northern England and in Wales—Scottish Arthurian place-names—Sleeping giants—Giants as Fians—Thomas the Rhymer as a giant—Inverness and other sleepers—Giants as family gods—Giants' vulnerable moles—Morven giant story—Banffshire giant story—Ciutach giant lore—Whale-fishing giants—English giants—" Long Meg "—Giant figures—Manx, Welsh and Irish giants—Fomorians originally pirates—Original name of giants lost.

Throughout Scotland there are a number of hills which, by reason of their situations rather than heights, might be referred to as positions of strategic importance. All of them command wide prospects, and from each another hill, or two hills of like character, may be visible. They have all distinctive names with folk-lore associations, and a number have archæological relics or are remembered as beacon hills. Some are referred to as " seats " or " chairs " of giants, or of heroes or saints who supplanted giants, and are connected in folk-tales with megaliths, or ice-carried boulders, supposed to be flung by giants.

As stated, these giants are in Gaelic referred to as the *Famhairean* (" Fomorians "). In the Gaelic Bible, *Genesis*, vi, 4 is rendered: *Bha famhairean air an talamh 'sna laithibh sin*, &c. ("There were giants on the earth in these days, &c.").[1]

The Fomorians of Scotland occupy not only hills, but caves among the mountains, while some come from the sea and others have strongholds in islands. As a rule hill giants are grouped in pairs, being rivals occupying opposing heights which may be only a mile distant, or from five to twenty miles or more, and separated by an inland loch or an arm of the sea. The opponents engage in the " Everlasting Battle ". Each giant takes his turn at throwing a boulder at his rival with purpose to strike and injure him. A throws the boulder at B to-day, and B throws it back to-morrow. The boulder is sometimes referred to as a " quoit ", and in the folk-tales it may sometimes be substituted by a stone hammer, a battle-axe or some other ancient or modern weapon. An Orkney giant flings a poker, but a Rousay giant flings a boulder to Westray.

The opposing headlands at Munlochy Bay in Ross and Cromarty are occupied by rival Fomorians who fling a battle-axe. A local folk-story tells that giant A had been severely wounded by the battle-axe and on the following morning was so weak from loss of blood that he was unable to fling back the battle-axe when B, his rival, appeared. His wife said, " I shall fling it myself against the boaster." She donned her husband's attire and took his place on the summit of the eminence. Then she flung the battle-axe across the bay. " Her aim was as true as her strength was great ", and the

---

[1] See also *Deut.*, ii, 10; *Numbers*, xiii, 33; II *Samuel*, xxi, 16; and I *Chronicles*, xx, 4. In I *Samuel*, xvii, Goliath is, however, referred to as a *curaidh* (a hero, champion or warrior).

axe " struck and stuck in the forehead of the giant ".

The giantess was well pleased and cried across the water, " That will keep you quiet for one day at any rate."

Hugh Miller [1] refers to the giant lore of the same county:

" There is a large and very ponderous stone in the parish of Edderton which a giantess of the tribe is said to have flung from the point of a spindle across the Dornoch Firth; and another within a few miles of Dingwall, still larger and more ponderous, which was thrown from a neighbouring eminence by a person of the same family, and which still bears the marks of a gigantic finger and thumb on two of its sides."

The eminence in question is that of Knockfarrel, Strathpeffer, on the summit of which is a vitrified fort.

A boulder at Glenmorangie, near Tain, is reputed to be a " bad throw " by a giant of a hill near Edderton. He had been married on the previous evening and feasted and drank so freely that he suffered loss of strength. His boulder was intended to strike a giant above Tain, but fell half way. Another giant, who dwelt in Kintail, Wester Ross, flung a boulder at a giant above Portree, Skye, but it did not reach him, falling near the village.

Hugh Miller tells of the giants of the two headlands (the Sutors) at the mouth of the Cromarty Firth. " The promontories of Cromarty," he writes, " served as work-stools to two giants of this tribe, who supplied their brethren with shoes and buskins. They wrought together; for, being furnished with only one set of implements, they could not carry on their trade apart;

[1] *Scenes and Legends,* Chapter I.

and they used to fling these to each other across the opening of the firth where the promontories are only about two miles apart." In my boyhood I heard that only the awl was flung across from one giant to the other.

Two boulders lying on the beach near Cromarty were reputed to have been flung by the giant on the hill of Struie (called Gilltrax[1] in Cromarty) in the parish of Edderton.

There are giants on three hills near Inverness, known as Torvean, Dunain and Craig Phadrick. They are said to throw a stone hammer from one to the other each morning. There is a vitrified fort on the summit of Craig Phadrick.

A boulder-flinging giant occupies Dun-Fhamhair (Fomorian's Hill) at Kilmorack, overlooking Beauly. Two famous Fomorians face each other on eminences on opposite sides of Loch Ness. The southern giant, according to a local folk-tale, became angered against the northern giant on Dùn Binniligh, Abriachan, and hurled a huge black boulder at him. The northern giant retaliated by flinging a huge white boulder. These boulders are still pointed out.

There are other boulder-flinging giants in Nairnshire, Morayshire, Banffshire, Aberdeenshire, Kincardineshire, Angus, Fife, Perthshire and the Lothians, and also along the western coast of Scotland.

A folk-story tells that the strongest giant in all Scotland is on Ben Ledi, near Callander. He challenged all the Scottish Fomorians to a trial of strength at

---

[1] The Gaulish form of this old place-name suggests that it was Pictish. Cromarty people tell that the sun sets behind Gilltrax when it has reached its farthest-north point. Fishermen used to regard the hill with some degree of reverence.

" putting the stone " and was the winner in the contest. A large boulder called " Samson's putting-stone " lies on the lower eastern slope of the Ben, and is said to have been flung from the summit by " Samson ". Not far from the stone is a hill fort.

Many of the giants are referred to simply as Fomorians, but some have been given personal names or are referred to as devils.[1] The Ben Ledi giant evidently acquired his name after the introduction of Christianity, having been compared to Samson. The giant of Norman's Law in Fife is the " devil ". He hurled a boulder across the Tay against the giant of Law Hill, Dundee, but it fell short. This boulder is known as the " de'il's (devil's) stane ", and is protected at Dundee by an iron railing. The giant of Eildon Hills in the east Lowlands has been named Wallace, after Scotland's hero of the War of Independence, and there is another Wallace giant at Easdale, a few miles distant from Oban. Alexander Stewart, son of King Robert II of Scotland, remembered as the " Wolf of Badenoch ", is a giant in Moray folk-lore. The Patrick giant at Inverness acquired his name from St. Patrick, Ireland's patron saint, who was probably a native of Strathclyde, and whose fame was celebrated by the missionaries of the Columban church. A Black Island giant is " Rory ". A giant on Arthur's Seat, Edinburgh, acquired the name of King Arthur after the Arthurian romances were popularized in the Edinburgh area. Some of the old maps give the place-name as " Arthur's Chair ". It is evidently not a name of great antiquity. Chalmers in his *Caledonia* remarks that " a late enquirer "

[1] The Gaelic word *samh* means both god and giant.

declared it " a name of yesterday ", but he notes that Arthur's Seat " had that distinguished name before the publication of Camden's *Britannia* in 1585, as we may see in page 478; and before the publication of Major in 1521, as appears in folio 28; Kennedy in his flyting with Dunbar mentions ' Arthur Sate, or ony hicher (higher) hill '."[1] Arthurian tales were current in Scotland in the fourteenth and fifteenth centuries. Sir David Lindsay (1490–1555) in his " The Dreme " tells that he entertained the young king (James V) " with antique storeis and deidis martiall " of

> Hector, Arthur and gentile Julius,
> Of Alexander, and worthy Pompeius.

The late John Stuart Glennie, who attempted to prove that Arthur was a Scottish king, notes in his *Arthurian Localities* (p. 67) that in the west of Northumberland there is an " Arthur's Chair ". It is one of the " Sewing Shields Crags ", another being the chair, or crag, of the queen. According to the local folk-tale, King Arthur and Queen Guinevere had a domestic quarrel.

"To settle the matter, the king, sitting on a rock called Arthur's Chair, threw at the queen an immense boulder which, falling somewhat short of its aim, is still to be seen on this side of the Queen's Crags. And on the horizon of the immense sheep farm of Sewing Shields, and beyond an outlying shepherd's hut very appropriately named ' Cold Knuckles ', is a great stone called ' Cumming's Cross ', to which there is attached another rude Arthurian tradition."

Another " Arthur's Seat " is in Cumberland.[2]

---
[1] *Caledonia*, Vol. I, p. 245.
[2] *Ibid.*, p. 68.

Welsh giants were similarly displaced by Arthurian heroes.

Glennie in his *Arthurian Localities* refers to " the famous cromlech called ' Arthur's Stone ' " in south Wales; it is situated " near the turnpike road from Reynoldstone to Swansea, on the north slope of Cefn Bryn ". " Arthur's Chair " is the name applied to the twin peaks of the Beacons, five miles south of Brecon, on the Usk. " Arthur's Table " is a cromlech on an eminence adjoining the park of Mocras in Brecknockshire. " Arthur's Table " is a name attached to the remains of a Roman amphitheatre upon the Usk. Merlin's Hill and Grove are four miles south of Caermarthen. A stone called " Maen Arthur " near Colomendy Lodge in Flintshire is said to bear an impression of the hoof of Arthur's steed. Near Denby twenty-four holes cut out of the rock were called the Round Table. Still another Round Table, an old camp, overlooks Redwharf Bay. A rocking-stone in Anglesey, in the grounds of Llwydiarth, is called " Arthur's Quoit ". The grave of Vortigern is Nant Gwrtheryn on the south of Caernarvon Bay. Cadbury Hill in Somersetshire is supposed to be a Round Table site. A little entrenchment near Camelford in Cornwall is " Arthur's Hall ", and " between Camelford and Launceston, on Wilsey Downs, is Warbelow Barrow, an ancient fortification of considerable size, in the centre of which is a large mound popularly called " King Arthur's Grave ". An " Arthur's Stone " lies between Camelford and Tintagel. " King Arthur's Bed " is a group of rocky tors some miles north of Liskeard.

Professor W. J. Watson[1] writes:

"The best-known 'Arthurian locality' is Arthur's Seat, Edinburgh. North of the Wall (of Hadrian) on the west are *Suidhe Artair*, Arthur's Seat, Dumbarton, on the right bank of the Leven; *Beinn Artair* (the Cobbler), at the head of Loch Long; *Aghaidh Artair*, 'Arthur's Face', a rock on the west side of Glenkinglas, in the same district, with the likeness of a man's profile; *Sruth Artair*, Struarthour, in Glassary, Argyll. In the east there are Arthur-stone near Cupar Angus; Arthouriscairne, apparently on the south side of Bennachie, Aberdeenshire; Arthur-seat in Aberdeenshire; and *Suidhe Artair*, Suiarthour, now *Suidhe*, in Glenlivet, Banffshire. There is, or rather was, also Arthur's Oven, in 1293 *Furnus Arthuri*, described in 1723 as between the house of Stenhouse (Larbert) and the water of Carron, 'an old building in form of a sugar loaf, built without lime or any other mortar'."

Other Arthurian names in Scotland suggest the influence of the metrical romances. " Ganore's Grave " is at Meigle in Perthshire, Ganore being a rendering of Guinevere. At Stirling is the " Tabyll Round ", referred to by Sir David Lindsay and still earlier by Barbour, who in his *The Bruce* calls it " the Rownde Tabill " (Book XIII, line 379). " Merlin's Grave " is a cairn on the Tweed. In the parish of Crawford, Lanarkshire, there is a well called " Arthur's Fountain ".

There are sleeping giants under various hills in Scotland. Those under Arthur's Seat, Edinburgh, are Arthur and his knights. In northern Scotland the sleeping giants have been named after the Gaelic hero Fionn,[2] folk-tales regarding whom were imported from

---

[1] *History of the Celtic Place-Names of Scotland*, pp. 208–9.
[2] Pronounced *fewn*.

Ireland. Both Arthur and Fionn have, however, been displaced by the later hero, Thomas the Rhymer, whose fame was spread by chap-books as far north as Cromarty.

The chief sleeping giant under Eildon Hills has been named Thomas the Rhymer, and Thomas sleeps also under Dunbuck Hill, near Dumbarton. "The last person that entered that hill found him resting on his elbow, with his hand below his head." Thomas asked, "Is it time?" and the man fled. The sleeping giants in Tomnahurich Hill, Inverness, are sometimes referred to as Fionn and his men and sometimes as Thomas the Rhymer and his company. Mac Codrum, the Uist bard, says in one of his poems:

> *Dar thigedh sluagh Tom na h-iubhraich*
> *Co dh' eireadh air tùs ach Tòmas?*

"When the hosts of Tomnahurich come, who should rise first but Thomas?"

Fionn and his men are the sleepers in the cave of Craigiehow,[1] near Munlochy, in the Black Isle and in the Smith's Rock in Skye. All these sleepers are supposed to be awaiting for the day of a great battle. In their cave is a whistle or horn, and when it is blown three times the heroes will come forth. Folk-stories tell of men who have blown the whistle or horn twice. The first sound caused the sleepers to open their eyes and shake themselves; the second made them rise, resting on their elbows. The visitor is afraid to blow a third blast, being terrified by the ferocious appearance of the warrior. As he retreats the chief giant calls

---

[1] In Gaelic *creag a' chobh* ("rock of the cave").

after him, " Wretched mischief-maker, you have left us worse than you found us ".[1]

Sir Walter Scott gives the version of the sleeping giants myth connected with the Lucken-hare hillock upon Eildon Hills. Thomas the Rhymer conducted a horse-dealer into an underground stable where armed warriors were seen sleeping beside their chargers. " All these men," said the wizard, " will awaken at the battle of Sheriffmuir." A sword and a horn hung on the wall at the end of the underground cavern. These were to be used to dissolve the spell.

" The man in confusion took the horn and attempted to wind it. The horses instantly started in their stalls, stamped and shook their bridles, the men arose and clashed their armour, and the mortal, terrified by the tumult he had excited, dropped the horn from his hand. A voice like that of a giant, louder even than the tumult around, pronounced these words:

Woe to the coward that ever he was born,
That did not draw the sword before he blew the horn.

A whirlwind expelled the horse-dealer from the cavern, the entrance to which he could never again find." [2]

Similar sleepers are found in Wales, Ireland, Scandinavia, Germany and eastward to Ephesus and Arabia. In the Arabian and Scottish stories a dog is associated with the sleepers. Among the sleepers in India are the five Indras.[3]

---

[1] J. G. Campbell, *Superstitions of the Scottish Highlands*, pp. 270 et seq.; J. MacDougall in *Waifs and Strays of Celtic Tradition* (Argyllshire Series No. III), pp. 73 *et seq.*; my *Finn and His Warrior Band*, pp. 245 *et seq.*, and my *Teutonic Myth and Legend*, pp. xliv *et seq.*

[2] *Letters on Demonology and Witchcraft* (London, 1831 edition), p. 133 (Letter IV).

[3] My *Myths of Babylonia and Assyria*, p. 101.

Some Scottish Fomorians were connected with families, as if originally family gods or goddesses. One at Gortlich, in Inverness-shire, was supposed to scream when a Fraser chief was about to die. His hill was pointed out to the writer by an elderly native. Sir Walter Scott mentions " that species of spirits to whom, in the Highlands, is ascribed the guardianship, or superintendence, of a particular clan, or family of distinction . . . Thus in a MS. history of Moray we are informed that the family of Gurlinbeg is haunted by a spirit called *Garlin Bodacher*; that of the Baron of Kinchardin by *Lamhdearg*, or ' Red-hand ', a spectre, one of whose hands is as red as blood; that of Tullochgorum by *Mag Moulach*, a female figure whose left hand and arm were covered with hair . . . a familiar attendant upon Clan Grant. These superstitions were so ingrafted in the popular creed that the clerical synods and presbyteries were wont to take cognizance of them."[1]

There are folk-stories of giants who are invulnerable to human attack unless wounded on a particular spot marked by a mole.

A Morvern giant of this type is described in a ceilidh story, taken down by the writer in Argyll, as follows:

" He was tall as an oak tree and very strong; his hands were so large that he could snatch up a bullock in one of them and make his fingers meet round the middle of it. There was not a giant in Mull who was a match for him, and two of them he killed with great boulders which he threw across the Sound.

[1] *Minstrelsy of the Scottish Border*, Introduction (1907 edition), Vol. I, pp. 208-9.

He used to sit on a hilltop with a great fishing rod made by stripping the branches from a tree. The line was a long rope he had stolen from fishermen in Ardnamurchan and he had for a hook the anchor of a large ship. The giant used to catch whales and it was a great sight to see him pulling one after another out of the water and throwing them on the beach!"

The giant one day thrust his great hand down a chimney of the castle of the king of Ardnamurchan and stole a pot of gold. He was chased as he went eastward to go round the end of Loch Sunart. The bravest of the king's men crossed the loch in a boat to intercept him as he came westward towards the eminence at Lon More (big meadow), the Morvern hill on which he dwelt. The giant flung a boulder at the boat and it caused the waters of the loch " to heave as if a storm were raging ". The men rowed hard and they landed on the other side as the giant was climbing the hill. As he drew near the summit he looked round. The king's champion archer bent his bow and shot an arrow which pierced a mole on the giant's forehead and immediately the monster fell down dead. The warriors cut off his head and rolled it down the hill to the shore, and they recovered the pot of gold. The champion archer was given the king's daughter as his wife, and when the king died he became the ruler.

W. Grant Stewart[1] records a folk-tale of a giant who had a mole over his heart. This giant, referred to as a " ghost ", lived in the wilds of Craig-Aulnaic, a romantic place in the district of Strathdown, Banff-

---

[1] *The Popular Superstitions and Festive Amusements of the Highlanders of Scotland* (Edinburgh, 1823), pp. 6 *et seq.*

shire. There was also a giantess. Stewart gives the name of the male as *Fhua Mhoir Bein Baynac*—his rendering of *Famhair* (giant) of the ben; and the name of the female as *Clashnichd Aulnaic*, evidently the *Glaistig* of Craig-Aulnaic.

The giant ill-treats the female nightly and her shrieks disturbed those who dwelt in the neighbourhood. The greatest sufferer was " James *Owre* (*odhar*) or Gray, the tenant of the farm of Balbig of Delnabo ". He and his family continually complained of the " cries and lamentations of the ' Clashnichd '."

One day Gray met this female and she told him that the giant had expelled her from her dwelling and beaten her severely. He followed her " for the purpose of inflicting on her person every degrading torment which his brain could invent ". She also told Gray that " Ben-Baynac was wholly invulnerable to all the weapons of man, with the exception of a large mole on his left breast ".

One moonlight night she came to Gray's house and induced him to go against the giant. He consented, and she carried him on her ample shoulders. When they reached the giant's dwelling " he came forth to meet them with looks and gestures which did not at all indicate a cordial welcome ".

Gray shot an arrow from his bow and pierced the mole, " large as a common bonnet ", on the giant's breast. The giant yelled and then " evanished into air ". The " Clashnichd " was so grateful that she " vowed to devote the whole of her time and talents towards his service and prosperity ". He set her to collect a herd of deer, saying they were his horses.

Then he returned home. Soon afterwards the " Clashnichd " entered to say that she had placed the " horses " in Gray's stable, but had found them unruly. " They shall be tame enough to-morrow," Gray remarked.

The writer heard from a Moray shepherd another version of this folk-tale. Two Fomorians occupied opposing eminences, and the dark one stole the bride of the other. He had a red mole over his heart and was mortally wounded by the wronged Fomorian, for, although " the dark fellow " could render himself invisible, the red mole remained.

Scotland imported from Ireland stories about Fionn (Finn, called " Fingal " by Macpherson) and his warrior band of Fians, or Fianna (Fenians). But in doing so the natives mixed the tales with their own lore. All the Fians became Fomorians, or giants, and acquired the characteristics of these Fomorians. They were thus transformed, as were Arthur of the romances, Samson, Wallace and the devil, into boulder-throwing giants.

In the Outer Hebrides a famous giant is known as the *Ciuthach* (pronounced " Kewach "). " At the present day in Lewis," writes Professor W. J. Watson,[1] " one expresses admiration of a young fellow's vigour (*tapachd*) by the expression *Bu tu fhéin an Ciuthach* (' It's yourself that's the Ciuthach ')." A legend connected with an ancient fort on Borronish (" fort point "), in Uig, Lewis, tells of a conflict between the Fians and this giant. Fionn was kept at bay by him, but Oscar took his place and slew the monster. The " Kewach " was " a giant and a real hero, a man not only of great

[1] *The Celtic Review* (January, 1914), pp. 193 *et seq.*

GIANT LORE OF SCOTLAND

size but great dignity . . . ' He would scorn to lay hand on a common man '." In the island of Eigg the " Kewach " lives in a cave. He is still remembered in Barra. On the north side of Loch Lomond a similar " hero " was associated with a circular fortress on a promontory which, according to Alexander Graham of Duchray, writing in 1724, was called " Gyants Castle ". His name was Keith, son of Doillus. Professor Watson shows that Keith is to be read as " Ciuthach " or " Cithich ". In a Scottish Fian story Grainne, who eloped with Diarmaid, was successfully wooed by a cave-giant referred to as " Ciach " and, in another version, as " Ciuthach ". Diarmaid slew him. J. F. Campbell in a prose tale says the giant's name was pronounced " Kewach " and explains that " Kewachs " were naked wild men living in caves.[1] J. G. Campbell refers to " Ciuthach mac an Doill " (Kewach, son of the blind man) in Tiree.[2] Other " Kewach " stories are given by Watson, who notes that a " Kewach " connected with a fort is associated with " Eibhinn and Trostan " and points out that " Trostan is a distinctively Pictish name" which occurs in Lewis, while "there was a Trostansfjord in Iceland ". Traces of the Ciuthach are found " from Clyde to the Butt of Lewis ".

Other giants are invulnerable against wounds, having their " souls " concealed in a stone, an egg, an animal or fish, or in a tree or a bush. The " soul body " must be discovered and destroyed so that an end may be made of the giant.

[1] *Popular Tales of the West Highlands*, Vol. III, p. 49.
[2] *The Fians*, pp. 53 *et seq.*

Giant lore similar to that of Scotland is found in England.[1] The whale-fishing giant, for instance, was known to Daniel Kenricus, the seventeenth century Worcester physician, who describes one in his poem included in Dryden's *Miscellany*:

> " His angle rod made of sturdy oak,
> His line a cable that in storms ne'er broke;
> His hook he baited with a dragon's tail,
> And sat upon a rock and bobb'd for whale."

Two giants connected with Norden Hill in Dorsetshire engaged in a stone-putting competition like the giants on Ben Ledi in Perthshire. The stone was thrown across the valley towards " Hanging Hill ". According to a folk-tale " he whose stone fell short was so mortified at the failure that he died of vexation and was buried beneath the mound, which has since been known as the ' giant's grave '."

From a giant's hill at Armley, near Leeds, a giant flung a boulder across the adjacent river and on it may be seen " the impression of the hero's fingers ". Fionn's " finger marks " are seen on a boulder he flung from Knockfarrel, Strathpeffer, Ross and Cromarty. Two small stone circles on Heathwaite in Furness, Lancashire, were called " giants' graves ". Giants once lived in the district. The last of them is said " to have been shot by an arrow upon the adjacent hill of Blawithknott ", as were the giant of Morvern in Argyll and the Banffshire giant.

A story regarding a giant's grave in Leicestershire was referred to by Ray in 1670. This giant was known

---

[1] E. J. Wood, *Giants and Dwarfs* (London, 1868).

as Bell and was famous for his three leaps. "At a place ever after called Mountsorrel, Bell mounted the sorrel horse and leaped a mile to a place since named Oneleap, now corrupted to Wanlip; thence he leaped another mile to a village called Burstall, from the bursting of both himself and his horse." He was buried in the place ever since called "Bell's Grave" or "Bell Grave". The amusing etymologies need not detain us. Apparently a story of a horsed giant, similar to the Scottish giant who pursues the Cailleach, has been localized.

Giants' caves are known in England. These include one near Edenhall by Penrith, the stronghold of the giant Tarquin slain by Lancelot; the "giant's cave" at Clifton, near Bristol; a barrow, similarly named, at Luckington in north Wilts; the "giant's cave" near Tolshill in the Scilly Islands and giants' caves in Cornwall, &c. Of special interest is the connexion between giants and giantesses and relics of the megalithic period. The Luckington "giant's cave" contained cists. Another sepulchral site at Uleybury in Gloucestershire was known as the "giant's chamber". The stone circle of Little Salkfield, near Penrith, is known as "Long Meg and her daughters". Meg may have originally been a giantess like the Scottish Cailleach, who is connected with standing-stones near Glasgow, as will be shown.

English figures of giants are evidently of considerable antiquity. One on a steep hill near Cerne in Dorsetshire is 180 feet long and 44 feet across the shoulders. In one of the hands is a club 120 feet in length. Two giants, Gog and Magog, were cut in the earth at the Hawe, Plymouth. " The Long Man of Wilmington " is on the side of the downs near Wilmington in Sussex. It is 240 feet long and has in either hand clubs or magic wands. A giant on the Cambridgeshire chalk hills represented " Atlas, Gomagog's cousin ".

William Cashen in his *Manx Folklore* tells of a giant " who flung a boulder from Peel Castle after his fleeing wife. This stone with the giant's finger-marks still lies poised on the Vaish Hill. The long mounds outside the wall of Peel Castle are supposed to be the graves of giants."

Miss Mary L. Lewis, author of *Stranger than Fiction*, informs me that in her Welsh home she has been familiar from childhood with the story that a Welsh giant flings a quoit into Ireland every morning. In her interesting book (p. 8) she tells that near her home " the highest hill is crowned by the grave of a mighty *cawr* (giant)—though archæologists will tell you that it is merely a British burial mound ". A big fortification called " Pen-y-Gair " at Llanderfell in Merionethshire is a fabled residence of giants.[1]

In Ireland the megaliths on the plain of Carrowmore, near Sligo, are connected with the Dananns and Fomorians. A stone circle at Lugna Clogh is the " giant's grave " and at Corren a " giant's house " is found to be a series of caves. The Danann deities have been connected with New Grange and other megalithic relics. A dolmen at Ballycandan, near Dundalk, is the " giant's load ", and there is a " giant's grave " not far distant. A dolmen near Drumboe Hill in County

---

[1] See also *Gossiping Guide to Wales*, published at Oswestry.

Down is the centre of an earthwork called the " giant's ring " and megalithic remains near Clayonagh bear the name " giant's grave ". Loch Neagh, according to contemporary lore, was formed by a giant who made a great excavation to fling missiles eastward across the land and ocean.

The Scottish Gaelic term *famhair* (Irish *fomhor*, early Irish *fomór*) signifies not only " giant " but " pirate ". Zimmer derived it from *fo-mór*, " submagnus "; Stokes referred *-mor* to the same origin as *mare* in night*mare*, and Rhys took *mor* from the root of *muir*, sea, but in his later years informed the writer that he had abandoned that view. Watson shows that the Fomorians were in old Irish accounts represented as pirates who ravaged the coasts of Ireland, laying the people under tribute. They were " huge and ugly ". In the *Táin Bó Cúalgne* Cuchulainn becomes " as huge as a *fomóir* or a sea man (*fer mara*) ". The form *fomóra* shows that the name is not from *muir*, sea. One of the Fomorian kings was *Indech mac Dé Domnand* (" Indech, son of the goddess Domnu "). The Fomorians were connected with the Hebrides.[1]

As we have seen, the hill giants of Scotland received in the course of time the names of heroes like Samson, Patrick, Arthur, Wallace, Thomas the Rhymer, " the Wolf of Badenoch " (Alexander Stewart, son of King Robert II), &c. At an earlier period they appear to have been compared with, and named after, the piratical Fomorians whose raids and invasions are reflected in Irish mythology. The original name of the giants has therefore been lost.

[1] W. J. Watson, *History of the Celtic Place-Names of Scotland*, pp. 41 *et seq.*

CHAPTER VI
A Scottish Beowulf

No Danann pantheon in Scotland, but Fomorians numerous—Mother giantess stronger than husband or sons—Her relations with Scottish goddess and *Beowulf* hag—Deities and demons of cardinal points—Finlay the Changeling—His unfaithful sister—Wise widow advises Finlay—The giant lover of sister—Finlay's dogs—Avenging giants slain—Conflict with mother giantess—Treasure in giants' cave—Magic wands and magic sword—Standing stone transformed by wand into warrior—Argyll and Badenoch versions of Finlay story—Scottish and Cornish giant lore—Grendel story in *Beowulf*—Fionn's conflicts with giant and giantess of the sea—Poet of *Beowulf* used British giant lore.

As has been stated, there is no trace in Scotland of the Irish Danann pantheon or of the myths regarding the Danann war against the Fomorians, whose leader was Balor, a demon slain by the young god Lugh. It has been assumed that the Irish myths refer to a struggle between the deities of light and summer and the deities of darkness and winter.[1]

Some of the Irish gods may have been imported from Gaul, but the process of culture blending operated in Ireland, and the pantheon was localized, reconstructed and transformed—another indication that the theory of a homogeneous Celtic religion is a hazardous one. Local elements entered into the Irish complex.

Although there is no Danann pantheon in Scotland, the Fomorians are found to be quite numerous, as has been shown in the previous chapter.

[1] H. D'Arbois de Jubainville, *The Irish Mythological Cycle*. Translation by R. I. Best (Dublin and London, 1903).

A SCOTTISH BEOWULF

A folk-story known as that of " Finlay the Changeling " throws much light upon the giant lore of Scotland and prepares us for the consideration of the ancient mythology that influenced it. This story was collected in Skye about thirty years ago and translated from Gaelic by Mr. Malcolm Mac Leod, a native of Plockton, Ross and Cromarty. It shows, as do others of like character, that the giant mother was reputed to be more cunning and dangerous than her husband or her sons, and this story will consequently be found to be of much value in dealing not only with the Cailleach Bheur, the Scottish Artemis, an ancient goddess, but with the problem presented by the ancient English epic *Beowulf*, in which the hero, having overcome Grendel, the son, has to wage a fierce struggle with the mother in her cave. Apparently a British folk-tale was incorporated in the Anglo-Saxon epic, which must therefore have been given its final shape in England. A famous old sword figures in the Skye story, as in the Grendel section of *Beowulf*. In addition, there are magic wands. The Gaelic hero strikes a standing-stone with a wand and it is transformed into a warrior, in whose right hand he places the cave sword. This Skye story opens with a reference to the haunting belief that good or evil influences issue from the cardinal points, as is indicated in the old Gaelic saying given by J. Gregorson Campbell:

" Shut the north window,
 And quickly close the window to the south;
And shut the window facing west,
 Evil never came from the east." [1]

---

[1] *Superstitions of the Highlands and Islands of Scotland* (Glasgow, 1900), p. 69.

The fairies were reputed to come from the west, and the evil-working giants came from the north, while men who returned from Paradise came from the south. There was a mountain paradise in the east. In Ireland certain deities are similarly connected with the cardinal or subsidiary points of the compass. The god Lugh, for instance, comes from the north-eastern quarter and the goddess Morrigan from the north-western. In all the old mythologies, indeed, including the Egyptian, Babylonian, Aryo-Indian, &c., there are deities of the east, west, north, south, &c.[1]

The first part of the Skye story, which is known as that of " Finlay the Changeling ", is as follows:

" There was once a man who was called Finlay Changeling, the widow's son. He was a hunter and lived with his sister in a solitary house among the mountains. Every morning Finlay went forth at an early hour to follow the chase, and before he took his departure he was wont to say to his sister, ' Open not the window to the north, nor let the fire go out.'

" His sister would answer him, ' I shall neither shut nor open any window, nor allow the fire to go out.'

" As it happened, however, the sister did not do as Finlay requested and she did what he asked her not to do. She would open the window to the north and shut the window to the south and she allowed the fire to go out while her brother was absent. In truth, the brother and sister were not ready to please one another and did not live very happily together.

" There came a day when Finlay, who was returning home by a route he was not accustomed to take, perceived a small dwelling he had never seen before. He was taken by surprise, and, wondering who might inhabit so lonely a place, went towards it and entered. Within this house he saw an old

[1] My *Migrations of Symbols* (London, 1926) pp. 18 *et seq.*

woman sitting on the floor. No one else was there.

"'Sit down, son of the widow,' said the old woman, and Finlay sat down.

"'I know well about your circumstances,' she told him, 'and of the treatment you are receiving. Alas! you have a most wicked sister and she is willing to have you put to death this very day.'

"'Is she?' exclaimed Finlay, taken by surprise.

"'Yes, indeed,' the old woman assured him. 'Pay heed to what I tell you. As a sign of her evil intention you will find when you return home to-night that she has prepared for you a floor-bed of rushes beside the fire, upon which she will ask you to sit. But do not do as she desires, because a giant is concealed under the rushes and in his hand he holds a sharp, blue sword with which to slay you.'

"After a pause the woman added, 'But, son of the widow, do as I instruct you and you will suffer no harm.'

"The old woman then gave Finlay certain instructions as to how he should act when he entered the house.

"Finlay left her and when he returned home his sister met him at the door with salutation and welcome. 'My darling,' said she, 'it is I who have provided for you to-night a resting place upon which you may lie and stretch yourself at your ease when you have eaten your dinner until the time comes for you to go to bed. I have made for you a soft bed of rushes and, my darling, it is indeed comfortable.'

"Finlay did not betray his suspicion or give any sign to indicate what he knew, but entered the house as usual.

"Now, it was Finlay's habit to wash his feet each evening before retiring to rest. He went towards the fire and lifted from it a large pot of boiling water, which he placed upon the bed of rushes made for him by his sister, but he did not sit down. He began to eat his dinner and he flung the first bone from which he had taken the flesh to his dogs, which lay near the bed of rushes. The three large dogs leapt upon the bed and so furiously did they fight for the bone that they upset the pot of boiling water. At once there sprang from under the rushes a giant who shrieked and bellowed, and he darted towards the door and ran from the house, followed by Finlay's sister. Together they made their way to the great cave of the giants.

"Finlay was left all alone in the house and his heart trembled with fear, because he expected that at any moment the giants would come to slay him.

"When the giant who fled from Finlay's house reached the cave, the other giants perceived that he had been scalded and burned. A young giant leapt up and exclaimed, 'It is I myself who will go forth and avenge my brother.'

"'No, it is not you but I who shall go,' the greatest of the giants said.

"'It is I myself who shall go,' growled the fierce, grey hag.

"'U! I must go,' exclaimed the young giant as he leapt out of the mouth of the cave.

"Finlay was waiting for certain death in his own little house, and he heard approaching a growing noise and disturbance that grew loud as thunder—small stones going to the bottom and big stones to the top and mud smiting the heavens in thuds.

"When the giant reached Finlay's house he cried out, 'Fith! foth! fugitive! There is hindrance to the poor, big stranger here. Let me in, son of the widow.' He threw in the door before him as if it were the leaf of a cabbage.

"Finlay thrust two bullets into his gun[1] and fired at the giant, but that did not kill him. Then the three dogs leapt against the monster, tearing and wounding him, while Finlay made fierce attack, and between them the dogs and Finlay slew the young giant.

---

[1] The weapon is here modernized. Originally he must have fired arrows.

"Finlay at once cut from the giant the five heads, the five humps and the five necks and, making a withy, tied them. He was still, however, in great fear and did not venture forth from the house that night.

"Long was the day without coming, but no longer than that did Finlay wait before he hastened to the little old woman of the little house. He carried with him a wheaten loaf [1] and a stoup of wine and these pleased her well; and he also carried the heads, the humps and the necks of the young giant.

"'Well then, valiant hand, how fared you yesternight?' the old woman asked him.

"Finlay related all that had taken place and how it was due to the dogs that the giant was killed.

"'There is need for the dogs,' said the old woman, 'but the day of their need has yet to come.'

"Finlay was as mannerly and courteous to the old woman as he could possibly be and there was good friendship between them.

"When Finlay returned home it was not to rest. The night came on and no sooner did it come than he heard approaching the hut a great noise and flurry and a sound as of thunder—small stones swept to the bottom and big stones to the top and mud thudding to the heavens.

"'Thoth! thoth! fugitive!' cried the voice of a giant. 'The smell of the foreigner is within. Let me in, son of the widow. Although you slew my son last night, you will not slay *me* to-night.'

"The giant threw in the door before him. The house trembled and the man in it trembled too. Finlay feared that the house would fall upon his back.

"He put two bullets in his gun and fired, but they made no impression upon the giant. Finlay then thrust his sword through him, but that did not kill the giant. Then the three big dogs

---

[1] A rare luxury to the story-teller.

leapt at the giant's scalp locks and between them they killed the big giant.

"Finlay cut off the five heads, the five humps and the five necks, and he carried them next morning to the old woman, taking with him also a wheaten loaf and a stoup of wine.

"'O clever hand!' exclaimed the old woman when Finlay reached her. 'What happened to you yesternight?'

"'I had great success,' Finlay said. 'An end has come to yon two at any rate. But it was the dogs who killed this one also.'

"'How well you have succeeded,' said the old woman, 'and how well have the dogs succeeded! There was need of them indeed. But the day of their need has yet to come. It is to-night that they will be put upon their mettle. The fierce grey Cailleach is coming to-night to avenge her husband and her sons. It is she who is indeed horrifying. She has a goad-like tusk for clearing her way of approach and a great tooth with which she rakes the fire to give heat. To-night will she visit you with gentle mannerliness; and, meekly and with mildness, she will ask you to let her in. It is her desire to take your life. But do as I instruct you and no harm shall befall you.'

"The old widow thereupon instructed Finlay how he should act when he returned home. But when he had left the widow and reached his house Finlay trembled, for oh! he was demented with terror.

"Night fell black, and, when it fell, the grey Cailleach came to Finlay's door and asked to be admitted. She spoke meekly, peacefully, patiently.

"'I shall permit you to enter,' Finlay said, 'if you promise that you will be mannerly until morning and give me no trouble.'

"'U![1] I shall not move,' the fierce grey Cailleach assured him. 'Permit me to enter.'

"Finlay admitted the Cailleach. She sat at the upward

---

[1] Pronounced *Oo*.

side of the fire and the hunter sat at this side. Before long the Cailleach arose and seated herself at the opposite side of the fire. Finlay arose (and it was well for him that he did) and sat at the other side of the fire.

"The three great dogs were prowling through the house and the fierce grey Cailleach said to Finlay, 'Arise, son of the widow, and tie your dogs with a thong.'

"'U! the dogs will not do any harm,' Finlay said.

"'U! you must tie them in any case,' insisted the Cailleach.

"'I have nothing with which to tie them,' Finlay said.

"Then the fierce grey Cailleach said, 'I shall give you three hairy, reddish ribbons from off the top of my shaggy, matted head. These would hold a great ship at anchor throughout the seven years.'

"Thereupon the Cailleach gave Finlay three rough, reddish hairs. He took them, but, instead of tying the dogs, he thrust them into his pocket, meantime making the dogs lie in a corner with their necks together as if they were on a leash.

"'Have you tied the dogs, son of the widow?' asked the fierce grey Cailleach.

"'I have,' he answered. 'Do you not see them in the corner?'

"Then they sat beside the fire as they were before—the widow's son at one side and the fierce grey Cailleach at the other.

"Suddenly Finlay exclaimed, 'I believe, O Cailleach, you are growing big!'

"'U! no, my darling,' said she, 'but my feathers and my quills are rising to the fire.'

"In a short time after that, the hunter said to the Cailleach, 'I will not credit it that you are not growing bigger.'

"'Oov! no,' she answered, 'my little son, it is but my feathers and my quills rising to the fire.'[1]

[1] In another version related to me by Mr. Alexander MacLennan, a native of Strathconon, the Cailleach enters as a partridge, which grew larger and larger and at length assumed her Cailleach shape.

"In a little while after that Finlay said, 'You are growing bigger, indeed, O Cailleach, however you may take it, well or badly.'

"At that the Cailleach exclaimed angrily, 'I am growing so big, son of the widow, that, although you killed, with your deceitfulness and trickery, my husband last night and my son the night before, I shall certainly kill you to-night.'

"Thereupon the fierce grey Cailleach sprang to her feet and the house shook under her. The widow's son also sprang to his feet and, if he was not the speediest, he was not the tardiest. They seized each other's scalp-locks and out of the door they went together in their conflict. The three dogs sprang after them.

"Fiercely did they wrestle—Finlay the Changeling, son of the widow, and the fierce grey Cailleach, the wife of the great giant and mother of the young giants. And, oh, my ruin alas! but that was the wrestling. For they would twist hither and turn thither, bend down and spring up, and they would plough the hard, grey, rocky ground with their feet as if it were the smooth, soft, fertile plain. They would make a quagmire on the face of each hard rock. When they would be the least under, they would be under to the knees; and when they would be most under, they would be under to the eyes.

"The widow's son thought of himself and of his kin and people, and he knew he was far from his friends and near to his enemy.

"Suddenly he made a swift and lively move and he threw the Cailleach upon her back, breaking a rib under her and an arm above her.

"'Permit me to rise to my feet,' cried the Cailleach.

"'I shall not permit you to rise,' Finlay answered, 'until you tell me what ransom you will give.'

"The Cailleach said: 'I have a trunk of gold and a trunk of silver in the cave, and they are yours, O son of the widow.'

"'U! Cailleach, these are mine in any case,' said Finlay. 'What is your ransom?'

"The Cailleach said: 'A trunk full of gold brooches and a trunk full of silver brooches which belonged to lords and gentlewomen. These are yours, O son of the widow.'

"'U! Cailleach, these are mine already,' said Finlay. 'What is your ransom?'

"The Cailleach said: 'There is in the cave a gold watch [1] which belongs to the son of the king of Tìr-fo-thuinn and his name is upon it; and there is a gold ring which belonged to the daughter of the king and her name is upon it. These are yours, O son of the widow. Permit me now to rise.'

"'O fierce grey Cailleach, these are mine in any case,' said Finlay. 'What is your ransom?'

"The Cailleach said: 'I have a gold sword in the cave and never was it drawn to man or to beast whom it did not overcome. It is yours, O son of the widow. Permit me now to rise up.'

"'The gold sword is mine in any case,' said Finlay. 'What is your ransom?'

"The Cailleach said: 'My ransom then is—and distressing it is!—two rods which are in the cave. If you will strike a blow with either of these rods, in any spot in the world whatsoever, on a stone pillar, that pillar will become a man; and if you will put the gold sword in the hand of this man, there is not another man under the sun who will stand up before him.'

"'Your cunning, magic wand is my own in any case, fierce grey Cailleach,' Finlay said. 'What is your ransom?'

"'Oov, oov! my darling little son,' the Cailleach cried, 'I have no more for you.'

"Thereupon the hunter and the three great dogs set upon the fierce grey Cailleach, and they killed her, leaving not a breath in her.

[1] Another modern touch. Tìr-fo-thuinn is "Land Under-wave".

"Finlay then fetched a hammer and took the two goad-like tusks out of the Cailleach. He measured them and each was five cubits long and three cubits in girth.

"When he had done that Finlay hastened to the little dwelling of the auspicious old woman, carrying with him the tusks.

"'Have you come, O strong-hand and clever hero?' exclaimed the old woman.

"'I have come,' Finlay said—'that and nothing more.'

"'And how feel you and how fared you yesternight?' she asked.

"'I am alive and nothing more,' Finlay said, 'but I was successful. Well,' he added, 'in yonder place there is an end to the riff-raff in any case. My dogs and I destroyed the fierce grey Cailleach and I have brought her tusks to you.'

"Finlay threw the tusks on the floor.

"'In the cave,' said he, 'there are heaps of wealth and precious treasure—jewels past reckoning, but how to get at them, I am at a loss to know.'

"'Nor do I any more than yourself,' the old woman said; 'but to-night I and my foster-child will go with you and assist you, and I believe we shall have success. I myself shall take with me my magic wand, and if everything else fails us the wand will not fail us in any case.'

"Thereafter they set out together—Finlay, son of the widow, and the one-eyed,[1] dark, grey old woman and her foster-child, who had bewitching eyes and fair, soft skin. In due course they reached the mouth of the cave of the giants.

"First, they plucked seven loads of grey heather, and, heaping these at the cave mouth, set fire to the fuel so that the giant within might be choked with the fumes and scorched with the flames. The dry grass was likewise set on fire and the cave was filled with smoke.

"The giant was panting heavily. When he inhaled his

[1] This is the first mention of the woman as one-eyed.

breath he drew in loose stones which were at the mouth of the cave; and when he exhaled he sent the flames, the heather and the stones smoking to the skies.

"Then they perceived a warning light appearing upon the giant's head.[1]

"'I shall fire,' said the son of the widow.

"'Do not fire,' the old woman warned him. 'That would only make him raging mad, and the dogs will be of no use to you here amidst the fire. Leave him alone so that I may get my chance against him with my cunning, black magic wand. If I can give him one smack, I will not leave a breath in his body; but if I am not successful, he must give me a single blow with the polished, light, bright grey sword which is in his hand.[2] With that he can make a lump of clay of me.'

"The giant stretched himself out from the mouth of the cave, but no sooner did he do that than the old woman gave him a thumping, hard smack on the head with her magic wand. She did not leave a breath in his body. At that moment there sprang up a gleam of light and the hunter perceived his sister crouching at the end of the cave. He fired and killed her.

"Then Finlay cut the five heads, the five humps and the five necks from the giant and bound them with a withy.

"'O clever hand and valiant hero!' cried the old woman, 'it is you who have performed the heroic deed that none ever did before you. Now the effects of it will be seen if you follow my advice.'

"'U! I will take your advice, woman,' Finlay said. 'It is I who will indeed take it, for to me it is of great worth. It is you who arranged every scheme in my head. Were it not for you, truly I should have been a lifeless creature at the hands of yon riff-raff. This part of the world will enjoy peace now that they have all been put to death.'

[1] Similar lights appear upon the heads of Cuchulainn and Achilles.
[2] Blow for blow as in combats between giants.

"Then Finlay, the old woman and the foster-daughter carried away each charm and amulet, the gold and silver and every other valuable thing that was in the cave. They conveyed everything to the house of the old woman.

"Finlay found the two rough black rods that had belonged to the fierce grey Cailleach and he carried them away. He was indeed very proud to have them.

"On his way he struck a stone pillar with one of the rods and the pillar immediately became a man. He then put the gold sword in the hand of the man. No eye ever beheld a hero more handsome than he. Although four thousand men came against him in armour, he would subdue them all.

"Finlay then struck the hero of the pillar a blow with the other rod and in the twinkling of an eye the stone pillar was as it was before.

"'What is this?' exclaimed Finlay. 'This is indeed a prodigious deed.'

"'U! it is that,' the old woman said. 'Never before was there ever the like of this.'"

A fragment of the Skye story, collected by Mrs. K. W. Grant in Appin, Argyll, tells of a hunter entering the house of a Cailleach accompanied by his two dogs. She says he must tie up his dogs and, plucking a long hair from her head, gives it to him, saying, "Here is a hair which could hold a five-masted gallant ship against the might of a seven-fold tempest".

The hunter pretends to tie the dogs, but, instead, winds the hair round the leg of a chair.

Soon afterwards he sees that the Cailleach is swelling and swelling bigger and ever bigger. She explains, "My featheries-and-fitheries are rising at the sight of the kilt". Then, having grown still larger, she cries out, "Tighten, O hair! Strangle, O hair!"

and attacks the hunter. The dogs spring at the Cailleach while the hair tightens round the chair leg, and as they hold her down the hunter hews her in pieces. But she is capable of coming to life again. The hunter " observed that the various parts of the hag's body were drawing nearer and ever nearer to each other. He thought it time to leave the hut along with his dogs. He gave another glance back as he reached the doorway and saw the pieces of the hag's body cementing and cementing, and he made off with all haste—and high time!"[1]

A Badenoch version, collected by W. Grant Stewart,[2] refers to a character known as " the wife of Laggan ", old giantess lore having been attached to the memory of a witch.

During a storm a hunter, accompanied by two dogs, takes shelter in a bothy. Suddenly the dogs bristle as " a miserable-looking, weather-beaten cat " enters. The cat speaks to the hunter, asking him to " restrain the fury of the dogs ", and claims protection according to the rule of " Highland hospitality ". She states that she is a witch who has " recanted her errors " and has taken flight from her " sisters ".

Fearing the dogs, she gives the hunter a long hair with which to tie them to a beam. The hunter pretends to do as she desires, but binds the hair round the beam instead.

[1] *Myth, Tradition and Story from Western Argyll*, pp.1–2. In an ancient Egyptian story the hero killed the " deathless snake " but it came to life again. He killed it a second time and it again revived. In the end he cut it in two and put sand between the parts. The snake perished. (*Egyptian Tales* (London, 1895, second series), pp. 98–9.)

[2] *Lectures on the Mountains, or the Highlands and Highlanders of Strathspey and Badenoch* (London, 1860), pp. 191 *et seq.*

The cat then squats beside the fire and begins to "expand her size into considerable dimensions".

"You are getting very large," the hunter remarks.

"Aye, aye," says the cat, "as my hairs imbibe the heat, they naturally expand."

She grows still bigger and then assumes human shape. The hunter then recognizes her as "the wife of Laggan" and she says angrily, "Hunter of the hills, your hour has come . . . Long have you been the devoted enemy of my persecuted sisterhood. The chief aggressor of our order is now no more; this morning I saw his body consigned to a watery grave, and now, hunter of the hills, it is your turn."

She then springs "at his throat with the force and fury of a tigress", but the dogs attack her. She cries out, "Fasten, hair, fasten!" The hair tightens and snaps the beam.

Wounded and thwarted in the struggle, the wife shrieks in her agony and, assuming the likeness of a raven, flies away in the direction of her home, where she ultimately expires. The dogs die soon after she has left the bothy, and the witch herself subsequently expires in agony, having had a breast torn off.

J. F. Campbell gives a story collected near Inveraray, entitled "The Sea Maiden", in which the hero slays sea-monsters. He afterwards visits a castle beside a loch and is welcomed by a flattering, little old woman, but, as he ascends the stairs, she strikes him with her *slachdan druidheachd* (druid wand) and he falls like one who has died. His brother searches for him, but meets with a similar fate. Then the third brother visits the castle. His dog springs at the woman, but is struck by her magic wand. In a wrestling match with the woman, the young man gets possession of the wand, smites her so that she becomes unconscious, and then uses the wand to revive his two brothers. Great treasure is found in the castle.[1]

The Finlay story is of interest in the first place when considered in connexion with the giant lore of England. Geoffrey of Monmouth and Layamon, author of *The Brut*, state that when Brute and his Trojans first reached Albion they found its only inhabitants were giants. " After exploring certain districts of the land," Geoffrey relates,[2] " they drove away the giants, who had to take refuge in the caverns of the mountains." In Cornwall nothing gave " greater pleasure " to Corineus " than to wrestle with the giants ". These giants killed many Britons, but in the end all were slain except Goemagot, who was " twelve cubits in height ". Corineus, " flinging away his arms, challenged him to a bout of wrestling ":

" At the start, on the one side stands Corineus, on the other the giant, each hugging the other tight in the shackles of their arms, both making the very air quake with their breathless gasping. It was not long before Goemagot, grasping Corineus with all his force, brake him three of his ribs, two on the right side and one on the left. Roused thereby to fury, Corineus gathered up all his strength, heaved him up on his shoulders, and ran with his burden as fast as he could for the weight to the seashore nighest at hand. Mounting up to the top of a high cliff, and disengaging himself, he hurled the deadly monster he had carried on his shoulder into the sea, where, falling on

---

[1] *Popular Tales of the West Highlands*, Vol. I, Tale IV.

[2] Chapter XVI, translation by Sebastian Evans.

the sharp rocks, he was mangled all to pieces and dyed the waves with his blood."

The place was afterwards known as " Goemagot's Leap ". Here Geoffrey evidently drew upon existing giant-lore.

In the *Beowulf* epic the warriors' hall is entered by a monster known as Grendel, who carries off men. He comes to the door, which, although "fastened by forged bands, opened straightway when he touched it with his hands. Thus, bent on destruction, for he was swollen with rage, he tore away the entrance of the building" (lines 715–20). One night Grendel seized a sleeping warrior and devoured him. Then he rushed at Beowulf, who, however, gripped him and held him tight. In the end Beowulf tore off one of Grendel's arms. The other warriors had attempted to assist Beowulf by using their weapons, but, like Finlay in the Skye story, they found that these could not injure the monster (lines 791–836).

Although Grendel was overcome, "an avenger" still lived. This was the mother of the monster, who "brooded over her misery". She resolved to "avenge the death of her son" (lines 1276–80). The poet declares regarding her that " the terror was less by just so much as woman's strength, woman's war-terror, is (measured) by fighting men " (lines 1280–1287). But as the story proceeds it is found that she is really more powerful and terrible than the son. Beowulf has to fling aside his sword when he enters her cave and trust to his " mighty hand-grip ", but he cannot overcome her as he overcame the son and in the end has to make use of the magic sword in the cave (lines 1512–1650).

Evidently the poet who composed the epic, drawing upon imported heroic lays, was unfamiliar, when using also local giant lore, with the belief that the mother was more powerful than the son.

In the Skye story the sword in the giant's cave is one of gold; in *Beowulf* the sword has a golden hilt (lines 1605–17 and 1677–98). There is treasure in the cave entered by Beowulf, and he carries some of it away (lines 1605–17).[1]

There is no trace in the north German cycle of romance of the type of story in which the mother of the giant avenges a son's death. In Scottish folk-lore, however, it is very common. Another story in which the mother is more to be feared than son or husband is that of " How Fin went to the Kingdom of the Big Men ".[2] The hero performs great feats, killing two giants who came from the sea, but has to meet the terrible Cailleach mhór, who has a great tooth which " would make a distaff ". She says, " You killed my husband and my son ", and then begins to fight, but the dog Bran slays her. The king says, " I and my kingdom will have peace ever after this. The mother herself of the brood is killed."

It would appear, as stated, that the epic *Beowulf* was given its final form in the north of England, the poet having made use in the Grendel section of old British giant-lore similar to that which has survived in Scotland, as well as of imported heroic lays.

[1] Quotations from prose translation of *Beowulf* by John R. Clark Hall (London, 1911).

[2] *Waifs and Strays of Celtic Tradition*, Argyllshire Series No. IV (London, 1891), pp. 176 *et seq.*

CHAPTER VII
A Scottish Artemis

Cailleach's links with Greek goddess—"Old wife" name—Nun connexion—The *Beur* wives—Reed as distaff—The staff—Cailleach's association with cold weather—" Daughter of little sun "—Boulder form—The loathly hag—Cailleach one-eyed with blue-black face—Her magic wand—The enemy of growth—Connexion with holly tree and whins (gorse)—Cailleach period in spring—Whirlpool and tempest connexions—Ben Nevis seat—The captive maiden—The elopement—Spring storms—Patroness of wild beasts—Cailleach's bird forms—Cailleach as a heron—Cailleach and witch lore—Artemis and Cailleach associated with swine—Boar hunt stories—Raven and corbie as oracular birds—Bird forms of Cailleach—Diarmaid slays Cailleach and boar—Human sacrifice—Gyre Carlin as Cailleach and as sow—Cailleach as " Nicnevin "—Birth from burnt bones—Myth of bone worm—Cailleach worm becomes water dragon—Cailleach's sheep and goats—Cailleach's cattle byre—Cailleach's wolves and wild pigs—Cailleach's herds of deer—Cailleach's fish connexion—Myths of origins of rivers and lochs—Artemis as " lady of the lake "—The river " black goddess ".

Memories of an ancient goddess cling to a giantess who in the folk-lore of Scotland is referred to as Cailleach Bheur,[1] Mala Liath, the Muilearteach and other names connected with localities. She resembles somewhat the Greek goddess Artemis, being associated with wild animals and capable of transforming herself into animal shape. Withal, she is a weather controller, like the Artemis to whom Iphigenia, daughter of Agamemnon, was sacrificed so that a favourable wind might be obtained for the fleet which was to set out from Aulis with the warriors who were to wage war against Troy.

In the Scottish goddess we appear to have glimpses of the fierce old Artemis who was ultimately idealized

[1] Pronounced *cal'yach vare* (*ch* guttural).

by Greek sculptors and accorded refining treatment by the poets after her character had been adjusted to changed social ideals and customs and after goats and boars were sacrificed to her instead of human beings.

Cailleach means in modern Gaelic " old wife " and originally signified a nun. Its oldest known form is *Caillech*, " veiled one ", from *caille*, " veil ", a rendering of the Latin *pallium*, the " p " becoming " c " in Q-Celtic. The supernatural Cailleach was distinguished from a nun by being referred to as Cailleach Bheur. J. Gregorson Campbell gives the qualifying adjective as *beura* or *bheura*, meaning " shrill, sharp, cutting ". He points out that the *beur* wives are sometimes spoken of in the plural number and referred to as staying in lochs and among rushes and as having been " very dangerous to come near ". In this connexion he reminds us that a tall reed found beside lochs is called " the distaff of the Bera wives " and that a species of flag or water plant is known as the " staff " of these " sarcastic wives ".[1]

The Cailleach Bheur is in the folk-stories associated with the coldest and stormiest period of the year. She is called " the daughter of Grianan " or " Grianaig "— that is, of the " little sun ". In the old Celtic calendar the " big sun " shines during the period from Beltane (1st May) till Hallowe'en, and the " little sun " is the sun of the winter period. " Daughter of the little sun " does not mean, however, that the sun was either her father or mother, but simply that she was born during the cold season. The Cailleach was supposed to have been transformed into a grey boulder at the end

[1] *The Scottish Historical Review*, Vol. XII, pp. 413 *et seq.*

of the period of the " little sun " and to have remained in that form during the period of the " big sun ". I have heard references to this boulder being " always moist ", an indication that it was reputed to contain " life substance ".

Another conception was that the Cailleach changed from a fierce old hag to a beautiful maiden. In a folk-story which was connected with the Fians, she appears one night as " a creature of uncouth appearance " who claims hospitality. Fionn and Oisean (Ossian) refuse to let her under their " coverings ". Diarmaid pleads that she should be allowed to " come to the warmth of the fire ". Soon afterwards she " sought to be under the warmth of the blanket together with himself ". Diarmaid " turned a fold of it (the blanket) between them ". Before long he " gave a start ", for the hag had transformed herself into " the most beauteous woman that men ever saw ".[1]

In the early poetic version of the Thomas the Rhymer legend given by Sir Walter Scott [2] the " fairy queen ", as she became known, appears as a lovely woman, worthy of being called " Queen of Heaven ". She subsequently appears as a blue hag, like Cailleach Bheur:

" Her heyre hang down about hyr hede,
The tane was black, the other gray,
Her eyne semyt onte before was gray,
Her gay clethyng was all away . . .
Her body as *blow* (blue) as ony bede (bead)."

[1] J. F. Campbell, *Popular Tales of the West Highlands*, Vol. III, Tale LXXXVI of " The Daughter of King Under-Waves ".

[2] *Minstrelsy of the Scottish Border* (London, 1907 edition), Vol. IV, pp. 122 *et seq.*

A SCOTTISH ARTEMIS

Scott gives another version of the folk-tale:

" The appearance of the beautiful lady is changed into that of the most hideous hag in existence; one side is blighted and wasted, as if by palsy; one eye drops from her head; her colour, as clear as virgin silver, is now of a dun, leaden hue." [1]

This is the story of the " loathly hag " of which a version is given in Chaucer's *The Wife of Bath's Tale*. The knight, under pain of death, has to discover what thing a woman most desires. He receives the answer from an ugly old hag on condition that he will marry her. It is that women desire to have sovereignty over husband and love and also mastery in married life. The knight marries the hag and, when he kisses her, she becomes as fair " as any lady, empress or queen ".

As the fair young woman, the Cailleach is the giver of luck and plenty during the summer.

The descriptions of the Cailleach Bheur heard by the writer in various parts of the Highlands agree in giving her " a blue-black face " with " one eye on the flat of her forehead, the sight of which is very keen ". In songs put into her mouth she is made to say, " Why is my face so black, so black?" Her teeth are red as rust and her hair matted, confused and long and " white as an aspen covered with hoar frost ". She wears a kerchief or mutch. All her clothing is grey and she is wrapped in a dun-coloured plaid drawn tightly about her shoulders. On her feet are buskins. She is of enormous stature and great strength, and capable of travelling very swiftly and of leaping from mountain to mountain and across arms of the sea. In her right

---

[1] *Letters on Demonology and Witchcraft* (letter IV, London, 1831), p. 129.

hand she carries a magic *slachdan*, " beetle ", " rod ", which is also referred to as a *farachan*, " hammer ". Dr. Macbain derives *slachd* from an early Irish word signifying " thrash ", " beat ", " strike " and connects it with English " slay " and Latin *lacerare*, " lacerate ". With her magic hammer or rod the Cailleach smites the earth, so that it may be hardened with frost and the grass prevented from growing. She is the enemy of growth.

The late Mrs. W. J. Watson (E. C. Carmichael) had heard in the Highlands and islands much about the Cailleach " as a wild hag with a venomous temper, hurrying about with a magic wand in her withered hand, switching the grass and keeping down vegetation to the detriment of man and beast ". She is baffled in the early spring period which bears her name:

"When ... the grass, upborne by the warm sun, the gentle dew and the fragrant rain, overcomes the Cailleach she flies into a terrible temper, and, throwing away her wand into the root of a whin bush, she disappears in a whirling cloud of angry passion."

The Cailleach then takes flight, saying as she goes:

" *Thilg mi'n slacan druidh donai
Am bun pris crin cruaidh conuis,
Far nach fas fionn no fionnidh,
Ach fracan froinnidh feurach.*

" I threw my druidic evil wand
Into the base of a withered, hard whin bush,
Where shall not grow *fionn* nor *fionnidh*,
But fragments of grassy *froinnidh*." [1]

[1] *The Celtic Review*, Vol. V (1908-9), pp. 65-6.

In other versions the Cailleach flings her magic rod or hammer under a holly tree, " and that is why no grass grows under hòlly trees ".

> " *Thilg i e fo'n chrasibh chruaidh chuilinn,*
> *Air nach do chinn gas feur no fionnadh riamh.*
>
> " She threw it beneath the hard holly tree,
> Where grass or hair has never grown." [1]

Like the Cailleach who is the mother of the giants in the Skye folk-tale " Finlay the Changeling ", the Cailleach Bheur carried a druidic or magic wand, which, however, she used chiefly as a weather controller. Some of the folk-tales in which she approximates to a human being refer to her, however, as wielding her wand as a weapon. She had apparently a connexion with the holly tree and whins (gorse), as with marsh reeds and water plants.

The period of spring called *A' Chailleach* is the one in which she pauses to prepare for her final effort in arresting growth, as is usually explained in the " céilidhs " (house " gossipings "). The " daughter of the little sun " of winter had been an active influence since her revival at Hallowe'en.

According to the folk-tales, our Cailleach Bheur ushers in winter by washing her great plaid in the whirlpool of Corryvreckan (*Coire Bhreacain*), " which may be translated either ' Breacan's Cauldron ' or the ' Cauldron of the Plaid '," writes Mrs. K. W. Grant, a native of Easdale, Argyll:

" Before the washing the roar of a coming tempest is heard

---

[1] J. G. Campbell, *Witchcraft and Second Sight in the Scottish Highlands*, p. 254.

by people on the coast for a distance of twenty miles, and for a period of three days before the cauldron boils. When the washing is over the plaid of old Scotland is virgin white."[1]

The Cailleach, Mrs. Grant notes, is associated with " wintry tempests " and the " bitter, stinging winds of spring ".

Her chief seat in Scotland is Ben Nevis and she keeps as a prisoner there a beautiful maiden, with whom her son falls in love. The young couple elope at the end of winter and the Cailleach raises storms to keep them apart. These, according to one account, begin in February, the " wolf " month (*Faoilleach*). Then comes the wind called *Feadag* (the " whistle "), which kills sheep, lambs, cattle and horses. It lasts for three days and is followed by *Gobag* (the sharp-billed one), which pecks in every corner and " lasts for a week " or, as some have it, " three, four " or " nine days ". Next comes *Sguabag* (the " sweeper "), and it is followed by *Gearan* (" complaint "), which lasts for a month and is associated with the period called *Caoile* (leanness). The next period is *A' Chailleach* (the Cailleach).[2]

Mrs. Watson and her father, Dr. Alexander Carmichael, give a different arrangement of the spring gales from J. G. Campbell of Tiree.

The " wolf " month (February) is the last month of winter:

" 'Mi Faoillich, month of ' Faoilleach '—sharp, ravenous, tearing wind.

---

[1] *Myth, Tradition and Story from Western Argyll* (Oban, 1925), p. 8.
[2] J. G. Campbell, *Witchcraft and Second Sight*, pp. 250 *et seq.*; A. Carmichael, *Carmina Gadelica* (2nd edition), Vol. II, pp. 288–9.

Naoi la Gearrain, nine days of ' Gearran '—galloping wind like a ' garron '.
Seachdain Feadaig, a week of ' Feadag '—sharp, piping wind.
Seachdain Caillich, a week of ' Cailleach '—a few semi-calm days.
Tri la Sguabaig, three days of ' Sguabag '—the soughing blast which ushers in spring."

The " Gobag " wind, the voracious one, began on the day before " Faoilleach ", and is called mother of " Faoilleach " (wolf month, from *faol*, wolf). A poetic reference is:

" Gobag! Gobag! mother of the wolf-month cold,
Thou didst kill the sheep and the lean lamb,
Thou didst kill the grey goat in two watches,
And the speckled stirk in one." [1]

Mrs. Grant refers to *Latha na Cailich* (Cailleach Day), 25th March (old style), as the date of the Cailleach's overthrow. Until December, 1599, 25th March was New Year's Day and is now " Lady Day ".

Some folk-stories tell that before the Cailleach had ceased her activities her son pursued her, riding a swift horse. According to Mrs. Grant, the Cailleach, having in her final storm caused the death of the wild duck and newly-hatched ducklings, " put out her eye ". Other versions heard by the writer state that her eye was " put out " by her son. To escape destruction at his hands, she transforms herself into " a grey stone looking across the sea ".

A place-name, " Horse Shoes ", on Loch Etive side is connected with this myth, which the writer heard

[1] Mrs. Watson, *The Celtic Review* (1908–9), Vol. V, pp. 66–7.

in his youth during his few years' residence in the neighbourhood. Another place-name is connected with the son's elopement. Mrs. Grant tells that " on Ben Hynish in Tiree there is a rocky chasm called *Leum an eich*, 'the horse's leap'. Over it Cailleach Bheur's son fled from her on horseback with his bride. The Cailleach pursued him; and, on leaping across, the forefeet of his steed, on alighting on the opposite brink of the fissure, struck a piece out of the rock; hence the name by which the gap is still known."[1] In Skye a fragmentary folk-tale tells of the Cailleach leaping from height to height to escape " the devil ". Her transformation into a boulder took place on *Beinn na Caillich*, and she is also associated with a prehistoric cairn on the summit of that mountain.

Another mountain connected with her activities is Schiehallion (*Sìdh Chailleann*, " fairy " or " sacred " hill of the Caledonians "—the Caledonian Olympus). On this eminence " there is ", as Mrs. Grant records, " *sgrìob na Caillich*, the ' Old Wife's Furrow ', where she unearthed huge masses of stones in her ploughing ".

The writer has heard references to the pursuit of the Cailleach by her son beginning when the day and night are of equal length. In the west this period, 17th to 29th March, the " middle day ", is known as *Feill Paruig* (St. Patrick's Day) and there is supposed to be a south wind in the morning and a north wind at night. The son who pursues the Cailleach is supplanted by St. Patrick, who is said to come from Ireland " to see his parishioners in Barra and other places on the west of Scotland ". His wife is a daughter

---

[1] *Myth, Tradition and Story from Western Argyll*, p. 8.

of Ossian, the last of the *Fianna* (Fians). After this day " the limpet is better than the whelk " and although " horses grow lean, crabs grow fat ". Vegetation is reviving. A Gaelic saying is " There is not a herb in the ground but the length of a mouse's ear of it is out on St. Patrick's Day ". High tides come on St. Patrick's Day. A swelling (*tòchadh*) in the sea is supposed to be caused by the increasing heat.[1]

The myth of the pursuit of the Cailleach appears to have been known in the Isle of Man. There the son is St. Patrick and the Cailleach " a sea-monster of great size ". The saint crosses from Ireland on horseback and the print of his horse's hoofs " is in the cliffs " and " can be seen still by anyone venturesome enough to go there to see it ". The saint cursed the sea-monster, which " was turned into a solid rock ". On Peel Hill, where the horse stood still, " a beautiful spring of pure water sprang out of the ground, whereby the saint and the horse were both refreshed. The well is called the Holy Well unto this day . . . The Holy Well is said to be the first well, or water, where the first Christian was baptized in the island, and was for ages resorted to as a healing well, and latterly it was called ' Silver Well ' on account of the small silver coins that were left there by persons seeking to be cured of some disease."

Before St. Patrick landed in Isle of Man he heard the cries of a curlew and the bleating of a goat whose kid had fallen down the rocks, " and he blessed them both ".[2]

[1] J. G. Campbell, *Witchcraft and Second Sight in the Scottish Highlands*, pp. 259–61.
[2] Wm. Cashen, *Manx Folklore* (Douglas, Isle of Man, 1912), pp. 48–9.

Like the goddess Artemis, the Cailleach, as has been stated, is the patroness of wild beasts. The theory that she is mainly or wholly a deer deity is urged by Mr. J. G. Mackay, but is not convincing to the writer, who agrees with Miss Eleanor Hull that it does not seem " to account for the various legends about her ". Mr. Mackay's view that some of the stories regarding the Cailleach reflect " the struggle between matriarchy and patriarchy " seems somewhat fantastic.[1]

Dr. Farnell shows that Artemis sometimes assumed the form of the wild animals with which she is associated. One of these was the quail.[2] In Highland folk-references the Cailleach is spoken of occasionally as a gull, cormorant, eagle or heron. Charles St. John, during his sojourn in Moray about a century ago, heard of the Cailleach in the form of a heron.[3] She was associated with " Loch A-na-Caillach " (*Lochan na Cailliche*), the Cailleach's small loch, " a bleak, cold-looking piece of water, with several small grey pools near it ". Donald, a gillie, who related a long story of the origin of the name of the lochan, drew St. John's attention to a large cairn of stones at the end of it. The Cailleach had been " spreading sickness and death among man and beast " and was opposed by the local clergyman by means of Bible and prayer, holy water and " other spiritual weapons ". It was subsequently discovered that she had her abode in the cairn and

---

[1] J. G. Mackay, " The Deer Cult and the Deer Goddess Cult of the Ancient Caledonians " in *Folk-Lore* (June, 1932), pp. 144 *et seq.*; Eleanor Hull in *Folk-Lore*, Vol. XXXVIII, pp. 225 *et seq.*

[2] Farnell, *Cults of the Greek States*, Vol. II, pp. 432 *et seq.*

[3] C. St. John, *Short Sketches of the Wild Sports and Natural History of the Highlands*, Chapter III.

was in the habit of flying through the air by night, especially when the moon was shining, towards " the inhabited part of the country ". At length she was shot by Duncan, an ex-soldier, who placed in his gun a crooked sixpence and some silver buttons. Everyone was convinced that the heron brought down was " the Cailleach herself". Donald added, " She hasna' done much harm since yon, but her ghaist is still to the fore, and the loch side is no canny after the gloaming ".

After beliefs in witchcraft were introduced into the Highlands, these were mixed with local beliefs. Memories of the Cailleach appear to account for the Highland beliefs regarding witches raising storms and drowning people, and appearing as various animals, including sheep, hares, wild cats, rats, ravens, gulls, cormorants, whales, &c.[1]

Artemis had a close connexion with the wild boar. In the story of Meleager " it was Artemis herself . . . who sent the boar ". Diodorus Siculus tells that Phintias, the tyrant of Acragas, " dreamed that while hunting the wild boar he was attacked and slain by the wild sow ". He appears to have sought the protection of Artemis and had coins struck with the head of the goddess on one side and a wild boar's head on the other. The untamed animals with which Artemis was " most frequently associated in cult and legend were the boar and the stag or fawn ".[2]

In the Gaelic story of Diarmaid hunting the wild boar, as located in the neighbourhood of Loch Glass

[1] J. G. Campbell, *Witchcraft and Second Sight in the Highlands and Islands of Scotland*, pp. 19 *et seq.*

[2] Farnell, *Cults of the Greek States*, Vol. II, pp. 432-3.

in Ross and Cromarty, the Cailleach referred to as *Mala Liath*[1] ("Grey Eyebrows") was protectress of a herd of swine. The writer has heard references in this area to the Cailleach and her swine. Dr. Arthur Sutherland[2] has turned into verse the local form of the legend of the boar hunt. He tells of the "venomous wild boar of Glen Glass" and the hag:

> "His lair on Meall-an-Tuirc's rough side
> Where Mala Lia' kept her swine—
> Witch Mala Lia', evil-eyed,
> Foul, shapeless and malign—
> Was all begrimed with filth and gore
> And horrid with the limbs of men
> The unclean monster killed and tore
> To feast on in his den."

Various warriors attempted in vain to slay the boar, but at length the heroic Diarmaid went towards its lair. He saw a raven pecking a dead hare and near it a corbie (hoodie-crow) perched upon a bare boulder. Both oracle birds warned him.[3] The raven said he was going to slay the boar but would meet with his death, while the corbie advised him to return to Grainne, the wife of Fionn, with whom he had eloped, because the boar would cause him to die.

Diarmaid raised and pursued the boar. Mala Lia', the Cailleach, attempted to thwart him. She followed in his footsteps, taunting and cursing him and urging him to return to Grainne. At length, greatly annoyed by her bitter tongue, Diarmaid paused, caught her by

---
[1] Pronounced *mala lee'a*.
[2] *The Highland Monthly* (Inverness, November, 1892), Vol. IV, pp. 491 *et seq.*
[3] These birds were forms of the Cailleach.

a foot and flung her over a cliff. After slaying the boar, he was fatally wounded by a venomous bristle which pierced a vital spot on the inner side of one of his heels.

The reference in this folk-tale to the swine devouring human beings suggests a memory of human sacrifices. There are, as stated, traditions of human sacrifice in connexion with the early worship of Artemis.[1] We meet with a similar reference in the Scottish Lowland lore regarding the "Gyre Carling" (Gay Old Wife), an undoubted form of the Cailleach Bheur. Sir Walter Scott wrote of her as "mother witch of the Scottish peasantry" and quoted a poem regarding her from the Bannatyne MS. in which occur the lines:

"Thair dwelt ane grit Gyre Carling in awld Betokis bour,
That levit (lived) upoun menis flesche (men's flesh)."

The Carlin carried "ane yren (iron) club", the Cailleach's druidical hammer or wand, and when she was attacked by "all the doggis (dogs)" from Dunbar to Dunblane and "all the tykis of Tervey" she fled in her pig form:

"The Carling schup (shaped) her on ane sow and is her gaitis (road) gane,
Grunting our (over) the Greik sie (Greek sea)."

In his poem "The Dreme" Sir David Lindsay, the Scottish poet, relates how he had been wont to carry in his arms and "hap" full "warme" in bed the young King James V and to entertain him with recitals of poems and stories about ancient heroes and

"The Reid Etin (red giant) and the Gyir Carlyng."

[1] Farnell, *Cults of the Greek States*, Vol. II, p. 439.

The Carlin was sometimes called "Nicnevin", an interesting Gaelic survival in the Lothian and Border counties. "Nic" is the female patronymic prefix, but "nevin" presents a puzzle. It was probably the genitive of the Gaelic word for "bone". Professor Watson has drawn my attention in this connexion to the remarkable story of a child conceived from the ashes of old burnt bones.[1] This child was called Gille Dubh Mac nan Cnàmh ("Black Lad, son of the Bones"), with an obscure added epithet. His place of origin was Annat in the parish of Kilmallie, Loch Eil. One has to go to India for similar births from sacrifices.[2] Apparently the "burnt bones" were sacrificial.

A north Irish folk-tale has an interesting bone reference. The Cailleach was slain and mutilated by the Fians and from one of her thigh bones crept out a long hairy worm. A red-headed dwarf warned the heroes that if this worm could find water to drink, it would destroy the whole world. Conan, the impulsive Fian, lifted the worm on the point of his spear and flung it into Lough Derg, saying, "There is water enough for you". The worm became "an enormous beast" which "overran the country, spreading destruction on every side and swallowing hundreds of people at a mouthful". Fionn knew that the monster had on its left side a mole, which was its vulnerable

---

[1] Macfarlane's *Geographical Collections*, Vol. II, p. 162.

[2] In the *Adi Parva* (Section CLXIX) of the *Mahābhārata* King Drupada prevails upon the two Brahmans Yaja and Upayaja to perform sacrifices so that he may get a son. A boy child arose from the flames on the sacrificial platform and was named Dhrista-dyumna. Then arose a daughter, one of whose names was Drupadi.

spot. He wounded it there, disabling it, and the monster's blood coloured the water red, so that it was called Lough Derg (Red Lake). The monster continued to haunt the lough.

As I have shown elsewhere, this story links with the dragon-lore of India and the Far East.[1]

Apparently the Cailleach had a water-dragon form. Other evidence in this connexion will be given further on.

Mrs. K. W. Grant makes mention of " the milking-fold of the Cailleach's sheep and goats—*Buaile nan Dròg̣h*", which is " a cave at Cailleach Point, that stormiest of headlands on the coast of Mull. There she sits among the rocks, ever gazing seaward. When she sneezes she is heard at the island of Coll." [2]

The writer often heard references to the rocks at the Falls of Lora at the mouth of Loch Etive, Connel Ferry, as the " stepping stones " of the Cailleach and her goats, which were at this place driven across the loch to Benderloch (Mrs. Grant [3] records this folk-story) and to *Acha-nam-bà* (cow-field) in Benderloch, where circular green hollows are referred to as " Cailleach Bheur's cheese-vats ".

J. G. Campbell refers to the Cailleach Bheur's cattle:

" A natural enclosure in the rocks above Gorten in Ardnamurchan is called ' the Old Wife's Byre ' (*Bàthaich na Caillich*), it being said that she folded her cattle there." [4]

Deer are not kept in byres.

[1] My *Buddhism in Pre-Christian Britain*, pp. 128–9; Thomas Wright, *St. Patrick's Purgatory*, pp. 3–4.
[2] *Myth, Tradition and Story from Western Argyll*, p. 8.
[3] *Ibid.*, p. 7.
[4] *The Scottish Historical Review*, Vol. XII, pp. 413 *et seq.*

Like the Irish Morrigan, the Cailleach had a cow which gave great quantities of milk. The writer has heard Highlanders tell of the Cailleach's assistants (*na Cailleacha Beura*) riding on wolves and wild pigs as storm-bringers. They raise the storms of " the wolf month " (February).

Thus we have among the Cailleach's animals deer, swine, goats, cattle and wolves.

There are many folk-stories regarding the Cailleach's herds of deer. One of the pastures to which she drove them is in the Ross of Mull. She also wandered with them by night on wild beaches where they devoured sea-tangle, especially in the winter season. The writer has seen wild goats feeding on seaweed in Skye.

Cailleach Bheinn a', Bhric is associated with the " speckled ben " in Lochaber. She pastured her herds of deer in Glen Nevis and milked them there, singing one of her songs the while. When hunters were unable to find deer, they blamed the Cailleach. J. F. Campbell gives a Sutherland folk-tale regarding the " Cailliach Mhor Chlibhrich ", who had enchanted the deer of Lord Reay's forest so that they eluded the hunters. A man named William kept watch one night and by means of some counter enchantments managed to be present when the Cailleach engaged in milking the hinds at the door of her hut in the early morning.

" They were standing all about the door of the hut till one of them ate a hank of blue worsted hanging from a nail in it. The witch (*Cailleach*) struck the animal and said: ' The spell is off you; and Lord Reay's bullet will be your death to-day.' William repeated this to his master to confirm the tale of his having passed the night in the hut of the great hag, which no

A SCOTTISH ARTEMIS 153

one would believe. And the event justified it, for a fine yellow hind was killed that day, and the hank of blue yarn was found in its stomach."[1]

The blue yarn is of interest, contrasting with the red cords, berries, &c., used by human beings to shield themselves against attack by the Cailleach, the fairies, &c.

Artemis had a connexion with fish and one of her forms resembled that of the mermaid, having been fused with a sea-goddess.[2] It is of interest therefore to find that in Lochaber the Cailleach " generally appeared to them (wanderers) in the form of a gigantic woman by a stream, in the act of cleaning fish ". She was, Mrs. Grant [3] says, " connected with good or evil luck in hunting and fishing ".

J. G. Mackay refers to a Gaelic song, *Cailleach Liath Ratharsaidh*, which tells of " the three Hebridean Cailleachs of Raasay, Rona and Sligachan as being fond of fish. They were probably," he adds, " fish-goddesses."[4] But the Cailleach was as complex a deity as Artemis. Her connexion with fish, the sea, rivers, &c., is not confined to the Hebrides.

The Cailleach's association with water is emphasized by a folk-tale located in various parts of the Highlands. One version given by J. F. Campbell is as follows:

" Where Loch Ness now is, there was long ago a fine glen. A woman went one day to the well to fetch water and she

[1] *Popular Tales of the West Highlands*, Vol. II, Tale XXVII; also Mrs. Grant, *op. cit.*, p. 10.
[2] Farnell, *Cults of the Greek States*, Vol. II, pp. 429–30 and Plate XXIX, facing p. 522.
[3] *Ibid.*, p. 10.
[4] *Folk-Lore* (June, 1932), p. 162.

found the spring flowing so fast that she got frightened, and left her pitcher and ran for her life; she never stopped till she got to the top of a high hill; and when there, she turned about and saw the glen filled with water. Not a house or field was to be seen." [1]

Mrs. Grant [2] gives an Argyll version which tells that the Cailleach was the guardian of a well on the summit of Ben Cruachan. She had to cover it with a slab of stone every evening at sundown and remove the slab at daybreak.

"But one evening, being aweary after driving her goats across Connel, she fell asleep by the side of the well. The fountain overflowed, its waters rushed down the mountain side, the roar of the flood as it broke open an outlet through the Pass of Brander awoke the Cailleach, but her efforts to stem the torrent were fruitless; it flowed into the plain, where man and beast were drowned in the flood. Thus was formed Loch Awe.... The Cailleach was filled with such horror over the result of her neglect of duty that she turned into stone. There she sits ... among the rocky ruins at the pass overlooking the loch, as on the rocks at Cailleach Point in Mull she gazes seaward."

The origin of Loch Tay in Perthshire and Loch Eck in Cowal is accounted for in the same manner. According to the folk-lore of Ireland the River Boyne was similarly brought into existence by a nymph who walked round a well three times by the left, with the result that the water rose furiously and drove her, as the river, towards the sea.[3]

[1] *Popular Tales of the West Highlands*, Vol. II, Tale XXXIV.
[2] *Myth, Tradition and Story from Western Argyll*, p. 9.
[3] Eleanor Hull, *Folk-Lore*, Vol. XXXVIII, p. 249.

A SCOTTISH ARTEMIS

The earliest form of Artemis was "connected with the waters and with wild vegetation and beasts". Farnell notes that in Arcadia, Laconia and Sicyon she was worshipped as "the lady of the lake". Near the lake of Stymphalus she "bred the deadly birds which Heracles slew". She was also "the goddess of the marsh" in Arcadia and Messene. " She was associated frequently with rivers as in Elis." Farnell comments, "The goddess of still and running water is also naturally a goddess of trees and fish."[1] As we have seen, the Cailleach was connected with the holly tree and whins and fish. No cultivated trees were associated with Artemis.[2]

It may be that the prototype of the Cailleach was connected with the River Lochy (*Lòchaidh*) in Lochaber, which Adamnan, in his *Life of Columba*, refers to as Nigra Dea ("black goddess"). Other river names of like character are the *Lòchá* and *Lòchaidh* in Perthshire and Lochy in Banffshire.[3]

[1] *Cults of the Greek States*, Vol. II, pp. 427-8.
[2] Farnell, *op. cit.*, p. 429.
[3] W. J. Watson, *History of the Celtic Place-Names of Scotland*, p. 50.

CHAPTER VIII

Ancient Goddess Forms

<small>Ocean Cailleach—Pleads for admittance to house—Theft of "Cup of Victory"—Dark and one-eyed like Cailleach Bheur—Cailleach as "Gentle Annie"—A storm demon—Enemy of fishers—Robbing the pot—Sailor saying about "Gentle Annie"—Calm before storm—Longevity of Cailleach—Renews her youth by drinking from "Well of Youth"—Her death—Tiree folk-tale—Poetic treatment of Cailleach—As mountain cairn and bridge builder—As bringer of thunder—Reference by the poet Dunbar—Wading the ocean—Cailleach's "fire-balls"—Cailleach as inhospitable housewife—Literary development of stories—William Sit-Down tale—Story of Cyclops—Fairy story links—Cailleach a complex deity—The magic wand—A ritualistic dance—Nature myth theory—Norse borrowing—Irish connexion of Cailleach—Bull turned into stone—Cairn building—Cailleach's black dog—Confusion of Cailleach with other deities—Cailleach not in Danann pantheon—Milton's blue hag—The English Black Annis—Morgan le Fay as the Cailleach—Welsh Cailleach—Norse fragment of Cailleach story—Danish fragment—Cailleach in central Europe—Greek demon-goddesses—Babylonian and Egyptian slayers—The complex Cailleach.</small>

An ocean form of the Cailleach is known as the Muileartach or Muireartach. Gregorson Campbell has suggested that this name means the "Eastern Sea", and that the monster was therefore a personification of the ocean which was regularly crossed by the intruding and hostile Vikings. His theory, however, can hardly be regarded as conclusive. It is questionable if we really meet in Scotland with any supernatural beings which can be regarded as local personifications of nature. Before the Celts or the earlier Bronze Age people arrived on our shores, they had definite ideas regarding the control of natural forces by anthropomorphic and shape-changing deities. They believed in the existence of deities and they imported and perpetuated them, imparting to them a degree of local colour.

A deliberate personification of natural forces would take us back to the very beginnings of early religion, and we find ourselves far from the beginnings when an intensive study is made of Scottish folk-lore and mythology, which are really of highly complex character. The idea of control in nature by supernatural beings arose after the family group had developed into an organized clan or state, and this development took place long before Britain was colonized by settlers from areas of ancient civilization—the Bronze Age people, whose burial customs and weapons indicate that they had definite religious beliefs and an advanced social organization, and the Celts with their pantheons and eastern chariots and other manifestations of the impress of cultures derived from areas of origin or characterization. It does not follow, however, that a pantheon in which a goddess was supreme necessarily reflected a state of society in which the females were supreme. The prominence accorded to the Great Mother was due mainly, it would appear, to the rise of a people who believed that life had " origin " when the first mother came into existence and gave birth to a fatherless son. Their theories regarding the riddle of life must not be confused with their social organization.

The Muileartach resembled the Sumerian Tiamat of Mesopotamia and certain old Egyptian goddesses in having a demon and reptile, or half-reptile, form and in being a slayer and destroyer as well as a giver of life. She could also appear as an anthropomorphic deity. Like the mother of the giants in the Finlay Changeling folk-story, the Muileartach assumes the form of an old woman after leaving the sea and visits a house to ask for a night's lodging, pretending to be a traveller who is cold and weary. .

In a well-known Gaelic folk-poem, of which there are several variants, she is represented as one who knocks at a door and calls upon Fionn to admit her. Although, as she approached in the darkness, she " pulled up a tree, swept off the branches and had it for a stick ", she cries in a plaintive voice:

" *Is mise Cailleach thruagh, thruagh*
(I am a pitiful, pitiful Cailleach)."

She wants only to warm herself at the fire and would be content to eat with the dogs (*B'fheàrr leam, a bhith am blàth 's do theine mhóir, 's a bhith an comith ri do chonaibh*). The door is barred against her, and when she finds that her deceitful pleading is in vain, she kicks it open. Then, entering quickly, she seizes with her " crooked claw " Fionn's " Cup of Victory " and runs away with it, having shown herself in her true colours as a Cailleach of great fury (*a' Chailleach bu mhór fearg*). The Fians pursue and struggle with the Cailleach:

" Thinman (Caoilte), son of Roin, caught
His big sword and his two spears;
And the active youthful Oscar caught
The embroidered skirt that was round her body.
They took the apple from the wretch."

This myth has not only been connected with the Fians, but the much later Manus (Magnus Bareleg), and in "the confused snowball of narrative" are fragments of ancient myths like the mystic apple and the "Cup of Victory" from which Fionn derived his mysterious powers, supplies of food, &c.

Like our Cailleach Bheur, the Muileartach has a blue-black face and a single eye:

> "There was one flabby eye in her head
> That quicker moved than lure-pursuing mackerel.
> Her head bristled dark and grey
> Like scrubwood before hoar frost."

A variant is:

> "Her face was blue-black of the lustre of coal,
> And her bone-tufted tooth was like red rust.
> In her head was one pool-like eye.
> Swifter than a star in a winter sky."

She had come across the ocean to demand the heads of Fionn and his chief warriors, but was herself slain.[1]

Our Cailleach acquired various names in different localities. She is *Cailleach uisge* ("water Cailleach") when she comes from the sea or haunts a swollen river ford, waiting to drown reckless and hurried travellers. Professor W. J. Watson tells me he has heard of *Cailleach na h-Abhann* ("the river Cailleach"), who haunted a ford on the River Orrin in Ross and Cromarty and drowned unwary people.

In the Cromarty Firth the south-westerly gales of

---

[1] J. G. Campbell, *Waifs and Strays of Celtic Tradition*, Argyllshire Series No. IV, pp. 131 *et seq.*; J. F. Campbell, *Popular Tales of the West Highlands*, Vol. III, pp. 136 *et seq.*; Mrs. Grant, *op. cit.*, p. 14.

spring are referred to as those of "Gentle Annie". Her stormy period is supposed to last for six weeks, and the fisher people of Cromarty have sayings regarding it.

The firth, called before 1300 Sykkersund ("safe sound"), is a natural, land-locked harbour, with abrupt headlands at its entrance, and is fringed by undulating hills. It is well protected from the east and north winds, but part of it is dangerous for small craft when the south-westerly gales blow in spasmodic gusts through a gap in the mountains. A particular point below the Cromarty coastguard station, which stands on Maryness, is feared by the boatmen, because there the tide runs swiftly and gusts of south-westerly wind sweep with great fury. The point of the promontory is called Heel of Ness, and the writer has seen fishermen lowering their sails as they rounded the point even in moderate weather, owing to the superstitious dread of this area of danger. "Gentle Annie" is deceitful and no risks should be taken!

The fishers speak an archaic dialect of Old English (or Scots), dropping the "h" and "wh" and using "thou" (thoo) and "thee" like the Quakers. According to local tradition, they came originally from the Firth of Forth area in the reign of James I and VI. The "h" is dropped or misused in like manner by the fishers of Newhaven, near Edinburgh.

In Cromarty the fishers have the following saying regarding the Cailleach of the south-westerly gales:

"When Gentle Hannie (Annie) is skyawlan (screeching) round the 'eel o' Ness, wi' a w'ite futher in her 'at, they'll (or she will) be 'arrying (harrying) the crook."

("When Gentle Annie is yelling round the Heel of Ness with a white feather (the foam) in her hat, she will be robbing the crook, i.e. the pot which hangs from the hook of the chimney chain.")

There is no food in the pot because the fishers cannot go to sea. A fish-wife once remarked to the writer: "We'll better hae (have) a shilling in oor pooch (our pocket) against the Gentle Hannie wuther (weather)."

The Cromarty fisher people have kept alive memories of former local superstitions and use some acquired Gaelic words.[1]

The seafarers of "windjammer days" used the expression "Don't come the Gentle Annie over me" when they suspected they were about to be deceived or cheated by a "mealy-mouthed" individual. "Gentle Annie" had the reputation of playing tricks with the weather. A morning broke peaceful and calm and men ventured to sea, lured by reason of her deceptive promise. Then suddenly a fierce storm came on and there were wrecks and drownings. In Gaelic lore the Cailleach period in spring is comparatively mild, but is only an interlude, because fierce storms follow. Mrs. Watson refers to the Cailleach period as "a few semi-calm days" which are followed by the *sguabag* sweeping storms.[2]

A sunken rock known as *Bogha na Caillich* is on the

[1] I dealt with "Gentle Annie" in her relation to other storm bringers in my article "A Highland Goddess" in the *Celtic Review* (1912), Vol. VII, pp. 336 *et seq*. My tentative suggestions of a connexion between goddesses and matriarchal customs and to fusions of beliefs and peoples have apparently inspired Mr. J. G. Mackay's rather extravagant theory of much later date in *Folk-Lore* (1932), pp. 144 *et seq*.

[2] *The Celtic Review* (1908-9), Vol. V, p. 66.

Inverness-shire coast. It is dangerous and is dreaded by seafarers. Other rocks, already referred to, at the mouth of Loch Etive, Connel Ferry, over which pour the Falls of Lora, are similarly a peril, although the Cailleach's " stepping stones " and the tides are very swift and treacherous. A dangerous sandy bar at the entrance to the Dornoch Firth is called " the gizzen brigs " (Norse, *gisnar bryggja*, " leaky bridge "). In the local Gaelic lore the bar is connected with a malicious female spirit.[1] The writer has heard references to her as a storm-bringer and drowner of seafarers. Hugh Miller in his story of the " Stine Bheag o' Tarbat ", who gives weather charms to sailors, appears to have preserved a memory of the dreaded hag of the " gizzen briggs ".[2]

The longevity of the Cailleach is accounted for in a group of stories which tell that she drinks the water of life. One of these, which locates the " Well of Youth " near Loch Ba in Mull, tells that she visited it at " the dead of night ", and drank " before bird tasted water or dog was heard to bark ". She thus " kept herself always at sixteen years of age ". J. G. Campbell, who gives a version of this story, continues:

" At last, when making her way to the well on a calm morning (and such mornings are very beautiful in the west Highlands) she heard a dog bark. She exclaimed:

' Little knows any living wight
When mischance may befall him;
For me early has the dog called
In the calm morn above Loch Ba.

[1] W. J. Watson, *Place-Names of Ross and Cromarty*, p. 37.
[2] *Scenes and Legends* (1st edition, 1835), pp. 304 *et seq.*

> ' I had enough of spells
> To serve the seed of Adam,
> But when the mischance was ripe
> It could not be warded off.'

Having said this, she fell, crumbling into dust. She lived so long that she had above five hundred children."[1]

A prior's daughter in Tiree is said to have met the Cailleach Bheur and asked her how old she was. She said her memory extended back to the time when the Skerryvore rocks, where the lighthouse stands, were covered with arable fields.

> " Little sharp old wife, tell me your age."
> " I saw the seal-haunted Skerryvore
> When it was a mighty power;
> When they ploughed it, if I am right,
> And sharp and juicy was its barley.
> I saw the loch at Balefuill
> When it was a little round well,
> Where my child was drowned,
> Sitting in its circular chair;
> And I saw Leinster lake in Ireland
> When children could swim across."

Beira sang in terms of affection regarding places in Tiree, and especially some on the farm of Valla:

> " The little dune, the big dune,
> Dunes of my love;
> Odram and the Raven's mound
> Where I was a young girl,
> Though I am to-day an old woman,
> Bent, decrepit and sallow."[2]

---
[1] *The Scottish Historical Review* (July, 1915), Vol. XII, No. 4, pp. 413 *et seq.*
[2] J. G. Campbell, *op. cit.*, pp. 413 *et seq.*

This is the late, poetical aspect of the Cailleach, reflecting the influence of Christian culture. Her fierceness of character is obscured and she is regarded merely as a woman of remarkable longevity and more a sentimentalist than a treacherous enemy of man who claims sacrifices of human life.

In numerous fragmentary folk-stories she is, along with her helpers, a shaper of Scotland. One given by Hugh Miller tells how she carried on her back a pannier filled with earth and stones and "formed almost all the hills of Ross-shire". Occasionally an accident happened.

"When standing on the site of the huge Ben Vaichaird, the bottom of the pannier is said to have given way, and the contents, falling through the opening, produced the hill, which owes its great height and vast extent of base to the accident."[1]

The eminence known as Little Wyvis was similarly formed while one of her assistants was leaping across a valley.

J. G. Campbell tells that when the Cailleach was constructing a bridge across the Sound of Mull, commencing at the Morvern side, the strap of her creel, filled with stones, snapped suddenly and the contents of the creel formed the cairn called in Gaelic *Càrn na Caillich*. "She intended to put chains across the Sound of Islay to prevent the passage of ships that way, and the stones are pointed out on the Jura side, to which the chains were to be secured." Other references by Campbell are:

"*Beinn na Caillich*, a hill in Kildalton parish, Islay, is called

---

[1] *Scenes and Legends* (1835 edition), p. 30.

after her, and a furrow down its side, called *Sgrìob na Caillich*, was made by her as she slid down in a sitting posture. In the parish of Strathlachlan and Strachur in Cowal, Argyllshire, there is also a hill called after her, *Beinn Chailleach Bheur*."[1]

In the eighteenth century *Statistical Account* of this parish, the Cailleach is referred to as "the Old Wife of Thunder". She is reputed to be a leaper from hill to hill and one who could "command terrific thunder and desolating deluges at pleasure and hence the dreadful apprehensions of incurring her ire that generally prevailed".

Although J. G. Campbell and others think that the parish minister of Strathlachlan and Strachur was mistaken in connecting the Cailleach with thunder, we find that the poet William Dunbar, who was familiar with her cantrips as a hill-shaper, &c., in Lothian, also refers to her as the source of thunder-storms. He makes her the wife of Fionn the giant, and writes:

"Scho spittit Lochlomond with her lippis;
Thunner and fyreflaucht (lightning) flew fra hir hippis."

When she "wald rift" the heaven "rerdit" (roared). Dunbar pictures her wading into the Spanish sea "with her sark lape (tucked up)".[2]

J. G. Campbell quotes a Gaelic poem with regard to a mountain loch in Mull, called *Crù-lochan* (horse-shoe lakelet), reputed to be "the deepest loch in the world". Cailleach Bheur says:

[1] *The Scottish Historical Review* (July, 1915), Vol. XII, No. 4, pp. 413 *et seq.*
[2] Poem "The Manere of the Crying of Ane Playe" in *The Poems of William Dunbar*, edited by W. Mackay Mackenzie (Edinburgh, 1932), pp. 170 *et seq.*

"The great sea reached my knee
And the horse-shoe tarn reached my haunch."[1]

A well-known Highland folk-tale is devoted to the Cailleach who came in a dark cloud from Lochlann and threw down fire-balls or thunder-bolts which set on fire the forests of Scotland.[2]

There are likewise folk-stories of our Cailleach as an inhospitable woman. She is visited by a man who wishes to reside for the night, and she gives him the head of one of her sheep to singe and then endeavours to deprive him of a share of it when it is cooked. But the man outwits her in a bardic contest, as the sea-captain outwitted the chief of the Blue Men of the Minch. Stories of this type were evidently of comparatively late literary development in the ceilidhs. They emphasize the meanness of the food-denying winter deity and the cleverness of men who make use of poetic charms.

In one of the stories a man named William declared he would compel her to give him lodgings and food. On entering her house she asked him his name, and he said it was "William Sit-Down". She repeated his name and he said, "Why should I not sit down when the mistress of the house asks it?" He thereupon sat down. After some lively passages he tricked her into giving him not merely a meal, but the whole meal.[3]

This type of story is of considerable antiquity.

---

[1] J. G. Campbell, *op. cit.*, pp. 413 *et seq.*

[2] *Transactions of the Gaelic Society of Inverness*, Vol. XXVI, pp. 277–9, &c.

[3] J. G. Campbell, *Scottish Historical Review*, Vol. XII (1915), pp. 413 *et seq.*; J. F. Campbell, *Popular Tales*, Vol. II, pp. 207–8.

Odysseus in the *Odyssey* (Book IX) tricks the one-eyed Cyclops by giving his name as " No-man ". In various Gaelic folk-stories a fairy is similarly deceived by a man who gives his name as " Me Myself " or, as Hugh Miller has it, " Mysel'-and-Mysel' ". In the development of the William Sit-Down narrative, it is obvious that other popular tales were drawn upon in the ceilidhs.

Our Cailleach Bheur and her assistants are evidently prominent figures in an imported mythology. In some respects, as has been shown, the chief Cailleach resembles the primitive Artemis of Greece. The view that she was merely a " deer goddess " ignores her associations with swine, goats, sheep, wolves, birds and fish as well as deer, her connexions with trees and plants, with mountain wells, rivers, lochs, marshes and the ocean, with tempests and thunder and with hills, rocks, cairns, boulders and standing stones.[1] An outstanding attribute is her druidic hammer or wand, which cannot be accounted for by any deer connexion. We gather from the folk-tales that it may be taken from her and that when she suffers loss of it she is powerless. There may have been a myth explaining how she recovered her wand after she emerged from her boulder, but, if so, it has been lost. As Finlay Changeling wields the hammer or wand for a time, so may have the Cailleach's son who " put out " her eye, apparently by making use of it.

We seem to detect a memory of some old ritual in a curious dance known in Gaelic as *Cailleach an Dùdain*

---

[1] The standing stones on Craigmaddy Moor between Glasgow and Milngavie are " the Auld Wife's Lifts ".

("Cailleach of the mill-dust"), which may throw light on this aspect of the problem. It is performed by a man and a woman and the man grasps in his right hand a wand known as the *slachdan druidheachd* ("druidic wand") or *slachdan geasachd* ("magic wand"). "The man and the woman," writes Dr. Carmichael,[1] "gesticulate and attitudinize before one another, dancing round and round, in and out, crossing and recrossing, changing and exchanging places." When the man touches the woman's head with the wand she falls at his feet as if dead. He laments over her, dancing and gesticulating.

"He then lifts up her left hand and, looking into the palm, breathes upon it and touches it with the wand. Immediately the limp hand becomes alive and moves from side to side and up and down. The man rejoices and dances round the figure on the floor. And, having done the same to the right hand, and to the left and right foot in succession, they also became alive and move. But, although the limbs are living, the body is still inert. The man kneels over the woman and breathes into her mouth and touches her heart with the wand. The woman comes to life and springs up, confronting the man. Then the two dance vigorously and joyously as in the first part. The tune varies with the varying phases of the dance."

Magic hammers were wielded by Greek satyrs apparently in connexion with the raising from the earth of Pandora as Ge, the earth goddess. An Armenian myth tells that Christ descended from the sky with a golden hammer. He smote the earth and evoked the virgin church.[2]

[1] *Carmina Gadelica*, Vol. I, pp. 206–7.
[2] Farnell, *Cults of the Greek States*, Vol. III, p. 26; *Hellenic Journal* (1900), pp. 106–7 and for 1901, p. 1, Plate I.

Our Cailleach cannot now be connected with any particular people who entered Scotland, and there is certainly no justification for confining her to the Caledonians. It is extremely hazardous to assume that she reflects an ancient state of society in Scotland in which " woman was supreme ". Although the Picts, for instance, recognized descent by the female line, no woman's name appears in the lists of Pictish rulers. There is really nothing in the Cailleach stories to justify the view that they reflect a " struggle between matriarchy and patriarchy ".[1]

Mrs. K. W. Grant regards the Cailleach stories as fragments of " nature myths " imported from Norway. There can be no doubt that the deity had a calendar significance in her association with the storms of winter and spring and that she was connected with the sea and the mountains. But Mrs. Grant's theory, like that of Mr. Mackay, fails to account for all the attributes of the complex Cailleach. The theory of Norse borrowing is far from convincing. Even the Norse material cannot be regarded as merely a collection of " nature myths ". Weather controlling was only one of the activities of the Cailleach.

Some would have it that the Cailleach was imported from Ireland. Miss Eleanor Hull comments, however: " The Scottish stories about the Cailleach are far more alive and more widely spread than those of Ireland . . . They do not seem to have any traditions about her in Aran."

In Ireland she has a " wizard's wand " with which,

[1] J. G. Mackay, "The Deer Cult and the Deer Goddess of the Ancient Caledonians " in *Folk-Lore* (June, 1932), pp. 144 *et seq.*

when herding her cows, she strikes a bull, turning it into a stone, and she is connected with cairns and dolmens. There is a "hag's chair" in County Meath. In Northern Ireland she formed a cairn on Carnbane by spilling stones from her apron, and she broke her neck when leaping from an eminence. "She lives in a cave on the hills above Tiernach Bran." Her black dog gives milk which imparts great strength to a man who drinks it. She is credited with some of the feats of *Aine an Cnuic* (Aine of the hill, Knockainy), "the Queen of the Limerick fairies", and she is the "banshee" of some Leinster and Meath families, as Cleena, Grian of Cnoc Grèine, Aine, Una and Eevil are of other families, there having evidently been "culture mixing" and the mixing of myths. Most of the Irish stories emphasize the Cailleach's great strength and longevity. She had "seven periods of youth" and was a great lover:

"It is riches
Ye love, it is not men:
In the time when *we* lived
It was men we loved.
My arms when they are seen
Are bony and thin:
Once they would fondle,
They would be round glorious kings." [1]

It may well be, judging from the late character of the Irish material, that the drift of lore regarding her was from Scotland to Ireland rather than from Ireland to Scotland. She plays no part in Danann myth and, as Miss Eleanor Hull, who has collected the Irish

[1] Kuno Meyer, *Ancient Irish Poetry* (London, 1911), pp. 88 *et seq.*

evidence, points out, "she is not mentioned in Cormac's glossary or in *Côir Anmann*, which contains the most ancient Irish existing traditions of the gods, nor yet in the *Dindsenchus* or *Agallamh na Senorach*."

Milton must have heard of her in England, for in his *Comus* he makes the First Brother refer to evil things that walk by night

" In fog or fire, by lake or moorish fen,
Blue meager hag, or stubborn unlaid ghost."

In Leicestershire she has been remembered as " Black Annis ", who is associated with the Easter " hare hunt " and has a " cat Anna " form. An eighteenth century title deed refers to land known as " Black Anny's Bower Close ". Her cave was in the Dane Hills, but was filled in. According to a local poet:

" An oak, the pride of all the mossy dell,
Spreads its broad arms above the stony cell;
And many a bush, with hostile thorns arrayed,
Forbids the secret cavern to invade."

She is credited in the local folk-lore with devouring lambs and young children. Like Cailleach Bheur, she has a blue face and only one eye. The poet continues:

" 'Tis said the soul of mortal man recoiled
To view Black Annis' eye, so fierce and wild.
Vast talons, foul with human flesh, there grew
In place of hands, and features livid blue
Glared in her visage; whilst the obscene waist
Warm skins of human victims close embraced." [1]

[1] *County Folklore* (Leicestershire and Rutland), Folklore Society's Publications, Vol. I (London, 1895).

In Arthurian romance Morgan le Fay, it is told, was chased by Arthur, whose scabbard she stole.

" Then she rode into a valley where many great stones were, and when she saw that she must be overtaken, she shaped herself, horse and man, by enchantment into a great marble stone." [1]

Lady Charlotte in her notes to the *Mabinogion* refers to two large rocks, reputed to be Arthur's " quoits ", which he flung from the summit of Pen Arthur. A rock was thrown from the same eminence " by a lady of those days, being a pebble in her shoe which gave her some annoyance ".[2]

A fragment of the Scottish Cailleach story of the imprisoned maiden is found in the Norse ballad of " Hermod the Young ", which tells of the hero liberating a beautiful maiden who had been taken captive by a giantess. Hermod visits the mountain dwelling of this hag and is permitted to remain for the night:

" Resorting to cunning, he persuades the giantess the following morning to visit her neighbours, liberates the fair maiden during her absence, and flees on his skis with her over the high mountains and down the low ones."

The giantess pursues the couple.

" When Hermod with his young maiden had come to the salt fjord (Elivagar) the giantess is quite near them, but in the decisive moment she is changed to a stone, according to the Norse version, by the influence of the sun, which just at that time rose; according to the Swedish version, by the influence of a cross which stood near the fjord and its ' long bridge '." [3]

[1] *Morte Darthur*, Book IV, Chapter XIV.
[2] Note on Porth Cleis in the story of Kilhwch and Olwen, Everyman's Library Edition, p. 335.
[3] V. Rydberg, *Teutonic Mythology*, translation by R. B. Anderson (London, 1889), pp. 573-4. The ballads are late.

In Danish lore the captured maiden is Sigrid, daughter of Siward. She is carried away by a giant who is slain by Ottar. The maiden is loved by the hero, but she declines to respond and takes refuge in the hut of " a certain huge woman " and undertakes the task of pasturing goats and sheep. In the end she consents to become the wife of Ottar, who carries her away.[1]

Mrs. K. W. Grant has collected in Rumania from a " Saxon-Hungarian woman ", named Malvinia, a folk-tale of a very great witch, who was head over eight witches. She was harsh to her son's wife, to whom she set the task of washing a brown fleece white. The young woman washes it at a brook, but old Winter took pity on her and, taking the fleece from her, made it white. When she returned home with the fleece and some mountain flowers, the old witch was enraged and she and the other witches mounted goats and began a contest against all growth, like the Scottish Cailleach and her helpers.

" Snow and hail, wind and rain were summoned to do battle, but the warm sun shone out, the south wind breathed, and Spring triumphed. The nine witches were turned into stone, and ' there they sit ', said Malvinia, ' on their goats, on the top of the mountain of Silash in Temesvar; and on the anniversary of their defeat the fountains in their heads overflow and their faces become blurred with weeping '."

The memory of an ancient savage goddess survives in the folk-lore of Greece. She is known as Lamia, Queen of Libya, whose children were robbed by Hera. She took up her abode " in a grim and lonely cavern, and there changed into a malicious and greedy monster,

---

[1] *Saxo Grammaticus*, Book VII, pp. 225-7.

who in envy and despair stole and killed the children of more fortunate mothers ". Another Lamia, the Gello, assumes the form of a fish, a serpent, a kite or a skylark and likewise devours babies. When one of these hags is slain, no grass grows where her blood falls.[1]

A primitive form of Demeter concealed herself in the cave of Phigalia, had a mare's head and was associated with snakes and other monsters. When the Phigalians neglected to sacrifice to her a famine afflicted the land. She was known as the Black Demeter.[2] Demeter cast a blight on the land when her daughter Persephone was carried away by Pluto. The Scottish Cailleach, as we have seen, beats the ground with her hammer, thus freezing it, to prevent the grass growing.

In Babylonia the demoniac forms of deities are referred to in metrical charms and incantations. Labartu (Sumerian " Dimme ") haunted mountain and marsh and devoured stray children, like the English Black Annis. The Egyptian goddess Sekhet was a slayer armed with a dagger. The mother goddess of Crete was associated with trees and mountains, snakes and wild beasts, and brandished a spear, or a staff which may have been a magic wand.

It would appear that our Cailleach Bheur of Scotland is a localized ancient deity of Cyclopean type and the Great Mother of giants. She shaped the mountains, gave origin to rivers, lochs and marshes, and had a sea connexion; she was the protector of fish and wild animals, whose forms she could assume; and she was

[1] Lawson, *Modern Greek Folklore and Ancient Greek Religion*, pp. 173 et seq.
[2] Pausanias, VIII, 42.

connected with uncultivated trees, and was possessed of a magic wand, with which she controlled the weather during the winter and spring; she was an enemy of man, but yet a mother of many children; and she had a boulder or standing-stone form. The outwitting of her by means of clever repartee appears to be a memory of incantations and charms which protected human beings and compelled her to render service.

The Cailleach has to be considered in her relation to human beings as well as to the calendar, and the various stories regarding her emphasize that she cannot be characterized as either a deer goddess or a central figure in a nature myth. The Scottish Cailleach had many specialized and local forms, like Artemis of Greece, whose primitive characteristics survived longer in one area than another. Like Artemis, the Cailleach had, as the lover of many kings and the mother of many children, a connexion with birth. Farnell refers to an "Artemis-Aphrodite". Although reputed to be a "virgin goddess", Artemis gave birth to children. Perhaps, like the Cailleach, she renewed her youth by drinking from a "well of life" and was supposed at the same time to renew her virginity.

CHAPTER IX

The Glaistig and Bride

Glaistig links with Cailleach—Glaistig as half woman, half goat—Connexion with water—Animal forms—Glaistig and yew tree—Glaistig as family guardian—Her green attire—Her magic wand—Cows transformed into stones—Glaistig fond of children—Attachment to individuals—Milk offerings—Glaistig as gruagach—Wader of deep sea—Islands as stepping stones—Glaistig and pirate—Swift crossing of Minch—Glaistig shrieks when pirate dies—Glaistig as river fury—Strathconon and Lochaber legends—Glaistig curses the Kennedys—As a house trickster—Ferry story—Glaistig patroness of domesticated animals—Goat lore—Urisk as a satyr—Urisk stories—Goddess Bride—A Great Mother—Bride and the seasons—Bride as prisoner of Cailleach—Bride's serpent-dragon—Link with Asiatic serpent-dragon—Bride and milk-yielding plants—Her dandelion nourishes early lamb—The Christianized Bride—As " aid woman " at Bethlehem—The foster-mother of Christ—Bride invoked at births—Bride's Eve ceremonies—Bride as oat sheaf—Dance of lads and girls—Women's Bride ceremony—Bride's magic wand—Invocation of Bride—Bride swastika—Birds of Bride—Bride and classical goddesses.

A supernatural being known as the " glaistig ",[1] " glaistic ", " glaisnig ", " glaislig ", " glaisric " or " glaislid " has features in common with Cailleach Bheur. She is credited, for instance, with an attempt to bridge the Sound of Mull. Mrs. Watson [2] summarizes this folk-tale:

" She gathered a huge creelful of stones among the hills to the north of Morvern and walked down to the Sound with her burden."

When near her destination, however, the creel-rope snapped, and down fell the stones. They are still

---
[1] Pronounced *gläsh'tik*. The Manx form is " glashtyn ".
[2] *Celtic Review*, Vol. V (1908–9), p. 61.

lying there, the heap being known as Carn-na-Caillich. The glaistig herself has related the incident in rhyme:

> "*An aithne dhuibh Carn-na-Caillich*
> *Air an leacainn ghlais ud thall?*
> *'S mise chruinnich sid le cliabh,*
> *A' h-uile spitheag riamh a th'ann.*
> *Drochaid a chur air Caol Muile,*
> *'S bha i furasd' a chur ann.*
> *'S mur briseadh an iris mhuineil*
> *Bha i nis gun teagamh ann.*

> " Know ye the Cailleach's cairn
> On that green hillside yonder?
> It was I that gathered it with a creel,
> Every pebble that is in it,
> To put a bridge on the Sound of Mull—
> And to put it there were easy,
> Had not the neck-rope broken,
> It were there now beyond doubt."

Mrs. Watson and her father, Dr. Alexander Carmichael,[1] have referred to the glaistig as " half woman, half goat " who frequents " lonely lakes and rivers ". Dr. Carmichael translated her name as " water imp ", from " glas ", water, and " stic ", imp. In the *Highland Society's Dictionary* the glaistig is " a she-devil, or hag, in the shape of a goat ". Some folk-tales refer to her as being very tall, while others depict her as a stout little woman. She has in widely scattered folk-tales various animal forms in addition to the goat, including those of the dog, mare, foal and sheep. Herding sheep and cattle was supposed to be one of

---

[1] *Carmina Gadelica* (2nd edition), Vol. II, pp. 302–3.

her chief occupations. She was fond of fish, her favourite fish-food being eels. In Mull she took refuge in a yew tree. Elsewhere she has her habitation in a cave or is supposed to be behind a waterfall, or at or in a ford of a river or a loch. Many folk-tales connect her with the strongholds of chiefs or with other old houses. As a family guardian she made merry when a marriage was about to take place, or wailed before a death. When unexpected visitors were coming, she could be heard at night in a house rearranging furniture and washing dishes. As a rule she was invisible, but when she permitted herself to be seen she was found to be attired in green like the fairies, and was consequently spoken of as *a' Ghlaistig uaine* ("the green glaistig").

She is sometimes referred to as having a magic or druidic wand like Cailleach Bheur. A Mull story tells that a glaistig who was attached to the family of Lamont at Ardnadrochit was herding the Lamont cattle when raiders from Lorne came to "lift" them. "She struck the cows and converted them into grey stones, which are to be seen to this day" in "the Heroes' Hollow" (*Glaic nan Gaisgeach*). She broke her heart over this incident, died and was buried by Lamont.

The glaistig was credited with being fond of children. Mrs. Watson writes in this connexion:

"While the township women milked their cattle in the *Bualie*, the glaistig would play hide and seek with the children. 'A ghlaistic duibh cha bheir thu oirnn,'[1] said the little ones, as they hid behind stones and bushes, and then the glaistig would

[1] "Thou black glaistig, thou shalt not catch us."

pretend to be angry and would shower twigs and daisies on the imps." [1]

She also protected people of weak intellect.[2] The writer has often heard her referred to as one who cared for lonely elderly people. J. Gregorson Campbell, dealing with her attachment to particular individuals, mentions an old woman named Mòr, resident on a farm. "When Mòr fell sick, the glaistig used to come to the window and wail loudly." [3]

Offerings of milk were made to the glaistig, being poured over, or into a hollow in, a boulder called Clach na Glaistig ("stone of the glaistig"). Those who forgot to give her milk found that the cattle were neglected by night.

Sometimes a glaistig was seen basking in the sun while seated on a rock. Her clothing was often wet, and stories are told of her entering houses by night to warm and dry herself at the fire. She had long golden hair, and was consequently often referred to as the "gruagach" (*gruag* meaning hair of the head). Gregorson Campbell tells that in Tiree "she was never called 'glaistig' but 'gruagach' and 'gruagach mhara' ('sea-maid')".[4] Like the Cailleach Bheur, she was sometimes a wader of the deep sea or crossed it by stepping from rock to rock or island to island. Dr. Carmichael tells of the "gruagach" taking offence and deserting the people of the township of Bennan whose cattle she had been accustomed to herd.

[1] *Celtic Review*, Vol. V, p. 62.
[2] J. G. Campbell, *Superstitions of the Scottish Highlands*, p. 166.
[3] *Ibid.*, p. 163.
[4] *Superstitions of the Scottish Highlands*, p. 165.

"She placed her left foot on Ben Bhuidhe in Arran and her right foot on 'Allasan' (Ailsa Craig), making this her stepping stone to cross to the mainland of Scotland or to Ireland. While the gruagach was in the act of moving her left foot, a three-masted ship passed beneath, the mainmast of which struck her in the thigh and overturned her into the sea. The people of Bennan mourned the gruagach long and loudly."[1]

She could pass from mountain to mountain or over the Minch very quickly. A glaistig was a "familiar" of Archibald Mac Ian Year (*Mac Iain Ghiorr*), a notorious Ardnamurchan pirate. His skill in thieving was said to have been bestowed upon him by the glaistig. He and his brother Ronald became annoyed with her because she always claimed a share of their spoil. On one occasion they went to Barra, thinking she could not follow them, but when they had taken possession of a dwelling and had kindled a fire to roast venison, she was heard calling to them through the smoke hole on the roof. When asked how she had discovered their whereabouts she replied, "*Bha mi air Sgùrr Eige*" ("I was on the height of Eigg Island"), an excellent point from which to keep watch. This saying became proverbial in the Outer Hebrides, being used when one made discovery of actions thought to be secret.

The glaistig crossed the Minch very rapidly. She said that when Mac Ian made the first clink (*snag*) while striking the flint to light the fire, she was on the highest point of the Coolin Hills in Skye. As soon as she entered the house she began to nibble at the roasting venison.

[1] *Carmina Gadelica* (2nd edition), Vol. II, pp. 307-8.

When Archibald Mac Ian died, the glaistig gave a shriek that roused the echoes of Ben Resipol (*Réiseapol*). The same night she was seen in the Coolin Hills in Skye, and after that neither her shadow nor her colour (*a du no dath*) was anywhere seen.[1]

The sinister aspect of the glaistig is brought out in folk-stories that tell of her attempts to waylay or kill travellers.

Mr. Alexander MacLennan, a native of Strathconon, told the writer of a glaistig that haunted the River Meig. A man met her as he was crossing a ford and she asked fiercely, " What have you against me?" If he named a weapon, he could not injure her with it. His first answer was " My sword ". She said, " It is harmless: what else?" The man next mentioned his black dagger in his right-foot stocking. " Anything else?" she asked. " Yes," the man made answer; " the long grey thing at my thigh." He referred to his dirk, but, not having named it, its virtue remained. He seized and overcame the glaistig and took her to his smithy, where he tied her to the anvil. She shrieked all night and those supernatural beings who came to give her aid took off the roof of the smithy, having raised a great storm. The man was glad to release her, and after she fled the wind fell.

A Lochaber story which the writer recently found to be still quite current in the vicinity of Roy Bridge tells of a glaistig being captured by a man named Kennedy (or Mac Cuaric, a local rendering of the surname [2]). The glaistig cursed the Kennedys, and

---

[1] J. G. Campbell, *Superstitions of the Scottish Highlands*, pp. 181-3; Mrs. Watson, *Celtic Review*, Vol. V, pp. 62-3.

[2] Also given as " Mac Ualrig ".

her curse is still supposed to cling to the family.

Mac Ualrig More (Big Kennedy) of Lochaber was a smith, and one night when going home on horseback he met the glaistig as he was crossing *Cùrr*, the ford of *Croisg*. She hailed him, asking if he would not be the better of a rider behind him, and he answered, " Yes, and a rider before ". Stooping, he seized the glaistig and, lifting her on to the back of his horse, threw round her " the wizard belt of Fillan ". Another version tells that he " put her on the saddle before him with his sword-belt round her waist". She could not effect her escape from the magic circle.

Shrieking and wailing, she asked to be released. " Let me go," she cried, " and I will give you a fold of speckled cattle and success on the hill (as a hunter)." He claimed what she offered but insisted that it was not sufficient. Then she said she would build at once a house and charm it against water, iron, arrows, poison, caterans and fairies. " Fulfil your words," said the smith, " and then you will be free ".

The glaistig shrieked and was heard over seven hills. From fairy mounds and cliffs " they " assembled and set to work speedily, calmly and orderly. A line of helpers was formed from Clianaig waterfall to the site of the house and passed slabs and stones from hand to hand. Others cut beams and rafters from the Knoll of Shore inlet, while the glaistig ordered them to fetch every timber except mulberry. At the grey dawning the house was ready and the smith had lit a fire, into which he thrust a coulter, which became red hot. He released the glaistig and as she passed a window she stretched out her " crooked palm " to bid him farewell, but he thrust the red-hot coulter into it and she was " burned to the bone ".

Uttering a shriek of agony, the glaistig leapt upon a grey stone (evidently a " cursing stone ") to pronounce the smith's doom. She " brought the curse of the people on him and the curse of the goblins ", saying,

> " Grow like rushes,
> Wither like fern,
> Turn grey in childhood,
> Change in height of your strength;
> May not a son succeed."

Then she fled to the peak of Finisgeig, where she spilled her life blood, " which is still visible in the discoloured russet vegetation of the spot ". Dr. Carmichael says that the curse on the Kennedys was uttered on the mountain:

> " Growth like the fern to them,
> Wasting like rushes to them,
> And unlasting as the mist of the hill."

It is said that the descendants of the smith grow grey while yet quite young and that the male succession is uncertain, the curse being still operative.

The glaistig is also spoken of as a trickster like Shakespeare's Queen Mab, who " plaits the manes of horses in the night ", and her fairies, who love cleanliness in a house and " pinch the maids as blue as bilberry " if they are guilty of " sluttery ". Folkstories tell of the glaistig giggling in the darkness and speaking with a lisp, expressing herself often in verse. She is reputed to sing melodiously and often plaintively.

Sometimes she has appeared at a ferry as a poor old

woman, asking to be taken across, although the tide might be running strong and the weather rough. It is told that one day she entered the boat of " Yellow Dougall of the Cave " (*Dùghaill Buidhe na h-Uamha*) to cross to Lismore and took the bow oar.

" ' A hearty pull, Dougall,' she cried. ' Another hearty pull then, honest woman,' said he."

She pulled so vigorously that Dougall had to row harder than ever he had done before. He marvelled at her strength, but on reaching the island realized who had been his helper, because she suddenly vanished, according to one version, or, according to another, plunged into the sea and swam back.[1]

Sometimes the glaistig is accompanied by a little son, who is quick witted and has a sharp tongue.

Our Cailleach Bheur, as shown, is usually associated with wild animals whose forms she is capable of assuming. The glaistig cares for domesticated animals instead, including cows, horses, sheep, goats and dogs, whose forms she can take at will. Gregorson Campbell [2] tells that in Mull she was " commonly seen in the shape of a dog and was said to carry a pup at the back of her head ". Yet, like the fairies and Cailleach Bheur, she fears dogs and takes flight from them. Gregorson Campbell objected to her association with the goat on the ground that only the devil assumed the form of a goat,[3] but in the north Highlands the goat is closely associated with fairies. Women were complimented

---

[1] Mrs. Watson, *Celtic Review*, Vol. V, pp. 61-2; J. G. Campbell, *Superstitions of the Scottish Highlands*, p. 174.

[2] *Superstitions of the Scottish Highlands*, p. 175.

[3] *Ibid.*, p. 157.

by having their eyes compared to those of the goat.

> "*Suil ghobhar ghean*
> *An aodann bhan*
> *Gu mealladh fhear.*
>
> "The eye of the sportive goat
> In the faces of women
> To wile the men."

A supernatural animal known as the "lame goat" (*gobhar bacach*) wandered through the country. It was supposed to lie down on the best land in a particular area. In Skye the "lame goat" was known as the *glas ghoibhle*. A rich grassy stretch in Strath is called *Leaba na glais-ghoibhle*, and the goat was also associated with Glendale. This supernatural animal was supposed to be "always in milk" and to have sufficient, indeed, to supply a large force of warriors.

Another supernatural being with a goat connexion is the urisk (*uruisg*), referred to by Dr. Carmichael as "a monster, half human, half goat, with abnormally long hair, long teeth and long claws". It was reputed to frequent "glens, corries, reedy lakes and sylvan streams". Like the glaistig, the urisk haunted waterfalls. Near Tyndrum there is a cascade called *Eas na h-uruisg* ("the urisk's waterfall"). St. Fillan is said to have banished the monster. It received offerings of milk which were poured out on the *Clach na h-uruisg* ("stone of the urisk") and not only herded cattle by night but did work about a farm. Like the glaistig, it was particularly friendly to some individuals and especially females. In the summer season it remained on the highest parts of certain hills; in winter it came down to the low-lying lands and sought shelter in houses and barns. "Its presence," says Gregorson Campbell, "was a sign of prosperity; it was said to leave comfort behind it."

Sometimes the urisk yearned for human company and accompanied travellers by night on the moors and among the hills, never seeking to do any harm, but greatly scaring those it followed.

According to Dr. Graham [1] "the urisks were a sort of lubberly supernaturals who, like the brownies, could be gained over by kind attention to perform the drudgery of the farm, and it was believed that many families in the Highlands had one of the order attached to them. They were supposed to be dispersed over the Highlands, each in his own wild recess, but the solemn stated meetings of the order were regularly held in this cave of Ben Venue." Dr. Graham was referring to a corrie in the mountain overlooking the southeastern end of Loch Katrine known in Gaelic as *Coire nan ùruisgean*. In some respects the urisks resemble the Fomorians who assembled on Ben Ledi to hold an athletic competition and were similarly associated with hill summits and caves.

Dr. Carmichael, dealing with *Gleann na h-uruisg* ("glen of the uruisg") in Killinver, Argyll, says that "the uruisg is not unfriendly to the friendly beyond showing them scenes and telling them of events above the world, upon the world and below the world, that fill them with terror". The urisks also haunted parts of the Coolin Hills in Skye, like the glaistig.[2]

[1] *Southern Confines of Perthshire* (1806), p. 19.
[2] Dr. A. Carmichael, *Carmina Gadelica* (2nd edition), Vol. II, pp. 372-3; J. Gregorson Campbell, *Superstitions of the Scottish Highlands*, pp. 195 *et seq.*, and the author's note-books.

Reginald Scott[1] refers to an urisk in the north of Scotland who was reputed to be a giant and the father of the fairies:

"Many wonderful and incredible things did he also relate of this Balkin ('lord of the northern mountains'), affirming that he was shaped like a satyr and fed upon the air, having wife and children to the number of twelve thousand, which were the brood of the northern fairies, inhabiting Southerland (Sutherland) and Catenes (Caithness) with the adjacent islands."

As there were various forms of the goddess Artemis in Greece, so apparently there were various forms of the ancient goddess of Scotland. It has been shown that Cailleach Bheur was associated with wild animals, while the glaistig's association was with domesticated animals, suggesting that she was the Artemis of the agricultural mode of life. Her interest in and kindness to children were evidently due to her connexion with birth. Farnell notes, as we have seen, that Artemis was in one of her phases a birth-goddess.

The urisks were, as satyrs, associated with the glaistig, as were the Fomorians with our Cailleach Bheur. Her partiality for a fish diet was shared by the Cailleach, and she was similarly connected with streams, marshes and the sea. Both the Cailleach and the glaistig could assume the forms of the animals they protected.

The specialized form of the goddess as a beneficent deity and a Great Mother was Bride, or Bridget, who appears to have been identical with the goddess of the Brigantes of south-eastern Scotland, the north and midlands of England and an area in Ireland, whence

[1] *Discoverie of Witchcraft*, Book II, Chapter IV (London, 1665).

they appear to have migrated from Celtic England. The Scottish Bride "is said", writes Dr. Carmichael, " to preside over the different seasons of the year and to bestow their functions upon them according to their respective needs ". The winter is the " dead season ", when nature is asleep, and Bride, who has a white wand, " is said to breathe life into the mouth of the dead Winter and to bring him to open his eyes to the tears and the smiles, the sighs and the laughter of Spring. The venom of the cold is said to tremble for its safety on Bride's Day (1st February, old style), and to flee for its life on Patrick's Day." [1]

The writer has heard Bride referred to as the maiden who is kept all winter a prisoner in Ben Nevis by big Cailleach Bheur. When the Cailleach's son elopes with her, the fierce old woman, as has been shown, raises storms to keep them apart.

Bride is associated with the serpent.[2] There are many folk-poems which refer to the awakening of Bride and her serpent:

> " The Day of Bride, the birthday of spring,
>   The serpent emerges from the knoll.
> " *La Bride breith an earraich*
>   *Thig an dearris as an tom.*"

Other translated versions are:

> " The serpent will come from the hole
>   On the brown Day of Bride,
>   Though there should be three feet of snow
>   On the flat surface of the ground.

[1] *Carmina Gadelica* (2nd edition), Vol. I, p. 172.
[2] It might be urged that the serpent is a form of Bride.

THE GLAISTIG AND BRIDE

" On the day of Bride of the white hills
The noble queen will come from the knoll;
I will not molest the noble queen,
Nor will the noble queen molest me.

" The Feast Day of Bride
The daughter of Ivor shall come from the knoll,
I will not touch the daughter of Ivor,
Nor shall she harm me.

" Early on Bride's morn
The serpent shall come from the hole;
I will not molest the serpent,
Nor will the serpent molest me.

" The daughter of Ivor will come from the knoll
With tuneful whistling."

A " propitiatory hymn " was sung to Bride's serpent, which was a form of the serpent-dragon and, like the goat-headed serpent of Cernunnos on the Gaulish sculptured stones, was evidently an importation from the East. The serpent-dragon was known in India as the *nāga*,[1] and it contributed, in consequence of Buddhist influence, to the complex dragon of China. The following Chinese text regarding the dragon which sleeps all winter and awakes in spring is remarkably like the Bride poems:

" If we offer a deprecatory service to them (dragons)
They will leave their abodes;
If we do not seek the dragons
They will not seek us." [2]

[1] A female *nāga* might appear as a beautiful girl.
[2] De Visser, *The Dragon in China and Japan* (1913), p. 46.

On the Celtic La Tène Gundestrup cauldron the serpent is associated with European and Asiatic fauna —the European red deer, the Asiatic gazelle and lion and the Indian elephant.

Bride was, like certain ancient European and Asiatic goddesses, connected, as a mother-goddess, with milk-yielding plants. The dandelion, for instance, is called in Gaelic *bearnan Brìde*, the " little notched (plant) of Bride ". One can still hear in the Highlands that " the plant of Bride nourishes with its milk the early lamb ".

The Christianized Bride has been identified with St. Bridget of Kildare and other St. Bridgets, and reputed to be an " aid woman " or midwife and a foster-nurse. She went to the stable at Bethlehem in which Christ was born " and was in time to aid and minister to the Virgin Mary ". Bride was therefore called *ban-chuideachaidh Moire* (the " aid-woman of Mary ") and *Muime Chriosda* (" foster-mother of Christ "), while Christ was referred to as *Daltan Brìde* (" little foster-son of Bride ").

The blessing and help of Bride were formerly invoked in many homes when a birth was taking place. She was the " knee wife ", the " aid woman " for all mothers—a kindly pagan goddess who had been Christianized in the early period.

A woman went to the door of the house and cried to the invisible Bride to enter the birth chamber:

" *Bhride! Bhride! thig a steach,*
Tha do bheatha deanta,
Tabhair cobhair dha na bhean,
'S tabh an gein dh'an Triana.

"Bride! Bride! come in,
Thy welcome is truly made,
Give thou relief to the woman
And give the conception to the Trinity."

Bride performed the baptismal ceremony. When Christ was born she " put three drops of water from the spring of pure water on the tablet of His forehead, in name of God, in name of Jesus, in name of Spirit ".

On Bride's Eve a sheaf of oats was fashioned in the likeness of a woman and dressed in female attire which was decorated with crystals, early flowers like snowdrops and primroses, cress, &c. Girls clad in white carried the " little Bride " from door to door, receiving gifts at every house, including oatmeal bannocks, rolls of butter and pieces of home-made cheese. The image was ultimately carried to a house occupied by women alone and after an interval young men called and pleaded for admittance. In the end the door was opened and they entered and bowed in honour of Bride. Then there were singing, dancing, fun and frolics. The collected food was eaten and when day broke Bride hymns were sung.

On Bride's Eve the older women plaited a cradle of rushes which was called " Bride's bed ". In it was placed a decorated " baby " made of oat-straw and called *dealbh Brìde* (" form of Bride ", or, as Dr. Carmichael renders it, " ikon of Bride "). Beside the *dealbh* was put a white wand, the bark having been peeled off. This was called *slachdan Brìde* (" rod of Bride ") or *barrach Brìde* (" birch of Bride "). Dr. Carmichael says that " the wand is generally of birch, broom, bramble, white willow or other sacred wood ".

Our Cailleach Bheur's magic wand or hammer is also referred to as a *slachdan*.

Martin [1] tells regarding the ceremony that "the mistress and servants of each family take a sheaf of oats and dress it up in woman's apparel, put it in a large basket and lay a wooden club by it, and this they call Briid's bed; and then the mistress and servants cry three times ' Briid is come, Briid is welcome '."

According to Gregorson Campbell, the call at the house door was " Bride, Bride, come in, your bed is ready ".

Dr. Carmichael states that on such an occasion one woman went to the door and, standing on the threshold, called softly in Gaelic into the darkness, " Bride's bed is ready ". A woman behind her said, " Let Bride come in, Bride is welcome ". Then the woman at the door cried, " Bride, come thou in, thy bed is made. Preserve the house for the Trinity ".

The writer saw the ceremony performed in Argyll. Girls nursed the Bride form, which was a swastika made of birch twigs, and after Bride was invoked at the house door, the swastika was placed in the cradle.

Another part of the ceremony given by Dr. Carmichael is the pounding on the doorstep of a stocking containing a fragment of peat, while a woman repeated:

> " This is the day of Bride,
> The queen will come from the mound,
> I will not touch the queen,
> Nor will the queen touch me."

Dr. Carmichael suggests that the pounding of the

---

[1] *Western Isles* (1716 edition), p. 119.

THE GLAISTIG AND BRIDE

peat in the stocking represented the destruction of the queen (serpent), but adds that the ceremony may have been " designed to symbolize something now lost ".[1]

The linnet is known as *bigein Brìde* (" little bird of Bride ") because it whistles a welcome to the goddess; the oyster-catcher, which greets her in its fussy manner on the shore, is called *gille Brìde* (" servant of Bride "). Evidently Bride comes across the sea.

Cock fighting took place on Bride's Day and in the Hebrides line-fishermen cast lots for fishing banks. The raven built its nest on Bride's Day and skylarks began to sing. Although there were still to be hardships and suffering, the coming of Bride inspired hope for better times, for she was the ultimate bringer of sunshine, warmth, growth and plenty.

There are links between Bride and the classical goddesses Artemis, Aphrodite and Kore-Persephone. No myth survives, however, regarding her abduction and imprisonment in the underworld of Ben Nevis. Like Kore, she was connected with trees and plants, but was something more than a " corn maiden ", although welcomed at the end of winter in connexion with a corn festival, as was Kore at Athens. Like Kore, she was " the first-born of the year ", but she was also the " aid woman " at birth and, as the giver of milk to the early lamb and to children, a " foster-mother "— a mother goddess. Rhea, the mother goddess of Crete, to whom the serpent was consecrated, may be a prototype of Bride. She was likewise associated with birth and appears to have had close connexions with the

[1] *Carmina Gadelica* (2nd edition), Vol. I, p. 170.

Phrygian Cybele as "a goddess of life and fertility". The dancing of lads and girls on Bride's Eve may have had a similar significance to the revels connected with the worship of the mother goddesses of Crete and Phrygia.[1]

[1] L. R. Farnell, *Cults of the Greek States*, Vol. III, pp. 294 *et seq.*

CHAPTER X

Fairies and Fairyland

Fairies of folk-belief and fairies of literature—No fairy queen or king in Gaelic stories—A complete republic—Introduction of Oberon—Shakespeare's Mab and Titania—Pluto and Proserpina as king and queen of fairies—Arthur as elfin king—Real folk-lore in Shakespeare—Teutonic elves—Gloom of Teutonic myth—Scott on elves and fairies—Fairies chiefly women—The Welsh fairies as " mothers "—Female fairies in Scotland—Groups of Celtic goddesses—Fairies come from west—Travelling on whirlwinds—Abduction story—Perthshire fairies visit England—Greek whirlwind nymphs—Widespread whirlwind lore—Underworld of Scottish fairies—Animals in fairyland—Fairies and deer—Water fairies—The Hebridean *loireag*—Little creatures from the sea—Fairies as " wee folk "—Small Highland and Lowland fairies—Invisible and noiseless fairies—Physical defects of fairies—Thefts of substance of food—Milk and meal offerings—Fairy raids—Fairy-lore and witchlore—Witchcraft of late importation.

It is necessary when we come to deal with the fairy-lore of Scotland to distinguish between the fairies of folk-belief and the fairies of literature. In the Border ballads, for instance, can be detected a blending of genuine tradition with elements introduced from the mediæval metrical romances and other sources. There is no " fairy queen " in the Gaelic folk-tales and her appearance in Gaelic fairy poems is of quite late date.

W. Grant Stewart, writing over a century ago, says in this connexion:

" The empire of Queen Mab, like that of the renowned Cæsar [*sic*], never was extended to the northern side of the Grampians, for she is entirely unknown in these countries. Indeed, it is believed that the Highland fairies acknowledge no distinction of this sort. As there were originally none such amongst them in Paradise, so they are not disposed to create any on earth, and a more complete republic never was." [1]

J. Gregorson Campbell expresses the view that the Banshee " is without doubt the original of the Queen of Elfland mentioned in the ballads of the south of Scotland ". He, too, emphasizes that in Gaelic folk-stories there is no mention of " an elfin king or queen ".[2] The genuine fairies of folk-belief are nameless and devoid of titles.

Spenser the English poet was the first to introduce Oberon, the elfin king, borrowing the name from French romance, in which the spelling is Auberon, a name derived from the German Alberich (*alb*, elf; *rich*, king), the guardian of the treasure in the *Nibelungenlied*. Shakespeare borrowed the Mab name for his fairy queen from Welsh and his Titania from a translation of Ovid's *Metamorphoses* (III, i, 173), Titania (Titan-born) being one of the names given in that work to Diana. Chaucer had set the fashion, by imitating from the metrical romances, of naming the fairies and giving them titles and identifying them with " the inhabitants of the classical Hades ":

> " Pluto, that is king of fayërye . . .
> . . . Pluto, and his quene
> Proserpina, and all his fayërye.
>
> " Pluto, that is king of fayërye,
> And many a lady in his companye,
> Folwinge his wyf, the quene Proserpyne." [3]

---
[1] *Popular Superstitions* (Edinburgh, 1823), pp. 72–3.
[2] *Superstitions of the Highlands and Islands of Scotland*, pp. 45–6.
[3] *The Marchantes Tale*, lines 794–5 and 983–5.

Chaucer also associates with his elfland, King Arthur, whom he regarded as a fairy king:

> "In th' olde days of King Arthour,
> Of which that Britons speken greet honour,
> Al was this land fulfild of fayere.
> The elf-queen, with hir joly companye,
> Daunced ful ofte in many a grene mede;
> This was the olde opinion, as I rede,
> I speke of manye hundred yeres ago." [1]

Here Chaucer drew upon genuine folk-belief, as did the later Shakespeare, although as a humorous sceptic. Of the two, however, Shakespeare was the more pronounced creator, contributing much to the folk-lore with which he must have been familiar in his boyhood, as is made evident in the renunciation speech of Prospero of *The Tempest*:

> " Ye elves of hills, brooks, standing lakes, and groves,
> And ye that on the sands with printless foot
> Do chase the ebbing Neptune and do fly him
> When he comes back; you demi-puppets that
> By moonshine do the green sour ringlets make,
> Wherof the ewe not bites, and you whose pastime
> Is to make midnight mushrooms, that rejoice
> To hear the solemn curfew."

Here the great poet-dramatist brings us into close touch with genuine tradition.

Partly as a result of literary influence and partly the intrusions of aliens and alien concepts, the Teutonic elves became associated with the fairies of the Celtic-speaking peoples. These elves are mainly of the male

---

[1] *The Tale of the Wyf of Bathe*, lines 857 *et seq.*

sex and include the dwarf, the troll, the brownie, the kobold and hobgoblin. They are of two outstanding classes: the light elves and the dark elves. Some abduct attractive girls and children. They are tricky, morose, shy and as ready to do evil as good. " They partake," writes Floris Delattre, " of that sad, sombre outlook on life which is the main characteristic of Teutonic mythology."[1]

Sir Walter Scott in his *Demonology and Witchcraft* (Chapter IV) has emphasized the difference between the elves and the fairies. He found from the evidence before him that these dwarfish northern elves were " spirits of a coarser sort, more laborious vocation and more malignant temper, and in all respects less propitious to humanity than the fairies ". His explanation of the difference is that the fairies " were the invention of the Celtic people and displayed that superiority of taste and fancy which, with the love of music and poetry, has been generally ascribed to their race ". His theory does not appear, however, to account for certain differences which are greater and more fundamental than he realized. The problem presented is one not really due to racial but to cultural influences. As Delattre has noted, the fairies are " chiefly women, wondrously fair, with their pale, long faces and flowing hair like ' red gold '."[2] Chaucer must have been aware of this when, although he introduced classical names into the old fairydom of the Britons, he wrote of " the elf-queen with her joly companye ". Sir John Rhys tells of Isaac Davies, the smith of *Ystrad Meurig*, who

---

[1] *English Fairy Poetry* (London, 1912, p. 18).
[2] *English Fairy Poetry*, p. 22.

declared that the fairies were "all women", and he states that "the idea was already familiar to me as a Welshman, though I cannot recollect how I got it".[1] The late Professor Anwyl, writing regarding grouped goddesses, pointed out that "in some parts of Wales *Y Mamau* ('the mothers') is the name for the fairies".[2]

Professor T. Gwynn Jones writes: "A Cardiganshire story (*Ystrad Meurig*), which seems to be unique in Welsh and reminds one of the Gaelic legend of *Tir na m-Ban*,[3] represents them (the fairies) as all women."[4] He makes no reference to the *Y Mamau* name.

In Scotland the knoll fairies are mainly women. Even in the Border ballads the females are in prominence. Tamlane is carried off by the elfin queen:

"Ae fatal morning I went out
Dreading nae injury,
And thinking lang, fell soun asleep
Beneath an apple tree.

"Then by it came the Elfin Queen
And laid her hand on me;
And from that time since ever I mind
I've been in her companie."

Thomas the Rhymer is similarly spirited away by "the queen of fair Elfland". It sometimes seems in some of the stories told by the folk, or used by the ballad makers, as if the only men in fairyland are

---

[1] *Celtic Folklore: Welsh and Manx* (Oxford, 1901), pp. 245, 661.
[2] *Celtic Religion* (London, 1906), p. 42.
[3] "Land of Women."
[4] *Welsh Folklore and Folk Custom*, pp. 54-5.

those who have been abducted by the queen or the other fairy women. The explanation may well be that in fairy-lore we have the elements of an old mythology in which females were in prominence. Anwyl, writing of the Celtic goddesses, says:

"Some are known to us by groups—Proximæ (the kinswomen), Dervonnæ (the oak spirits), Niskai (the water spirits), Mairæ, Matronæ, Matres or Matræ (the mothers), Quadriviæ (the goddesses of cross roads)."[1]

In "Fiacc's Hymn"[2] it is stated that before St. Patrick arrived in Ireland the pagans there were wont to worship the *síde* (fairies).

An important fact regarding the Highland fairies is that, as J. Gregorson Campbell[3] states, they "come always from the west", and often in the folk-tales it is told of one who, when departing, "went westward". They travelled through the air in whirlwinds. J. Gregorson Campbell writes in this connexion:

"In this climate these eddies are among the most curious of natural phenomena. On calm summer days they go past, whirling about straws and dust, and as not another breath of air is moving at the time their cause is sufficiently puzzling. In Gaelic the eddy is known as 'the people's puff of wind' (*oiteag sluaigh*), and its motion 'travelling on tall grass stems' (*falbh air chuiseagan treòrach*). By throwing one's left shoe at it, the fairies are made to drop whatever they may be taking away—men, women, children or animals. The same result is attained by throwing one's bonnet, saying, 'This is yours, that's mine' (*Is leatsa so, is leamsa sin*), or a naked knife, or earth from a molehill."

[1] *Celtic Religion*, p. 41.
[2] Whitley Stokes, *Goidelica*, p. 127.
[3] *Superstitions of the Highlands and Islands of Scotland*, pp. 19, 24–5 and 105.

People are lifted by night as well as by day on these eddies of wind and carried from island to island or to the summit of a distant hill.[1]

W. Grant Stewart, who refers to the whirlwind as the fairies' "engine of robbery", tells of John Roy, Glenbrown, parish of Abernethy, Perthshire, having rescued a woman by throwing his bonnet into a whirlwind and demanding an exchange by exclaiming: " Mine is yours and yours is mine ".[2] The fairies had to comply with the demand and they " abandoned the burden ", which proved to be a " Saxon lady " whose husband and son were Hanoverian officers in charge of men engaged in road-making. She had been carried by the Perthshire fairies from " the south of England ". Grant Stewart states " that the Saxon lady was again restored to her affectionate husband ", and John Roy was " gratified by the only reward he would accept of —the pleasure of doing good ".[3]

In north-eastern Scotland the whirlwind that raises dust on roads is called " a furl o' fairies' ween (wind) ".[4]

The nymphs of Greek folk-lore similarly travel through the air on eddies of wind. Lawson [5] writes of these:

" The habit of travelling on a whirlwind, or, more correctly perhaps, by stirring up a whirlwind by rapid passage, has gained for the nymphs in some districts secondary names which might seem to constitute a new class of wind nymphs.

[1] *Superstitions*, pp. 24–5.
[2] Or *Is leatsa so; is leamsa sin* (" This is yours; that is mine ").
[3] *Popular Superstitions* (Edinburgh, 1823), pp. 116 *et seq.* and p. 122.
[4] W. Gregor, *Folklore of the North-east of Scotland*, p. 65.
[5] J. G. Lawson, *Modern Greek Folklore and Ancient Greek Religion* (Cambridge, 1910), pp. 131 *et seq*.

"In Athens whirlwinds are said to occur most frequently near the old Hill of the Nymphs; and women of the lower class, as they see the spinning spiral of dust approach, fall to crossing themselves busily and to repeating, 'Honey and milk in your path!' This incantation is widely known as an effective safeguard against the Nereids in their rapid flight, and must in origin, it would seem, have been a vow."

Sir James G. Frazer in *The Golden Bough*[1] gives various examples of the widespread belief that eddies of wind contain witches, wizards or evil spirits. Breton, German, Slavonian and Esthonian rustics throw knives, sickles or forks, sticks or stones into a passing whirlwind. Of the Bedouins of eastern Africa it is said that " no whirlwind ever sweeps across the path without being pursued by a dozen savages with drawn creeses, who stab into the centre of the dusty column in order to drive away the evil spirit that is believed to be riding on the blast ".

The poet Keats heard of the English folk-belief regarding fairies riding on whirlwinds, for he wrote in his *The Eve of St. Agnes*:

"Hark! 'tis an elfin-storm from fairyland
Of haggard seeming."

In Egypt the belief that a pharaoh's spirit was carried to the sky-world by a whirlwind is as old as the pyramid age. In one of the pyramid texts it is declared:

"King Unis goes to the sky! On the wind!
On the wind!"[2]

---

[1] *The Magic Art*, Vol. I, pp. 329 *et seq.* (1911 edition).
[2] Breasted, *Religion and Thought in Ancient Egypt*, p. 110. Unis, the last king of the fifth dynasty, died about 2625 B.C.

FAIRIES AND FAIRYLAND 203

The whirlwind is a carrier of spirits in central and south Africa. There are biblical references to the ancient belief that the whirlwind was a carrier of souls and deities. " He shall take them away as with a whirlwind," says the psalmist. Zechariah declared that "the Lord God shall blow the trumpet, and shall go with whirlwinds of the south ".[1]

India has much whirlwind lore. In China and Japan whirlwinds are carriers of the dragon gods.[2] The Maori of New Zealand believed, like the ancient Egyptians, that the spirits of the dead ascended to the " sky-Parent " by means of " the gyrating whirlwind ".[3]

The Ainu of Japan imagine that " little whirlwinds " that " play among the trees of the forest during the summer months " are carriers of supernatural beings. " They say that when one is seen approaching, the best thing is to hide behind a tree or bush till it has safely passed by. And, while in hiding, one should expectorate profusely in order to drive the demons away." [4]

The Scottish fairies are connected with the underworld which is reached through mounds, mountains, rocks or lochs. They never dwell in caves like the giants and giantesses. To this fairy underworld the flowers and plants which fade at the approach of the winter season are supposed to descend. There are always

---
[1] *Psalm* lviii, 9; *Jeremiah*, xxiii, 19, and xxv, 30–2. See also *Job*, xxxviii, 1; and xl, 6; *Nahum*, i, 3, and *Zechariah*, ix, 14.
[2] De Visser, *The Dragon in China and Japan* (Amsterdam, 1913), pp. 117, 233.
[3] Elsdon Best, *Maori Myth and Religion* (Wellington, New Zealand, 1922), pp. 16–7.
[4] Rev. John Batchelor, *The Ainu and their Folklore* (London, 1901), pp. 385, 593.

sunshine and growth in fairyland. Migrating birds are reputed to take refuge there. The cuckoo is called in Gaelic *eun sìth* (" fairy " or " supernatural bird "), because it is reputed to dwell in the underworld during the winter.

Other animals that dwell in fairyland and are occasionally seen in the land of men are the *cu sìth* (" supernatural dog "), which is as big as a stirk and has a dark green coat; the *cait shìth* (" supernatural cats "), which are large and black and have a white spot on the breast; the *lucha shìth* (" supernatural mouse "), the " lesser shrew ", which is credited with paralysing the limb of a human being which it runs over during sleep, while engaged in *marcachd shìth* (" fairy riding "); *crodh sìth* (" supernatural cows "), also called *crodh mara* (" sea cows "), which are hornless; the *each sìth* (" supernatural horse "), also called *each uisge* (" water horse "); the *lacha shìth* (" supernatural duck "), the teal, common in the Hebrides during winter but rare in summer; teals are supposed to herald storms and are associated with swans, which are reputed to be transformed human beings under spells; the snipe is likewise supposed to have associations with the fairies. Deer are spoken of as " the cattle of the fairies ", being milked by them. A fairy lullaby, known as " Bainne nam fiadh ", given by Dr. Carmichael,[1] is translated by him as follows:

" On milk of deer was I reared,
On milk of deer was nurtured,
On milk of deer beneath the ridge of storms,
On crest of hill and mountain.

[1] *Carmina Gadelica*, Vol. II, p. 232.

Dr. Carmichael suggests that we have here a memory of domesticated reindeer. The reindeer survived in Scotland till the beginning of the thirteenth century, the Gaelic name being *brāc*.

Fairies that came from or across water are referred to in various Scottish areas. According to J. F. Campbell, " the Highlanders distinguish between the water and land, or *dressed*, fairies ". A water fairy on being informed by an old man who was reading a Bible that it made " no mention of salvation for any but the sinful sons of Adam " was greatly distressed, " flung her arms over her head, screamed and plunged into the sea ".[1]

A story of a fairy changeling tells of an Irishman who paid a visit to Gaolin Castle on the island of Kerrera, near Oban. When he saw the child in a cradle he recognized her as " a fairy sweetheart of an Irish gentleman of his acquaintance ". He addressed her, mentioning this gentleman's name, Brian Mac Braodh. The fairy was offended and, running out of the castle, " leaped into the sea from the point called *Rudha na Sirach*, ' the fairies' point ', to this day ".[2]

W. Grant Stewart in his Strathspey collection of folk-tales tells of a clergyman who, when returning home one night, " had to pass through a good deal of uncanny ground ". When he reached the end of a lake he heard music and saw a light coming across the water towards him.

" As the light and music drew near, the clergyman could at length distinguish an object resembling a human being

[1] *Popular Tales*, Vol. II, p. 75.
[2] *Popular Tales*, Vol. II, p. 62.

walking on the surface of the water, attended by a group of diminutive musicians, some of them bearing lights and others of them instruments of music, on which they continued to perform those melodious strains which first attracted his attention. The leader of the band dismissed his attendants, landed on the beach, and afforded the minister the amplest opportunities of examining his appearance. He was a little, primitive-looking, grey-headed man, clad in the most grotesque habit he ever witnessed and such as led the venerable minister all at once to suspect his real character."

The fairy man wished to know if there was any hope of salvation for him, and on learning that pardon was impossible " uttered a shriek of despair " and " plunged headlong into the loch ".[1]

In the Hebrides Dr. Carmichael found that the water fairy is referred to as the *loireag*, a term applied elsewhere to a pretty girl. A Benbecula informant explained that the *loireag* is " a small mite of womanhood that does not belong to this world but to the world thither ". She is " a plaintive little thing, stubborn and cunning ". Although connected with water, like others of her kind, one dwelt in a hill. The *loireag*, during the manufacture of homespuns, " presided over the warping, weaving and washing of the web, and if the women omitted any of the traditional usages and ceremonies of these occasions, she resented their neglect in various ways ". Her punishment was to make the web as thin as it had been before the " waulking " process, and then all the work would have to be repeated. The *loireag* was made angry if a woman had a hard voice or sang out of tune.

---

[1] W. Grant Stewart, *Popular Superstitions* (Edinburgh, 1823), pp. 58 *et seq.*

FAIRIES AND FAIRYLAND

In one of the forms of the *Taghairm* (invocation) ceremony described by Martin it is stated that " a number of little creatures came from the sea, who answered the question and disappeared suddenly ".[1]

Fairies are invariably referred to as " wee folk ". The Rev. John Gregorson Campbell, Tiree, discussing the size of the fairies, says:

" The true belief is that the fairies are a small race, the men about four feet or so in height, and the women in many cases not taller than a little girl (*cnapach caileig*)." [2]

Cromek, quoted by Thomas Keightley, refers to the Lowland fairies as being " of small stature, but finely proportioned; of a fair complexion, with long yellow hair hanging over their shoulders and gathered above their heads with combs of gold. They wear a mantle of green cloth, inlaid with wild flowers; green pantaloons, buttoned with bobs of silk; and silver shoon. They carry quivers of ' adder slough ' and bows made of the ribs of a man buried where three lairds' lands meet; their arrows are made of bog-reed, tipped with white flints and dipped in the dew of hemlock; they ride on steeds whose hoofs ' would not dash the dew from the cup of a harebell '." [3]

Dr. Carmichael quotes a typical Gaelic description of a fairy—" the slender woman of the green kirtle and the yellow hair " (*bean chaol a' chota uaine 's na gruaige buidhe*), and tells that " she can convert the white water of the rill into rich red wine, and the

---

[1] *A Description of the Western Islands* (1884 edition), pp. 110-1.
[2] *Superstitions of the Highlands and Islands of Scotland* (Glasgow, 1900), pp. 9-10.
[3] Thomas Keightley, *The Fairy Mythology* (1850 edition), pp. 351-2.

threads of the spider into a tartan plaid. From the stalk of the fairy reed she can bring the music of the lull of repose and peace."

As a rule, the fairies are invisible, but they occasionally appear to certain individuals. Their motions are noiseless and they glide, as Gregorson Campbell puts it, rather than walk: they " come and go with noiseless steps . . . The wayfarer, resting beside a stream, on raising his eyes sees the fairy woman, unheard in her approach, standing on the opposite bank."

Although very comely, fairies have often a physical defect. " In Mull and the neighbourhood," writes Gregorson Campbell, " they are said to have only one nostril."[1] The banshee (*bean shìth*) has but a single nostril, a large, protruding front tooth and long, hanging breasts, and she is web-footed or has one web foot. Fairies sometimes take the form of the deer. They can cross running water, but knoll dwellers are unable to follow a human being on to a beach below high-water mark. They enter houses and steal the substance (*toradh*) of food unless certain preventive measures are taken. A baking, for instance, may be protected against them by sprinkling salt on the bannocks (cakes), or by making with the remnants of a baking a *bonnach fallaid* ("remnant bannock"), which is shaped between the palms of the baker, holed in the middle, toasted on a " bannock stone " in front of the fire and sprinkled with water from a certain well. The bannocks must not be counted; fairies extract the substance from counted bannocks.

Offerings of meal and milk are supposed to appease

---

[1] *Superstitions of the Scottish Highlands*, pp. 3-4 and pp. 15 *et seq.*

the fairies. All milk spilled upon the ground is supposed to reach either them or the small subterranean demons known as the *fridean*.

A herb called *mothan* protects human beings against fairy spells. The milk of a cow which has eaten the *mothan* is similarly efficacious. According to W. G. Stewart,[1] the *mothan* is given to a cow and of this cow's milk cheese is made. " Whoever eats of that cheese is for ever after, as well as his gear, perfectly secure from every species of fairy agency." Fairy raids take place on the last night of every quarter, " particularly the nights before Beltane, the first of summer, and Hallowmas, the first of winter ".[2]

In the west and north the writer has heard references to the quarterly raids. These are worst when the sun is being changed, the " big sun " being put in place on 1st May (old style) and the " little sun " on the day after Hallowe'en. Fairies, demons, giants, &c., are supposed to flit at the time of change and to take advantage of the general confusion by attacking human beings. Houses have to be specially protected by herbs, holly, &c., iron and charms. Red cords and red berries are attached to the tails of domesticated animals. On Friday of each week the fairies are likewise at liberty and very bold. It is as well, when referring to fairies, to call them " good folk " or " good neighbours ".

Fairies steal women and children and especially children who have not been baptized, substituting a peevish old fairy in child form—a " changeling ".

[1] W. G. Stewart, *Highland Superstitions and Amusements*, p. 90.
[2] J. G. Campbell, *Superstitions*, p. 18.

To those human beings whom they favour the fairies give skill in music and the crafts and sometimes gold, or cups, banners, staves, &c., possessed of magical virtues.

Theorists who have not lived among the fairy-believing folk would have it that the fairy legends are really memories of an ancient people—Stone Age man or Bronze Age man. Miss Margaret A. Murray, for instance, favours this view and asserts that the fairy godmother is identical with the witch.[1] Witchcraft was, however, of comparatively late introduction into the Scottish Lowlands; it reached the Highlands at a much later period. The Gaelic word for witch (*buitseach*) is derived from English, as Dr. Macbain has shown.[2] In the records of Scottish witch trials there is evidence that imported beliefs regarding witches were mixed with local beliefs regarding fairies, hags, giants, &c. Highland witch-lore, outside the burghs, is of very diluted character. There is " no mention of incubus and succubus, midnight meetings and dances with the devil, dead men's fingers . . . riding through the air on broomsticks, nor, like the witch of Endor, raising the dead ".[3] Fairy-lore was rife in Scotland long before witches were ever heard of by the folk. A contrary view is found to be favoured by those whose knowledge of Scottish folk-lore and ancient history is quite superficial or tainted by preconceived theories of the rationalizing order.

---

[1] *The God of the Witches* (London, 1933), &c.
[2] *Etymological Dictionary of the Gaelic Language.*
[3] J. G. Campbell, *Witchcraft and Second Sight in the Scottish Highlands*, p. 2.

CHAPTER XI

Fairies as Deities

Nine ages of fairies—Tree spirits—Fairy blows—Where fairies assemble annually—Isle Maree nail tree—Nail tree in Egyptian sacred grove—Hebridean fairy tree spirit—Milk of wisdom for women—Milk trees and plants—Near Eastern links with Scotland—Milk lore—Milk offered to dead and fairies—Milk poured on hills—Inverness milk famine and milk stream—Fairies as spirits—Hosts travelling by night—The Everlasting Battle—Northern Lights—Fairies non-human—Dead in fairyland—Vision of Osirian fairyland—The fairy eye-salve—Welsh and English links—Kirk on souls in fairyland—Supernatural lapse of time—Story of Thomas the Rhymer in Inverness—The fairy revels—Brownies—The male gruagach—The gunna—Highland barn brownie—Prayer for protection against fairies.

Fragments of old mythology and glimpses of antique ideas regarding the destiny of the soul are found embedded in the fairy-lore of Scotland. There is much evidence, too, which emphasizes the essentially non-human character of the fairy.

Like our Cailleach Bheur, the fairy is not an immortal, but is noted for great longevity. Our Cailleach, as we have seen, is reputed to have had seven successive periods of youth; the fairies live through nine ages, " with nine times nine periods of time in each ". Dr. Carmichael gives these in detail, translating from Gaelic:

" Nine nines sucking the breast,
Nine nines unsteady, weak,
Nine nines footful, swift,

Nine nines able and strong,
Nine nines strapping, brown,
Nine nines victorious, subduing,
Nine nines bonneted, drab,
Nine nines beardy grey,
Nine nines on the breasting-beating death,
And worse to me were these miserable nine nines
Than all the other short-lived nine nines that were." [1]

We have seen that there are fairies of land and water. There are also fairies who figure as tree spirits, not only as haunters of woodlands but as actual tree-dwellers. A north-country story told me by Professor W. J. Watson of the University of Edinburgh has been known to him from boyhood. It tells of a Highlander, named Hugh Ross, who went out one morning to work on his farm at Dola, near Lairg, in the county of Sutherland. At the foot of a field were some trees in which he saw two or three little women dressed in green. They were disporting themselves among the branches and, not realizing they were supernaturals, Ross said to them that they would be better employed at home attending to their housework. One of the little women came down, grasping a twig in her right hand, and with it she struck Ross's face. The man was stunned, went home, lay down and never rose again. His death took place about 1812.

A somewhat similar story is known in Ireland as " The Sick Bed of Cuchulainn ". It relates that there once came towards Cuchulainn two fairy women, one wearing a green mantle and the other a mantle of purple. The woman in green smiled and then struck

[1] *Carmina Gadelica* (2nd edition), Vol. II, p. 334.

Cuchulainn with a horse-switch; then the other woman, who likewise advanced smiling, struck him in the same manner. They continued to attack Cuchulainn for a long time, each striking him in turn, so that he was almost dead. Thereafter Cuchulainn lay in bed for a whole year without speaking to any man.

Fairies are associated with " wishing trees " and wells. Isle Maree in Loch Maree, Gairloch, Ross and Cromarty, is reputed to be a haunt of fairies, while an adjoining island, Eilean Suthainn, is the place of their annual assemblies. Isle Maree has a sacred tree and sacred well, the ruins of a small chapel and a graveyard. The tree, an oak, is a " wishing tree " and when visited by Queen Victoria in September, 1877, was studded with nails. The queen had a coin offering attached to the tree after " wishing a wish ".

Evidently this fairy island was one of the pagan sacred places taken over by the early Christians, as Iona, a druidical centre, was by St. Columba. The saint whose name clings to Loch Maree and Isle Maree was Maol Rubha, born in A.D. 640, who migrated from Ulster to Scotland in 673 and founded the monastery of Applecross, where he died in 722. His name became softened to " Mourie " and " Maree ".

The " wishing tree " had evidently been a sacred one in pagan times, like the ancient Egyptian " tall sycamore . . . whereon the gods sit "—the " tree of life in the mysterious isle " in the sky world.[1]

The habit of driving nails into a tree to ensure luck was evidently imported into Scotland with the associated beliefs. As much is suggested by nail-trees found

[1] J. H. Breasted, *Religion and Thought in Ancient Egypt*, pp. 104, 133.

elsewhere. In Egypt, for instance, a nail-tree may be seen in a sacred grove of long-thorned acacias at the village of Nezlet Batrân, in the Gizeh area, south of Cairo and not far from the great pyramids. This grove is sacred to *Sukkân es-Sunt*, the " Inhabitants of the Acacias ", supernatural beings " who lived underground " like the fairies of Scotland. Mr. G. D. Hornblower,[1] the Egyptologist, says that the grove is visited on Friday mornings. The leaves of the acacias are dried and powdered and used as incense for healing the sick, and the wood must not be used as fuel lest there should be sickness or loss of cattle or crops. " Mysterious lights may be seen flitting through the grove at night." Mr. Hornblower says that when the local gods were replaced first by Christian and then by Moslem saints the trees were allotted to them. St. Mourie similarly displaced the local gods in the Loch Maree area.

A fairy who inhabits a tree on a knoll, and comes forth to give " milk of wisdom " to women, figures in an old Gaelic myth recovered by Dr. Carmichael. She is referred to in a poem by a MacDonald bard of which a translated verse states:

> " The maiden queen [2] of wisdom dwelt
> In Beauteous Bower of the single tree,
> Where she could see the whole world
> And where no fool could her beauty see."

The Gaelic word *cnoc*, a knoll, has the secondary meanings of " council ", " court ", " wisdom " and " sense " (good sense). It was anciently the custom

[1] *Man* (February, 1930), Vol. XXX, No. II, pp. 16-8.
[2] The " queen " is here a literary importation.

FAIRIES AS DEITIES

to have meetings on a particular *cnoc* in a district at which disputes were settled and cases tried, the clansmen acting in trials as the jury and the chief of a clan as judge. In some areas the judge might be a hereditary *breitheamh* (Anglicized " brehon "). The Hebridean Morrisons were usually " the Lewis brehons ".

Carmichael gives interesting examples of the use of *cnoc* in Gaelic prose and poetry, including *cnoc na comhairle* (" hillock of counsel "), *duine cnocach* (" a shrewd man "), and *cho glic ri cnoc* (" as wise as a council knoll ").

The fairy of the *cnoc* with single tree summoned the daughters of men to gather at her residence on a certain day. Some women sneered, the foolish women laughed and the thoughtful women sighed. Many, however, assembled at the knoll, " some to be seen and some to seek wisdom ". Then the fairy woman appeared, " holding in her hand the *copan Moire* (' cup of Mary '), the blue-eyed limpet-shell containing the *ais* (milk) of wisdom ".

A Gaelic poet describes the fairy, whom he refers to as " queen ", as a lovely woman " arrayed in all the beauteous, iridescent hues of silver, emerald green and mother of pearl.

> " Loveliness shone around her like light
> Her steps were music of songs."

The fairy invited the assembled women to drink of the " *ais* (milk) of wisdom ", and she gave to each " according to her faith and desire till none was left ".

Several women arrived at the knoll too late, " and there was no wisdom left for them ".

Here we have evidently a memory of a milk goddess. The arbitrary association of milk with a tree and a sea-shell is suggestive of the importation in early times of a complex deity with a history rooted in a distant area of origin.

In ancient Egypt, Greece, India and elsewhere trees and plants that yield the milk-like fluid known as latex were, as indicated in connexion with Bride, associated with the mother goddess. The milk- (latex) yielding sycamore fig of Egypt was the tree of the cow-goddess Hathor and the many-breasted Artemis of Anatolia, the Diana whom " all the world worshipped ", according to St. Paul. The Ephesian Artemis impersonated the fig tree, the fruits of which were referred to as " teats ". In Greece the first food given to children, even in modern times, is the " milk of the fig ", which is sometimes mixed with honey. Sir Arthur Evans [1] has shown that in Minoan Crete libations of milk and honey were offered to the mother goddess. The association of the bee with Artemis [2] is of interest in this connexion.

The " milk-goddess " cult spread eastward and westward. India has much lore regarding " milk-yielding trees " and " milk-yielding plants " which are regarded as the daughters and descendants of the cow mother goddess called " Surabhi ", and the Hindu elixirs " amrita " and " soma " were milk mixtures.[3]

The very name of Rome is connected with the

---

[1] *The Palace of Minos*, Vol. I, pp. 625 *et seq.* Zeus is as a babe fed by nymphs with milk and honey. Diodorus Siculus, V, 70.

[2] Farnell, *Cults of the Greek States*, Vol. II, p. 481.

[3] *The Mahábhárata* (*Vana Parva*), § CI, and *Adi Parva*, Roy's translation, p. 163.

FAIRIES AS DEITIES

ancient milk cult. Anciently the Tiber was " Rumon ", a word derived from " ruma " and " rumen ", signifying milk and the teat that produced it. The milk goddess was Deva Rumina of the " Milky Way ", and on earth she was represented by the ruminal, or milk-yielding, fig tree under which the twins Romulus and Remus were suckled by the she-wolf, a cult animal and also a form of the goddess.

Pliny explains that the vegetable world receives " milk " (latex) from the Milky Way.[1]

In Scotland the milk-yielding tree is the hazel, the " milk " being in the green nut. An elixir given to weakly children is *cìr na meala is bainne nan cnò* (" comb of honey and milk of the nut "). Those children who were born in autumn were regarded as particularly fortunate because they could be given " milk of the nut " as their first food. Honey mixed with the milk of a cow or a goat was given to the newly born babe when " milk of the nut " could not be obtained. In our own day the custom of giving honey or sugar-sweetened water as baby's first food is quite common.

The Gaelic folk-poem *Ora Ceartais* (" Invocation for Justice ") refers to the washing of the infant Christ in milk:

" I will wash my face
In the nine rays of the sun,
As Mary washed her Son
In the rich fermented milk." [2]

---

[1] The milk cult is dealt with at length in my *The Migration of Symbols*, Chapter IV, and my *Myths of Pre-Columbian America*, Chapter XI; Pliny, Book XVIII, Chapter LXIX. In Gaelic the Milky Way is *A bhainne-shlighe*.

[2] *Carmina Gadelica*, Vol. I, p. 3, and Vol. II, pp. 253 *et seq.*

In the Irish epic *Táin Bó Cúalnge* the goddess Morrigan is wounded by Cuchulainn in her various shapes of eel, grey she-wolf and hornless red heifer. To obtain healing she must be blessed by him. The Morrigan comes from a knoll and milks a cow with three teats.

Cuchulainn, "maddened with thirst" and also in need of healing for his wounds, begs for milk. He is given a drink from each teat and not only expresses the wish, "May this be a cure in time for me", but blesses the milker, whose wounds are consequently healed. Then the Morrigan makes known who she is and Cuchulainn exclaims, "Had I known it was thou, I would never have healed thee".[1]

Milk was offered to the dead. J. Gregorson Campbell tells that after a coffin had been carried out of a house water was left on the boards upon which it had rested "in case the dead should return and be thirsty". Some, however, "put the drink of water or of milk outside the door".[2] The writer was informed in Argyll of the custom of placing a bowl of milk beside the grave.

Milk was similarly offered to the mummy in ancient Egypt. In the *Book of the Dead* (Chapter CLXXII) it is stated: "Thou offerest the water of Rē in a *snbt*-ewer (and) two great vessels of milk."

Libations of milk had to be offered to the water fairy called *loireag*. "If," Carmichael states, "this were omitted, she sucked the goats, sheep and cows of

---

[1] Joseph Dunn, *The Ancient Irish Epic Tale Táin Bó Cúalnge* (London, 1914), pp. 177–8.

[2] *Superstitions of the Scottish Highlands*, p. 241.

FAIRIES AS DEITIES

the townland, placing a spell upon them so that they could not move."[1]

Milk, as we have seen, was offered to the glaistig-gruagach. In the seventeenth century records of the Presbytery of Dingwall various pagan practices in Gairloch, Ross and Cromarty, are exposed and condemned. Bulls were sacrificed on 25th August, and there was also the " pouring of milk upon hills as oblationes ".[2] The offerings were to St. Mourie, who had evidently displaced a pagan god.

It was believed that if milk offerings were not made to the fairy folk they might work evil with the cows. An Inverness folk-tale tells of an eighteenth century " milk famine " in which Simon Lord Lovat, who was executed for high treason in the Tower of London, figures as a man suspected of being in league with the evil powers.

Lovat had ejected one of his tenants named John Fraser, better known as John Barron, from a mill and land near Beaufort Castle. John subsequently became the tenant of a farm with a mill on the estate of Robert Chevis of Muirtown in the vicinity of Inverness. This led to a quarrel between the two proprietors, and in December, 1746, Chevis gave evidence for the prosecution at Lovat's trial before the House of Peers.

John Fraser prospered for a time and supplied milk of excellent quality to his Inverness customers. Then suddenly " a famine of milk set in "; the cows gave little or no milk. At last no more could be supplied for sale to Inverness. The very bairns in the town

---

[1] *Carmina Gadelica* (1928 edition) Vol. II, pp. 320-1.
[2] Presbytery record of meeting at Kinlochewe on 9th September, 1656.

cried out for milk which could not be had. " Through summer, autumn, winter and spring the scarcity of milk continued."

One evening " early in the summer of the year following that when the dearth began ", Fraser was standing beside a rowan tree near his mill. He saw approaching a strange dwarfish man clad in curious attire. The careworn and elderly aspect of his face contrasted with his " youthful locks of brown hair ". This stranger carried over a shoulder " a long tapering sapling of hawthorn that seemed as if it would break beneath the load of some invisible burden that was attached to its slenderest end ". He did not speak to Fraser when he reached the rowan tree, nor did Fraser speak to him.

Fraser suddenly suspected that the stranger had some evil intent and, seizing the end of the hawthorn sapling, severed a portion of it with his gulley knife. The old man walked on as if unaware of Fraser's action and " disappeared over the rising ground towards the Leachkin ". The narrative continues: " As he vanished from the sight of Fraser, a rushing sound came from the cut twig that had fallen . . . Rich, creamy milk flowed as in a stream—it overspread in all directions the field where the miller stood." A rivulet of milk flowed towards the River Ness, giving it for a time " a milky appearance ". Thus did John Fraser " cut the fairy spell and let loose the milk that had been stolen from the cows of the valley for so many months. No longer did the cows refuse their milk, but gave it even more plentifully than before, and it was noticed that the field where the switch had

FAIRIES AS DEITIES

been cut from the old man's wand yielded a richer crop of grass for years after."[1]

The essentially spiritual character of the fairy folk is emphasized by the references to them as the " sluagh ", a term signifying a people, a host, a multitude, and especially as " sluagh eutrom ", the " light ", " airy ", " gay " or " giddy " folk. Dr. Alexander Carmichael was familiar with the application of " sluagh " to the " spirit world " and explains that the " hosts " are " the spirits of mortals who have died ",[2] while the Rev. John Gregorson Campbell gives both " sluagh " and " sluagh eutrom " as names of the fairy folk.[3]

According to Carmichael, the " sluagh " fly like the starlings " in great clouds up and down the face of the world ", returning " to the scenes of their early transgressions "; they cannot enter heaven " till satisfaction is made for the sins of earth ".

Stories are told of individuals who have been carried through the air by the " sluagh " as by the fairies. Carmichael took down several stories of persons who went with the " hosts ", disappearing mysteriously from among their companions and ultimately reappearing " utterly exhausted and prostrate ". An Uist woman told him of one man who feared to cross the threshold of his house after dusk. " When the spirits flew past his house, the man would wince as if undergoing a great mental struggle, and fighting against forces unseen of those around him." Dr. Carmichael writes regarding the " sluagh ":

[1] *The Witch of Inverness and the Fairies of Tomnahurich* (Inverness, 1891), pp. 38 *et seq.*
[2] *Carmina Gadelica* (1928 edition), Vol. II, p. 357.
[3] *Superstitions of the Highlands and Islands of Scotland*, pp. 8, 9.

"They fight battles in the air as men do on the earth. They may be heard and seen on clear frosty nights, advancing and retreating, retreating and advancing, against one another. After a battle, as I was told in Barra, their crimson blood may be seen staining rocks and stones. (*Fuil nan sluagh*, ' the blood of the hosts ', is the beautiful red *crotal* of the rocks melted by the frost.) These spirits used to kill cats and dogs, sheep and cattle, with their unerring venomous darts. They commanded men to follow them, and men obeyed, having no alternative. It was these men of earth who slew and maimed at the bidding of their spirit-masters, who in return ill-treated them in a most pitiless manner. . . . They would be rolling and dragging and trouncing them in mud and mire and pools."

The " Everlasting Battle " is also fought by the *Fir Chlis* (Aurora Borealis), and the blood of the wounded " falling to the earth and becoming congealed, forms the coloured stones called ' blood stones ', known in the Hebrides also by the name of *fuil siochaire* (fairy blood)".[1] The writer has heard stories of the " nimble men ", or " merry dancers ", engaging in clan fights for the possession by the rival chiefs of a fairy lady. The red cloud seen below the streamers when they are particularly vivid is called " the pool of blood ".[2]

Many other folk-stories of the Lowlands and Highlands reveal the non-human character of the fairies.

A Kirkcudbright story states that one day while she rocked her cradle a housewife suddenly saw an elegant and courtly lady standing in the middle of the room. " She had not heard anyone enter." The visitor

---

[1] J. G. Campbell, *Superstitions of the Highlands and Islands of Scotland*, p. 200; MacBain in his *Etymological Dictionary of the Gaelic Language* gives the early Irish form of *siochair* as *sithchaire*, from *sìth*, fairy, and *cuire*, host.

[2] My *Elves and Heroes* (Inverness, 1908), p. 85.

FAIRIES AS DEITIES

wore a dress " of the richest green, embroidered round with spangles of gold, and on her head was a small coronet of pearls ... One of the children put out her hand to get hold of the grand lady's spangles, but told her mother afterwards that she felt nothing. The mother was afraid the child would lose the use of her hands, but no such calamity ensued."[1]

There are stories which tell of the dead being resident in fairyland. They are seen feasting with the little green folk or gathering fruit and reaping crops, like the departed in the Egyptian underworld paradise of Osiris.

In a tale from Badenoch a man who had travelled from Inverness reached in the night-time a solitary place called *Sloc-muic* (" pigs' hollow "). There he was met by " crowds of people, none of whom he could recognize ". He asked one of them who they were and received the reply, " None of the seed of Abram nor of Adam's race; but men of that party who lost favour at the Court of Grace." [2]

W. Grant Stewart, in his collection of Strathspey folk-lore,[3] tells of an interview which a " pious clergyman " had with a fairy, who told he had been " originally angelic in his nature and attributes " but had been " seduced by Satan to join him in his mad conspiracies " and, having been cast out of heaven, " was now doomed along with millions of fellow sufferers to wander through seas and mountains until the coming of the great day—the Day of Judgment."

---

[1] J. F. Campbell, *Popular Tales* (Paisley edition, 1890), Vol. II, pp. 67–8.
[2] J. F. Campbell, *Popular Tales* (1890 edition), Vol. II, p. 77–8.
[3] *Popular Superstitions* (Edinburgh, 1823), pp. 58 *et seq.*

Hugh Miller in his *Scenes and Legends* (Chapter V) tells of a farmer who was reading his Bible while keeping watch over his sheep, the herd-boy having been sent to church. " A strong breeze was eddying within the hollow " and there appeared " a beautiful sylph-looking female ... attired in a long, flowing mantle of green which concealed her feet, but her breast and arms, which were of exquisite beauty, were uncovered." She asked the farmer regarding the Bible he was reading " if there be any offer of salvation in it to us?" His reply was, " The gospel of this book is addressed to the lost children of Adam, but to the creatures of no other race." The fairy shrieked and vanished.

J. F. Campbell gives another version of this tale " which," he says, " shows that they (the fairies) are supposed to be 'spirits in prison '."[1] He notes that " the fairies of the Isle of Man are believed to be spirits ".[2]

Dr. Alexander Carmichael provides a Hebridean version of the story of the war in heaven. Many angels followed Satan and suddenly the gates of heaven and hell were closed. Those who were out flew into holes in the earth and became fairies.[3]

M. Martin, dealing with the precautions taken to prevent the abduction of women and children, refers to the fairies as " evil spirits ".[4]

In a Badenoch story " a man sees fairies carding and spinning in a sheal (shieling) where he is living at the

[1] J. F. Campbell, *Popular Tales*, Vol. II, p. 75.
[2] *Op. cit.*, p. 81.
[3] *Carmina Gadelica* (2nd edition), Vol. II, pp. 352-3.
[4] *A Description of the Western Islands* (1884 edition), pp. 117-8.

FAIRIES AS DEITIES

time. Amongst them is Miss Emma Macpherson of Cluny, who had been dead about one hundred years." Another story tells of a lad who recognizes his mother, believed to be dead, beholding her in fairy company. She was ultimately rescued and taken home. Yet another Badenoch story of like character relates that an old woman met among fairies her deceased landlord and landlady. They told her that the fairies had " just carried off a young man supposed to be dead ".[1]

A Nithsdale young man one night heard " delicious music " in a lonely place and, advancing towards the spot whence it issued, saw a fairy company partaking of a banquet.

" A green table with feet of gold was laid across a small rivulet, and supplied with the finest of bread and the richest of wines. The music proceeded from instruments formed of reeds and stalks of corn. He was invited to partake in the dance, and presented with a cup of wine. He was allowed to depart in safety and ever after possessed the gift of second sight. He said he saw there several of his former acquaintances, who were become members of the fairy society."

Another Nithsdale story concerns a woman who acted as the " wet nurse " of the baby of a pretty fairy lady in a " green mantle ". The baby thrived and the fairy came one summer day on a visit and asked the woman to follow her and then led her to a green hill, which they entered on the sunny side, a sod lifting and revealing a door.

" The fairy then dropped three drops of a precious liquid on her companion's left eyelid, and she beheld a most delicious

[1] J. F. Campbell, *Popular Tales*, Vol. II, p. 77.

country whose fields were yellow with ripening corn, watered by looping burnies (small streams) and bordered by trees laden with fruit. She was presented with webs of the finest cloth and with boxes of precious ointments.

"The fairy then moistened her right eye with a green fluid and bade her look. She looked and saw several of her friends and acquaintances at work, reaping the corn and gathering the fruit.

"'This,' said the fairy, 'is the punishment of evil deeds!'

"She then passed her hand over the woman's eye and restored it to its natural power.

"Leading her to the porch at which she had entered, she dismissed her; but the woman had secured the wonderful salve. From this time she possessed the faculty of discerning the fairy people as they went about invisibly; till one day, happening to meet the fairy lady, she attempted to shake hands with her.

"'What ee (eye) d'ye see me wi?' whispered she.

"'Wi' them baith (both),' said the woman.

"The fairy breathed on her eyes and the salve lost its efficacy, and could never more endow her eyes with their preternatural power."[1]

In a Welsh folk-tale of similar character the fairy mother gives a woman who acted as midwife and nurse a "certain ointment" to rub over the eyes of the fairy baby. The woman did as directed and thought she might try it upon her own eyes. When she did so she saw the fairy mother as a beautiful lady attired in white, while the babe was seen "wrapped in swaddling clothes of a silvery gauze". On either side of the bed's head were repulsive-looking imps with flat noses.

She left the fairy dwelling without telling that she

[1] Thomas Keightley, *op. cit.*, pp. 352–4.

FAIRIES AS DEITIES

had used the magic ointment. On the next market day she saw the fairy husband and asked regarding the mother and child. He asked her with which eye she saw him and she said with the right. He struck that eye, which was made blind.

An English folk-tale tells that a human nurse, while anointing a fairy child with the ointment, felt an itch in one of her eyes and rubbed it with a finger that had touched the mysterious substance. "A new scene forced itself upon her astonished vision," the cottage becoming a tree and the lamps glowworms.

Later at a market she saw an old fairy woman stealing butter and spoke to her. The fairy blinded the woman's eye which had been touched by the ointment with a puff of her " withering breath ".[1]

The Rev. Robert Kirk in his *The Secret Commonwealth of Elves, Fauns and Fairies*[2] states that a man with the power of " second sight " averred that the subterranean people (fairies) were " departed souls, attending awhile in this inferior state and clothed with bodies procured through their almsdeeds in this lyfe; fluid, active, ætheriall vehicles to hold them, that they may not scatter, or wander, and be lost in the Totum, or their first Nothing; but if any were so impious as to have given no alms, they say when the souls of such do depart, they sleep in an unactive state till they resume the terrestrial bodies again."

Folk-tales which tell of the supernatural lapse of time in fairyland further emphasize that we are really dealing with a community of spirits and ghosts. One

---

[1] Thomas Keightley, *op. cit.*, pp. 302, 311.
[2] London edition, 1893, p. 18.

of these is connected with the Inverness hillock named Tom-na-hurich (*Tom na h-Iubhraich*, meaning, Watson states, " knoll of the yew wood "). It has been recorded by W. Grant Stewart [1] and by the author of *The Witch of Inverness and the Fairies of Tomnahurich*.[2] The former dates it " about three hundred years ago ". It relates that two Strathspey fiddlers paid a visit to Inverness. " A venerable-looking old man, grey-haired and somewhat wrinkled, of genteel deportment and liberal disposition," employed them to provide music at a dance. He led them to Tom-na-hurich in the dusk and when they entered it they found themselves in a large hall brilliantly lit, in which " tables were profusely laden with viands, fruits and liquors of every description ". There they ate and drank among hundreds of small and lovely women. After the feast there was dancing. " The night passed on harmoniously, while the diversity of reels and the loveliness of the dancers presented to the fiddlers the most gratifying scene they ever witnessed."

When, as they supposed, morning came they left the hillock dwelling, receiving from the little old man a purse of gold. They found that Inverness and its surroundings had greatly changed and that there had been " strange innovations of dress and manners ". Many of the Inverness people " jeered at their appearance " and, feeling puzzled and offended, they made their way back to their native place. They arrived on a Sunday and entered the church in which they had been accustomed to worship. The clergyman was

---

[1] *Popular Superstitions* (Edinburgh, 1823), pp. 98 *et seq.*
[2] Inverness, 1891, pp. 23 *et seq.*

reading the Bible and when he came to the name of God the two fiddlers were observed by the congregation to crumble into dust.

In one of the versions of the folk-tale an Inverness man who conversed with them after leaving Tom-na-hurich said, " You are the two men my great-grandfather lodged, and who, it was supposed, were decoyed by Thomas Rhymer to Tom-na-hurich. Sore did your friends lament your loss—but the lapse of a hundred years has now rendered your name extinct."

Other stories tell of some individual entering a fairy knoll, the door of which happened to be open, to join in dancing a merry reel. A year and a day elapse and then a rescuer, who has affixed a knife or other article of steel or iron to the knoll door, or is wearing a rowan cross, enters the fairy dwelling at midnight, seizes the lost one and forces him to leave. Many versions of this story are found throughout Scotland and are fairly common elsewhere.[1]

Brownies were reputed to attach themselves to families, doing the work of man-servant or maid-servant. They were of short stature, had wrinkled faces and curly brown hair and wore a brown mantle and hood. Some haunted the ruins of old castles or dwelt in the hollows of old trees. They lived to a great age. One was reputed to have dwelt in Leithin Hall in Dumfriesshire for three centuries, and when he deserted it the owners of the hall met with ruin.

A male gruagach is referred to in some parts of the Highlands and resembles a brownie. He usually wears a beaver hat and carries a wand. Many tricks

[1] E. S. Hartland, *The Science of Fairy Tales* (London, 1891), pp. 161 et seq.

are played by him. Like the female gruagach, he receives offerings of milk, which is poured into a hollowed stone called *clach na gruagaich*, or over a slab called *leac gruagaich*.

Another fairy of this class is known as the *gunna* (pr. " goo′na "). He is supposed to watch the cattle by night so that they may not stray or fall over rocks. This supernatural is not clad in green like a female fairy, but is nude save for a fox's skin drawn around his body, and he has long yellow hair like the gruagach. When nights are cold, the people sitting about warm fires pity the little gunna. One who has the faculty of " second sight " laments the fate of this solitary.

> " For he'll see him perched alone
>   On a chilly old grey stone,
>   Nibbling, nibbling at a bone
>   That we'll maybe throw away.
>
> " He's so hungry, he's so thin,
>   If he'd come we'd let him in,
>   For a rag of fox's skin
>   Is the only thing he'll wear.
>
> " He'll be chittering in the cold
>   As he hovers round the fold,
>   With his locks of glimmering gold
>   Twined about his shoulders bare." [1]

The " little old man of the barn " (*bodachan sabhaill*) is another kind of brownie, who takes pity on old men and during the night threshes corn and ties the straw into bundles.

[1] *Elves and Heroes* (Inverness, 1908), pp. 29–30.

"When the peat will turn grey and the shadows fall deep,
And weary old Callum is snoring asleep . . .

> The Little Old Man of the Barn
> Will thresh with no light in the month of the night,
> The Little Old Man of the Barn."

The dread of fairies as supernatural beings is emphasized by the prayer of a Skye centenarian named Farquhart Beaton, given by the Rev. Alexander MacGregor:[1]

"*Gleidh an t-aosda agus an t-òg, ar mnathan agus ar paisdean, ar sprèidh agus ar feudal, o chumhachd agus o cheannas nan sithichean, agus o mhi-run gach droch-shùla.*"

"Preserve the aged and the young, our wives and our children, our sheep and our cattle, from the power and dominion of the fairies and from the malicious effects of every evil eye."

---

[1] *Highland Superstitions* (Stirling, 1901), p. 15.

CHAPTER XII

Demons of Land and Water

St. Columba and the demons—The Fuath—Cailleach as a Fuath—Fuaths of streams, cascades and glens—The Peallaidh as the Devil—Peallaidhs of Perthshire—Shellycoat—The Fideal—Female vampires as beautiful dancing girls—The water-horse takes human form—The kelpie—Banshee as a Fuath —Banshee as raven and hoodie-crow—The night mourner—Washers at fords as ghosts—Glaistigs as ghosts—Glaistig as cave monster—Glaistig and birds —Green ghosts—The green ladies—Ghosts as dogs, cattle and deer— Ghostly hunters—Rock-dwelling beings—Underground demons—The " blood one " and " killing one "—Black king of death revels—The demon of lightning—The gigantic cat demon—Cat roasting and other Taghairm ceremonies —Monster of the sea loch—King's daughter as sacrifice—Slaying of the monster—Fraoch myth—The dragon guardian of rowan tree—Salmon form of dragon—Juice of salmon or white serpent imparts knowledge—Serpent lore —Cailleach and the serpent—Monsters of the night—Mermaid lore—" Shony " the sea-god or demon.

When St. Columba was engaged in converting the pagans in Scotland, he substituted for magic wands, finger-signs, charms, &c., the Christian blessing and the sign of the cross. Demons were thus worsted and expelled in a new and easy manner.

Adamnan tells that one day a youth who was carrying a vessel of new milk asked the saint to bless his burden. The saint did so, raising his hand and making " the saving sign ". When he did so the lid of the vessel fell off and the greater part of the milk was spilled. The youth was informed that he had neglected to banish the demon lurking in the empty vessel by making the sign of the cross before the milk was poured into it.

The saint then blessed the vessel, which was immediately filled with milk again by " divine agency ".[1] A wild boar was slain and an aquatic monster in the river Ness thwarted by the saint making the sign of the cross and praying. Demons lurked everywhere, ready to do injury to mankind.

Some of these demons have been included in vague traditions among the fairies simply because they were supernatural. But they differ from the knoll dwellers in many respects.

The *fuath* (pronounced foo'ă), for instance, was a term applied to various monsters. The *muileartach* form of the Cailleach was a *fuath*.

> " 'S gum b'ainm do'n fhuath nach robh tìom
> A mhuireartach maol, ruadh, muing-fhionn.
>
> " The name of the daring *fuath*
> Was the bold, red, white-maned *muileartach*."

J. G. Campbell [2] thought the *fuath* had no particular connexion with water and considered that J. F. Campbell was wrong in asserting that it had. But the Tiree Campbell was in error in this connexion. The *fuath*, as Dr. Carmichael and others, including the writer, have found, haunted streams, waterfalls and glens. Watson has provided conclusive evidence in this connexion. " Glen Cuaich in Inverness-shire," he writes, " is, or was till lately, haunted by a being known as Cuachag, the river sprite." The spirit of Loch Etive in Argyll was reputed to have been seen in Glen Salach. When the northern Nethy rose in flood the people said

[1] *The Life of St. Columba*, Book II, Chapter XV.
[2] *Witchcraft and Second Sight in the Scottish Highlands*, pp. 188–9.

in Gaelic, " The Nethy sprites are coming ". Offerings appear to have been made to these supernatural beings. " A stream in Benbecula is called *a' Ghamhnach*, ' the farrow cow ', and the custom in crossing it was to throw a wisp of grass into the water with the formula *fodar do'n Ghamhnaich* (' fodder for the Gamhnach ')." [1]

Peallaidh [2] was a *fuath*, and in Lewis, Professor Watson tells me, *Peallaidh* is dialectically *Piullaidh* and applied to " the devil ". There are many demons of the *peallaidh* type in Perthshire folk-lore, and Aberfeldy is in Gaelic *obar pheallaidh*. Our *Peallaidh* (" shaggy one ") was reputed to have been the chief of the urisks, some of whom were harmless and friendly to individuals, while others were hostile and dangerous as water demons. Watson refers to a footprint on a Glen Lyon rock (*caslorg Pheallaidh*) reputed to be that of *Peallaidh*, and a cataract called *eas Pheallaidh*. An urisk might also be called a *fuath*, although all the demons referred to as *fuath* were not necessarily urisks. John Macdiarmid, Killin, has given a list of urisk names in Perthshire, one of which is *Fuath*.[3]

A form of *Peallaidh* or the urisk on the east coast of Scotland and in the Lowlands was shellycoat. Sir Walter Scott [4] has referred to him as a " water spirit " who has " given his name to many a rock and stone upon the Scottish coast ". When shellycoat appeared " he seemed to be decked with marine productions, and, in particular, with shells, whose clattering an-

[1] *History of the Celtic Place-Names of Scotland*, pp. 426–7; *Carmina Gadelica*, II, p. 83.
[2] Pronounced pyaw'le.
[3] *Transactions of the Gaelic Society of Inverness*, Vol. XXV, p. 133.
[4] Introduction to *The Minstrelsy of the Scottish Border*, written in 1802.

DEMONS OF LAND AND WATER 235

nounced his approach. From this circumstance he derived his name." Scott gives the following folk-tale regarding shellycoat:

" Two men, on a very dark night, approaching the banks of the Ettrick, heard a doleful voice from its waves repeatedly exclaim, ' Lost! Lost!' They followed the sound, which seemed to be the voice of a drowning person, and, to their infinite astonishment, they found that it ascended the river. Still they continued, during a long and tempestuous night, to follow the cry of the malicious spirit; and, arriving before morning's dawn at the very sources of the river, the voice was now heard descending the opposite side of the mountain in which they arise. The fatigued and deluded travellers now relinquished the pursuit; and had no sooner done so, than they heard shellycoat applauding, in loud bursts of laughter, his successful roguery. The spirit was supposed particularly to haunt the old house of Gorinberry situated on the River Hermitage in Liddesdale."

A shellycoat was reputed to haunt a rock on the shore of Leith and according to local writers the boys were wont to run round the rock three times, repeating the couplet,

" Shellycoat, shellycoat, gang awa hame,
I cry na' yer mercy, I fear na' yer name."

The demon was reputed to thrash severely those who offended it. Urisks and glaistigs similarly dealt with those individuals who had incurred their displeasure. Water demons had various local names, including " smiter ", " brounger ", " clootie ", &c.

A female impersonation of entangling grasses, known as the *fideal*, haunted *Loch na Fideil* in Gairloch, Ross and Cromarty. A folk-tale tells of a strong man named

Ewen who wrestled with her. "Ewen killed the *fideal* and the *fideal* killed Ewen."[1]

A particularly fierce female demon called *baobhan sìth* might appear as a hoodie crow or raven, or as a beautiful girl of human stature clad in a long, trailing, green dress which concealed the deer hoofs she had instead of feet. Like a vampire, she drank the blood of her human victims.

There are many stories regarding this class of demon. The Rev. C. M. Robertson, in a paper on "Folk-lore from the West of Ross-shire",[2] tells of four men who had been hunting and sought shelter for the night in a lonely shieling. One supplied vocal music (*puirt-a-beul*) and one of the others, who danced, expressed the wish that they had partners. Four women entered the shieling and three of them danced with the men, while the fourth sat beside the music maker. One of the men saw blood drops falling from a companion and fled from the shieling, taking refuge in a horse-fold. His demon partner pursued him, but "once he got in alongside of the horses she was powerless to harm him". When daylight came he and others went to the shieling and found the lifeless remains of the other hunters. "The creatures with whom they had associated had sucked the blood from their bodies."

Another story is told regarding three hunters. One of them saw that the women had hoofs and took flight. He was pursued by one of them, who referred to him as her *dubhach*, a word now obsolete but

[1] W. J. Watson, *Place-Names of Ross and Cromarty*, pp. 239 and 281.
[2] *Transactions of the Gaelic Society of Inverness*, Vol. XXVI, pp. 262 *et seq.*

supposed to mean something she was to devour.

A Kintail version is given by Mrs. Watson [1] in which the musician plays a " jew's harp ", and it was he who perceived that the strange and comely women had deer hoofs for feet. He effected his escape. Next morning it was found that the other hunters had had their " throats cut and chests laid open ".

Some Argyll versions of the story are detailed by J. Gregorson Campbell.[2] The hunters take refuge in a cave. Each of the young men said he wished his own sweetheart were there that night, but Macphee, who was accompanied by his black dog, said he preferred his wife to be in her own house. Young women entered the cave and the men who had wished for sweethearts were slain. Macphee was protected by his dog, who drove the women from the cave. Then a great hand was thrust into the cave and it groped for Macphee, but the dog fought with the hand and drove away the demon.

A greatly dreaded demon was the *each uisge* ("water-horse"), which lived in a loch but never in a stream or river, like our *Peallaidh*. This demon might assume the form of a handsome young man, but could be detected by his horse hoofs and by green water-weeds or sand in his hair. Stories are told of water-horses in human form making love to girls. Some discovered in time the real character of the lover and escaped. Others were taken to a loch and devoured. Children who saw a horse grazing on a green bank mounted it. The demon then rushed into the loch and next day

---

[1] *Celtic Review*, Vol. V, p. 164.
[2] *Superstitions of the Scottish Highlands*, pp. 109 *et seq.*

the livers or entrails of its victims were washed ashore.

A woman herd was alone in a shieling on a small island off the Rhinns of Islay, and one night a tall, large, rough and hairy man with a livid face entered. He asked her name and she answered "*mise mi fhìn*" ("me myself"). She threw boiling water at him and he was scalded and ran outside yelling. When asked by his companions who had harmed him, he answered "*mise mi fhìn*" and they laughed. The water-horse had apparently ferocious as well as comely forms.[1]

A similar story is told in Sutherland [2] regarding the *brollachan*, son of the *fuath*, an untidy creature like the urisk, *Peallaidh* and shellycoat.

The kelpie resembled the water-horse, but was more associated with rivers than with lochs. It was heard yelling or calling by night like the urisk and shellycoat and, in human form, was untidy and shaggy. Sometimes the kelpie in man shape attacked wayfarers, leaping up behind them as they rode on horses, gripping them in his arms and hurting as well as scaring them. The kelpie's commonest form was that of a young horse which scampered on a river and, striking the water three times with his tail so heavily that each splash sounded as loud as thunder, disappeared in a flash of fire in a deep pool. The kelpie had a magic bridle, and a bold MacGregor, known as Wellox, who attacked one, struck off the bit, which he seized and kept. Apparently the kelpie's power was weakened by this loss, but it pleaded in vain that it

---

[1] J. G. Campbell, *Superstitions of the Scottish Highlands*, pp. 203 et seq.; J. F. Campbell, *Popular Tales of the West Highlands*, Vol. II, pp. 205-6.

[2] J. F. Campbell, *op. cit.*, pp. 203-4.

should be restored. Wellox subsequently worked magic with the kelpie's bit.[1]

Another *fuath* was the "banshee" (*bean shìth*), also called the *bean nighe* ("washing-woman"), *nigheag bheag a bhròin* ("little washer of sorrow") or *nigheag an àth* ("little washer of the ford"). She sang a mournful dirge as she washed the "death clothes" of someone doomed to meet with a sudden end by violence. When a human being seized hold of her after stealthy approach, she revealed who was about to die and also had to grant three wishes.[2] The banshee, like the *baobhan sìth*, sometimes appeared as a raven or hoodie crow.[3]

The spirit known as the *caoineag* or *caoidheag* (*caoin*, "weep"; *caoidh*, "lamentation"), the one who weeps and mourns, foretells death like the banshee, or "washer", but is rarely seen and cannot be approached or questioned or forced to grant wishes. She is heard wailing in the darkness at a cascade or stream, or in a glen or on a mountainside. If a foray or battle is about to take place, sorrow is in store for those who listen to her wailing and mourning. "It is said," writes Dr. A. Carmichael, "that she was heard during several successive nights before the massacre of Glencoe. This roused the suspicions of the people and, notwithstanding the assurance of peace and friendship of the soldiery, many of the people left the glen and thus escaped the

---

[1] W. Grant Stewart, *Popular Superstitions* (Edinburgh, 1823), pp. 147 *et seq.*; *Minstrelsy of the Scottish Border*, Vol. IV; Dr. Jamieson, "Water Kelpie" poem; Sir Thomas Dick Lauder, *Tales of the Highlands*, Chapter I.

[2] A. Carmichael, *Carmina Gadelica*, Vol. II, pp. 227 *et seq.*; J. G. Campbell, *Superstitions of the Scottish Highlands*, pp. 42 *et seq,*

[3] J. G. Campbell, *op. cit.*, pp. 107-8.

fate of those who remained." Dr. Carmichael collected and translated surviving fragments of dirges of the doomful glen:

"Little caoineachag of the sorrow
Is pouring the tears of her eyes,
Weeping and wailing the fate of Clan Donald,
Alas, my grief! that ye did not heed her cries."[1]

There was a widespread belief that some of the supernatural washing-women were the ghosts of women "dreeing their weird":

"Women dying in childbed were looked upon as dying prematurely, and it was believed that, unless all the clothes left by them were washed, they should have to wash them themselves till the natural period of their death."[2]

A similar belief obtained regarding some of the glaistigs:

"Many people use banshee and *glaistig* as convertible terms and the confusion thence arising extends largely to books. The true *glaistig* is a woman of human race who has been put under enchantments and to whom a fairy nature has been given. She wears a green dress."[3]

Gregorson Campbell is here highly controversial. As we have seen, he rejected the evidence that the true *glaistig* was "half woman, half goat" and overlooked the fact that, although some *glaistigs* were tutelary beings, others were enemies of man and had links with Cailleach Bheur. The *gruagach*, connected in Tiree with the sea, was *gruagach mhara* (sea-maid) and was

---
[1] *Carmina Gadelica* (2nd edition), Vol. II, pp. 244-5.
[2] J. G. Campbell, *op. cit.*, p. 43.
[3] J. G. Campbell, *op. cit.*, p. 44-5.

undoubtedly a *glaistig*.[1] Dr. Carmichael has provided evidence which emphasizes the sinister aspect of her character. In East Bennan in Arran is a cave called *uamh na gruagaich* (" cave of the gruagach ") and *uamh na béiste* (" cave of the monster "). But, although she was a cave-dweller like the Cailleach, she herded cattle and sang beautifully. She crossed the sea regularly and in her song referred to this habit:

" A night in Arran, a night in Islay,
And in green Kintyre of the birches." [2]

The *glaistig* is referred to as a " monster " in the story of Mac Mhuirich More, which links with the Lochaber story of Big Kennedy (Mac Ualrig Mór) of Lianachan. Mac Mhuirich had seized *isean*[3] *na béist* and she begged for the return of her young one, promising to perform any task he desired. Mac Mhuirich demanded that she should build in a single night " a house of nine couples " which would be thatched " with the down and feather of birds, no two feathers to be alike ". She performed the task before cock crow, singing as she darted about:

" Turf! divot! and splint!
To the side of the house of the rogue! "

The song was varied:

" Any tree in the forest save the wild fig tree,[4]
Any tree in the forest save the aspen tree,
The thorn of pain, the crooked yew and the wild fig tree." [5]

[1] *Ibid.*, p. 165.
[2] *Carmina Gadelica* (2nd edition), Vol. II, pp. 306-7.
[3] *Isean*, a chicken, the young of any bird; here it signifies " the child " of the monster.
[4] *Fiodhag*, the bird cherry.
[5] *Carmina Gadelica* (2nd edition), Vol. II, p. 290.

Here the *glaistig* has a connexion with birds, like the Cailleach Bheur.

Green ghosts which are distinguished from *glaistigs* are known in the folk-lore of the north as " green ladies ". The writer in his boyhood heard many stories regarding them. Some " green ladies " were so common that people became quite accustomed to them, remarking, " There she goes again ". They appeared sometimes in broad daylight, but usually at dusk and in the night-time.

Hugh Miller tells of a " green lady " in Banffshire who was " tall and slim and wholly attired in green, with her face wrapped up in the hood of her mantle ". She was the former mistress of the laird's house. For nearly a year " scarce a day passed in which she was not seen by some of the domestics. The maids could see her in the grey of the morning flitting like a shadow round their beds, or peering in upon them at night through the dark window-panes or at half-open doors . . . Though always cadaverously pale and miserable looking, she affected a joyous disposition and was frequently heard to laugh, even when invisible." Sometimes she had " the roguish, half-humorous expression of one who had just succeeded in playing off a good joke ". In this respect she resembled the *glaistig*.

One day she appeared at noon and told of children who were on a tidal rock and in danger of being drowned, and they were rescued just in time.

It was after that incident that the " green lady " told that she had been concerned in the robbery and death of a pedlar who had been buried under an ash-tree. She revealed where the pedlar's gold had been

DEMONS OF LAND AND WATER 243

hidden and directed that it should be sent to his widow in Leith. Then she vanished and the woman who had been informed of the crime saw only " a large black greyhound crossing the moor ". The gold was sent to Leith as directed and the " green lady " was never again seen.[1]

Although some " green ladies " were harmless, others might be fierce and dangerous.

The reference to the " green lady " assuming the form of the greyhound is of special interest. Mr. James Macdiarmid, dealing with Breadalbane folk-lore, has recorded:[2]

" It was firmly believed that ghosts could appear in many different forms, sometimes in human shape, at other times in the shape of dogs, cattle and deer. Probably about ninety years ago it was rumoured that a ghost haunted the neighbourhood of the farm-house of Claggan, on the south side of Loch Tay, and that it occasionally at least took its nightly rambles in the shape of a dog."

Macdiarmid tells of a man who was followed by a " big grey dog " which appeared at *An Carn mòr* (" the big cairn "). Yet although a ghost might assume dog-form, an ordinary dog, especially a greyhound, was considered to be " an efficient protector against a dog or witch ".

In the Hebrides the supernatural greyhound (*cu gorm*) and other dogs accompanied the ghostly hunters who, with hawks on hand, went westward through the air towards *Tìr na h-òige* (" land of youth ") and *Tìr fo thuinn* (" land under-wave "). Although some would have it that we have in folk-beliefs of this character

[1] Hugh Miller, *Scenes and Legends*, Chapter XXV.
[2] *Transactions of the Gaelic Society of Inverness*, Vol. XXVI, pp. 32 *et seq*,

traces of Norse influence, it has to be recognized that similar hunts are depicted on the pre-Norse sculptured stones of Scotland.

The *frid, fride*, is a supernatural which dwells under or inside rocks and feeds on the milk and crumbs of bread that fall to the ground. There are references to human beings making regular offerings to the *fridean* and it may be that the oblations of milk poured upon the hills in Gairloch, Ross and Cromarty, were originally intended for these invisible beings. There are many stories of pipers accompanied by dogs exploring underground passages. Listeners hear the music for some time; then it ceases suddenly. The pipers are never seen again, but their dogs return in a hairless condition and die, having fought with the underground fiends.

Widespread but somewhat vague references are made in Gaelic to demons known as the *cear* ("blood one"), and the *cearb* ("killing one"), which attack human beings and cattle.

A boys' rhyme preserved in Creich, Sutherland, runs in Gaelic:

> "I came from small peril,
> I came from great peril,
> I came from *Geigean*,
> I came from *Guaigean*,
> And I will come from thee if I can."

Dr. Carmichael, who has recorded it, tells that the term "King Geigean" was applied to a man who presided over "death revels" which were held in winter. When he was chosen after lots were drawn he reigned from midnight to cock crow.

"A tub of cold water was poured over his head and down his throat, after which his face and neck were smeared with soot. When the man had been made as formidable and hideous as possible, a sword, scythe or sickle was placed in his hand as emblem of office."[1]

Evidently " King Geigean " impersonated some old forgotten demon. Certain of the supernatural beings remembered as urisks were black. One of them was known in Perthshire as *Triubhas-dubh* (" black trews "). The *dubh-sìth* (" black supernatural ") is another hostile demon.

A ferocious and gigantic cat demon appeared in connexion with the *Taghairm* ceremony. Martin, in his seventeenth century *Description of the Western Isles*, refers to one mode of it as the roasting of a live cat on a spit until a very large cat appeared and answered certain questions. A later version of the ceremony was related at some length in the *London Literary Gazette* for March, 1824. It tells that the last time the *Taghairm* was performed was in Mull at the beginning of the seventeenth century. Allan MacLean, son of Hector, was assisted by Lauchlan MacLean, and their aim was to secure two boons.

" The sacrifice consisted of living cats roasted on a spit while life remained, and when the animal expired, another was put on in its place. This operation was continued for four days and nights without tasting food. The Taghairm commenced at midnight between Friday and Saturday, and had not long proceeded when infernal spirits began to enter the house or barn in which it was performing, in the form of black cats."

A cat protested against the proceedings, but the

[1] *Carmina Gadelica* (2nd edition), Vol. II, pp. 300–1.

men paid no heed. Other cats entered and yelled fiercely like the cat on the spit.

"A cat of enormous size at last appeared and told Lauchlan MacLean that if he did not desist before his great-eared brother arrived he never would behold the face of God.

"Lauchlan answered that if all the devils in hell came, he would not flinch until his task was concluded.

"By the end of the fourth day there was a black cat at the root of every rafter on the roof of the barn, and their yells were distinctly heard beyond the Sound of Mull in Morvern."

In the end the men were asked what they wanted. Allan, greatly agitated, asked for wealth, and Lauchlan asked for progeny and wealth. Both got what they demanded.

The gigantic cat which appeared to grant their wishes was called "Big Ears". It perched upon a stone which, according to the writer in the *London Literary Gazette*, was still pointed out in his time; the marks of Big Ear's claws were "visible in small pits upon its surface".

Some time before the Mull ceremony, the Taghairm was performed by Cameron of Lochiel, who received "a small silver shoe which was to be put on the left foot of every son born in that family". The shoe apparently brought good luck and ensured personal courage. It fitted all the Camerons of Lochiel but one; "and he afterwards turned his back to the foe at Sheriffmuir, having inherited a large foot by his mother".

M. Martin tells of other modes of the Taghairm ceremony. One was performed by carrying a man to a boundary stream and bumping him against a bank

DEMONS OF LAND AND WATER 247

till there came from the sea small beings who gave an answer to a certain question. Another was performed by wrapping a man in the skin of a cow and leaving him all night at a lonely spot. Supernatural beings visited him during the night and revealed what was desired to be known.

According to Professor W. J. Watson, *Taghairm* (Irish *Toghairm*) means " invocation ". The ceremony is evidently a survival of paganism. Watson draws attention to Keating's *History of Ireland*, in which, writing of the Druids, he says:

" But when all these expedients failed them, and they were obliged to do their utmost, what they did was to make round wattles of the rowan tree, and to spread thereon the hides of the bulls offered in sacrifice, putting the side that had been next the flesh uppermost, and thus relying on their *geasa* (magical injunctions) to summon the demons to get information from them."

In the original " to summon the demons " is *do thoghairm na ndeamhnan.*

A destructive demon known as the *beithir* haunted " caves, corries and mountain fastnesses ". The name was also applied to lightning, the thunderbolt and the serpent. Another name for the serpent was *nathair.*

A monster is reputed to haunt Loch Morar, Lochaber, the deepest loch in Scotland. It is known as " Morag " and has been described as " a huge, shapeless, dark mass, rising out of the water like an island ". According to local belief, the monster never rises " save when some MacDonald or a Gillies is about to exchange the barren hills of Morar for a fairer and more salubrious clime ".[1] Another form of the belief is that " it appears only when one of the natives of the place dies " and is therefore referred to as *Mórag dhubh* (" black Morag ") and *Mórag odhar* (" dun Morag ").[2]

A large group of Gaelic stories tell of the monster of the deep which came into a loch, causing a high tide; it claimed a human sacrifice and when lots were drawn the king's daughter was the victim. The young and beautiful princess had to go to a selected spot and await the coming of the monster so that the whole realm might not be ravaged. Like Iphigenia, daughter of King Agamemnon, who was sacrificed to the Artemis of Aulis, she was to be the salvation of her people.

The Gaelic stories tell that the king's daughter was accompanied by warriors to a green mound by the seaside, but these armed men fled at the first hint of peril. A brave young man who had been acting as herd came to defend the princess and lay down to sleep until the monster appeared. To awaken him from his " magic sleep ", during which he acquired " power ", the princess had to cut off a portion of his ear or a joint of his little finger or a portion of his scalp.

As the young hero slept, the princess saw the three-headed monster approaching in a squall of wind, while the tide rose and the loch grew stormy. She awoke the young man by slightly mutilating him as instructed, and on the first day he cut off one of the monster's heads. The combat was repeated on the second day,

[1] W. T. Kilgour, *Lochaber in War and Peace* (Paisley, 1908), pp. 173-4.
[2] *Highland News* (Inverness, 14th April, 1917).

DEMONS OF LAND AND WATER 249

when another head was cut off. On the third day the hero cut off the last head and the monster was slain.[1]

Another monster, which guarded a rowan tree, dwelt in a pool. Fraoch, the hero, is asked to pluck a branch of the tree with its red berries and is seized by the monster. Fraoch fights with the monster and cuts off its head, but he dies from his wounds, as does Ewen who fought the *fideal* in the Gairloch loch.[2]

The monster which guarded the sacred rowan tree with its life-giving red berries was usually seen in salmon shape. This salmon swallowed the berries that fell from the tree and thus acquired its red spots. If the salmon were caught and roasted, the one who first tasted of its juice acquired the power to prophesy and to make revelation of the unknown.

The white serpent found under a hazel tree possessed similar virtues. When it was cooked the man who first tasted the juice became a great physician and magician. The Beaton and Farquhar leech physicians, Michael Scott and others are reputed in various folk-tales to have obtained their knowledge and power from the juice of the serpent, or serpent-dragon.

A dreaded white snake in Sutherland was reputed to form itself into a ring and run swiftly like a wheel over moor and mountain. It is referred to by J. F. Campbell,[3] who does not, however, give any of the stories regarding it. This serpent killed human beings and was slain by a hero.

[1] J. F. Campbell, *Popular Tales* ("Sea Maiden" story), Vol. I, No. IV.
[2] George Henderson, *The Celtic Dragon Myth* (Edinburgh, 1911), gives various versions of the story, which received in Ireland somewhat elaborate literary treatment. Harland also deals with it in his *Legend of Perseus*.
[3] *Popular Tales*, Vol. II, Tale XLVII and notes.

J. Gregorson Campbell, writing regarding Highland serpent superstitions which appear to survive from a body of ancient serpent-dragon lore, says:

"A serpent, whenever encountered, ought to be killed. Otherwise, the encounter will prove an omen of evil. The head should be completely smashed and removed to a distance from the rest of the body. Unless this is done, the serpent will again come alive. The tail, unless deprived of animation, will join the body, and the head become a *beithir*, the largest and most deadly kind of serpent. A person stung by one should rush to the nearest water. Unless he reaches it before the serpent, which also makes straight for it, he will die from the wound."[1]

As we have seen (p. 131) Cailleach Bheur was in an Argyll story slain by a hunter, but after she was hewed to pieces the various parts of her body came together again. It may well be that our Cailleach Bheur, as has been suggested,[2] was connected with the serpent-dragon of the loch—that, in fact, the serpent-dragon was one of her forms. She was associated with the holly tree, the red berries of which were, like the red berries of the rowan, reputed to be "life-givers".

Most of the Scottish lochs have their monsters. There were also monsters in passes which came from a loch or the sea. The Skye monster of Odal Pass (*Biasd Bealach Odail*) appeared in various shapes.

"Sometimes it bore the form of a man, sometimes of a man with only one leg; at other times it appeared like a greyhound

---

[1] *Superstitions of the Scottish Highlands*, pp. 223-4.
[2] Chapter VIII., pp. 150, 151, 157, 158.

or beast prowling about; and sometimes it was heard uttering frightful shrieks and outcries which made the workmen leave their bothies in horror. It was only during the night it was seen or heard. . . . It ceased when a man was found dead at the roadside, pierced with two wounds, one on his side and one on his leg, with a hand pressed on each wound. It was considered impossible these wounds could have been inflicted by human agency."

A female demon, known as *Luideag* (the " Rag "), who was slovenly in attire, haunted the shores of *Lochan nan dubh bhreac* (" small loch of the black trout ") in Skye and similarly slew human beings.[1]

Bòchdan is a term applied to a terrifying apparition which may be a demon or ghost. A *bòchdan* may appear as a headless man, a he-goat, a black or grey dog, a one-legged, one-armed and one-eyed being, &c. In Glen Etive the *Direach Ghlinn Eitidh Mhic Calain* is a monster " with one hand out of his chest, one leg out of his haunch and one eye out of the front of his face ". A *fachan* had one hand out of the ridge of his chest and one tuft out of the top of his head. These and other monsters are usually referred to under the generic term *athach* (" monster ", " giant ").[2]

The mermaid is known in Gaelic as the *ceasg*, *maighdean na tuinne* (" maid of the wave ") and *maighdean mhara* (" maid of the sea "). A *ceasg* is a half-woman, half-grilse, who haunts rivers and streams and is said to be very beautiful but dangerous. The " maid of the wave ", if caught, can be prevailed upon to

[1] J. G. Campbell, *Witchcraft and Second Sight in the Scottish Highlands*, pp. 207–8.
[2] J. F. Campbell, *Popular Tales of West Highlands*, Vol. IV (1893 edition), pp. 297–8.

grant three wishes. There are stories of men marrying mermaids who had left off their skin coverings. Like the swan maidens, they recover their hidden skins and escape, but they always take an interest in their human descendants, shielding them in storms or guiding them to the best fishing grounds. Families of pilots are reputed to be descended from mermaids.

The " maid of the wave " is in some tales a fierce demon. She swallows a hero and he remains alive in her stomach. The hero's wife plays her harp, charming the mermaid until she " gapes " and the hero escapes. Then the mermaid swallows the hero's young bride. The hero consults a wizard, who informs him that " the mermaid's life . . . is in an egg, which is in a fish, which is in a duck, which is in a ram, which is in a wood, under a house on an island, in a lake ".

The hero, aided by animal helpers, obtains the life-egg and the mermaid gives him back his bride. Then he crushes the egg and the mermaid perishes.[1]

The hero had been promised to the mermaid before birth. His father had been childless and the mermaid rose in the sea as he was fishing and promised him sons on condition that the first born was given to her.[2]

It may be that the " maid of the wave " was originally a sea-goddess to whom human beings, especially children, were sacrificed.

Martin in his *Western Isles* tells that in seventeenth century Lewis " the inhabitants . . . had an ancient

---

[1] G. Henderson, *The Celtic Dragon Myth*, pp. 78 et seq.
[2] *The Celtic Dragon Myth*, pp. 34 et seq.

custom to sacrifice to a sea-god called ' Shony ' at Hallow-tide ". The people gathered at the church of St. Mulvay with a supply of ale brewed from malt supplied by the various families. One of their number waded into the sea carrying a cup of ale. In a loud voice he cried, " Shony, I give you this cup of ale, hoping that you will be so kind as to send us plenty of sea-ware for enriching our ground the ensuing year ". Then he poured the ale into the sea.

The ceremony took place at night. When the man waded back to the shore, all the people entered the church. A candle burning on the altar was suddenly extinguished. Thus was the god invoked. The remainder of the night was spent in drinking ale, dancing, singing, &c.

Dr. A. Macbain, writing of this ceremony, says that after the sacrifice had been repressed, some people " proceeded in spring to the end of a long reef and invoked ' Briannuil ' to send a strong north wind to drive plenty sea-ware ashore ".[1]

Attempts have been made to connect " Shony " with Norse mythology on the assumption that the seafaring Picts and Scots had no sea-beings. There was, however, a Gaelic sea-god called Ler, known to the Welsh as Llyr, who passed into historical romance as " King Lear ".

A goddess called " Dumna ", a feminine form of early Celtic *dubnos, dumnos* (" deep "), had the same name as the " Long Island " (Outer Hebrides). Professor W. J. Watson believes that " Dumna ", like Orcas, Ebuda and Thule, goes back, as a place-name, to the

[1] *Celtic Mythology and Religion*, p. 171.

fourth century B.C., having originally been recorded by Pytheas.[1]

The Scottish sea-deities and demons are evidently of considerable antiquity, although they may have in the process of time acquired secondary names.

[1] *History of the Celtic Place-Names of Scotland*, pp. 6, 40, 70, 72.

CHAPTER XIII

Sacred Rocks and Stones

Power derived by contact with stone—Cursing stones—Stones used in weather ceremonies—Stones as " soul bodies "—" Telling the stones "—The " worship stone " and " bowing stone "—Boundary stones—Royal coronation stone—MacDonald chief installed in contact with stone—The chief's wand—Stone at coronation of King Alexander III—Gaelic bard as forerunner of Lyon king—MacLaren stones and necklace—Edinburgh and other " spitting stones "—The " holed rock " of Brahan—Getting the answer—Oracular bird—Children cured at " holed rock "—Cakes used in divination ceremony—Ceremonial lighting of fire—Fear of removing standing stones—Wishes wished on prehistoric tomb—Raising the devil at stone circle—Child-getting stones—Burghead " cradle stone "—" Cup marked " stones—Relics of divination ceremonies—Loch Maree record—Healing stones—God stone broken in pulpit—Kelpie and Pict stone—Giant of Pictish broch in Berwickshire.

There is much evidence to show that certain stones or rocks were anciently believed to be sources of magical influence. Vows, invocations and curses were supposed to be made effective by reason of contact with stone. At Cromarty there is a big boulder known as the *Clach na Mallachd* (" Stone of Cursing "). Curses were delivered when an individual stood or knelt barekneed upon it. In the old Gaelic poem regarding Kennedy of Lianachan in Lochaber it is told of the glaistig whom he compelled to build a house that before departing

" She sprang . . . on a grey stone
Of the field to pronounce his doom." [1]

[1] J. G. Campbell, *Superstitions of the Scottish Highlands*, p. 171.

Ceremonies were performed with stones to control wind and rain. M. Martin tells that when fishermen were detained by contrary winds in the island of Fladda, near Skye, they made use of a blue stone which was always moist and lay on the altar of a chapel dedicated to St. Columba. They washed the stone all round, " expecting thereby to procure a favourable wind ". This stone was also an " oath stone " and " curing stone ".

In Sinclair's *Statistical Account of Scotland*[1] it is told that a saint was wont to dispense favourable winds at the columnar rock called " Kempock Stane " in the Firth of Clyde. A confession in a witch trial at Auldearn in Nairnshire in 1662 was, according to the surviving record:

" When we raise the wind we take a rag of cloth and wet it in water, and we take a beetle and knock the rag on a stone and we say thrice over—

> I knock this rag upon this stane,
> To raise the wind in the devil's name.
> It shall not lie until I please again."

Certain stones were reputed to be " soul bodies " (*coach anama*) of famous men. In the story of Finlay Changeling, as we have seen, a standing stone struck by a magic wand became a warrior, and when the warrior was struck by the wand he was transformed into a pillar stone.

The lingering sanctity of some standing stones is emphasized by names like *clach aoraidh* (" worship stone ") and *clach sleuchda* (" genuflexion " or " bowing stone ").

[1] Vol. VIII, p. 52.

SACRED ROCKS AND STONES

A Highland folk-saying, "telling it to the stones" (*ga innseadh do na clachan*), is given by Dr. George Henderson.[1] It looks as if the stones were, like the bees, told of a death in former times. Henderson says that the phrase is repeated by a woman " under her breath " when narrating some untoward disaster, and that its use is supposed to avert any harm arising either to the speaker or the listener.

Stones were erected to mark clan boundaries and were ceremonially visited when " riding the marches " once a year. Chiefs met at boundary stones when disputes were settled. A clansman who went beyond a boundary stone did so at his own risk and could not claim the protection of his chief. It may be recalled in this connexion that the Roman god Terminus was a sacred boundary stone.

Courts of justice were held in historic times at stone circles.[2]

The ancient " coronation stone " of Scotland, carried away to London by King Edward I of England, still remains in Westminster Abbey and is an interesting relic of the ancient belief that a sacred stone confers power and ensures that justice will be done.

Clan chiefs as well as kings took vows when in contact with stone. Dr. Alexander Carmichael states that when a chief of Clan Donald (MacDonald clan) was installed as " Lord of the Isles " at Loch Finlaggan in Islay he stood upon a stone " with the footmarks cut in it " and was proclaimed " MacDonald " and " high prince of the seed of Conn ". The eighth

[1] *Survival in Belief Among the Celts* (Glasgow, 1911), p. 199.
[2] See my *Scotland: The Ancient Kingdom*, p. 37.

"Lord of the Isles" was, however, installed with ceremony at Kildonan in the island of Eigg. An account of the MacDonald installation ceremony by Hugh MacDonald, the Seanchie (Recorder) of Sleat, states:

"At this (ceremony) the Bishop of Argyll, the Bishop of the Isles and seven priests were sometimes present, but a Bishop was always present, with the chieftains of all the principal families and a Ruler of the Isles. There was a square stone seven or eight feet long, and the track of a man's foot cut thereon, upon which he stood, denoting that he should walk in the footsteps and uprightness of his predecessors, and that he was installed by right in his possessions. He was clothed in a white habit to show his innocence and integrity of heart, that he would be a light to his people and maintain the true religion. The white apparel did afterwards belong to the poet by right. Then he was to receive a white rod in his hand, intimating that he had power to rule, not with tyranny and partiality, but with discretion and sincerity. Then he received his forefathers' sword, or some other sword, signifying that his duty was to protect and defend them from their enemies in peace or war."[1]

M. Martin tells that a "young chief stood upon a cairn of stones, while his followers gathered around him in a circle, his elevation signifying his authority over them, and their standing below their subjection to him". After the proclamation of the chieftain, "the chief druid or bard performed a rhetorical panegyric setting forth the ancient pedigree, valour and liberality of the family as incentives to the young chieftain and fit for his imitation".

[1] *Carmina Gadelica* (1928 edition), Vol. 1, p. 323.

SACRED ROCKS AND STONES

When Alexander III of Scotland was, in March, 1249, declared king at Scone, the Latin coronation formulas were recited in the abbey church and translated into Norman French. Then the royal heir, a boy of seven, was conducted into the old burial ground and seated upon the " coronation stone ", which was covered with " cloth of gold ". An old Gaelic bard, wearing a scarlet robe, performed the ancient druidical custom of reciting the pedigree of the king. The Lyon King of Scotland, in making royal proclamations at the stone cross of Edinburgh, is perpetuating an immemorial Celtic rite. In former times he wore a scarlet robe. The stone market cross of old burghs is a relic of the times when vows, bargains and proclamations were made in contact with stone.

The late Mr. MacLaren of Anie, Callander, possessed two dark stones shaped somewhat like kidneys, which, he told the writer when he exhibited them on the palms of his hands, had been handed down in his family for generations. He informed the writer that he had inherited them as rightful chief of the MacLarens, along with a necklace of large amber beads, black with age, for the chief's wife.

Near Edinburgh market cross is the " heart of Midlothian ", formed by granite setts in the street. The custom of spitting on the centre of it is still practised. In former times luck was secured, increase ensured and compacts made by spitting upon a stone. Fishwives spat upon the first silver coin received when vending fish; livestock dealers spat on their palms when a bargain was arranged and before they shook hands. Brand refers to the spitting custom in the north of England when asseverations were made. Colliers who combined to demand an increase of wages spat upon a stone " by way of cementing their confederacy. Hence," adds Brand, " the popular saying, when persons are of the same party or agree in sentiments, that ' they spit upon the same stone '." [1]

There is a " spitting stone " at Forres. On Cromarty hill a " spitting stone " lies near a mountain ash (rowan tree) which is known as " the rock tree ".

An interesting glimpse into the past is afforded by the surviving lore connected with a dolmen-like holed rock called " gara howl " (Gaelic, *garadh tholl*) in Brahan wood, a few miles distant from Dingwall. Contact with it was of importance in connexion with divination ceremonies. A curiously vague but significant folk-tale tells of a man from the Loch Ness area who was advised to visit " gara howl " to obtain his answer. On his arrival he sat beside it for a long time but nothing happened, and he began to think his visit was in vain when, all at once, he heard a bird warbling the words, " Go to Epack—go to Epack!"

He went down to a neighbouring village and asked if anyone there knew of an " Epack " and was informed that a " wise woman " so named lived on the Mulbuie in the Black Isle. He visited Epack and " from her he got the answer ".

Until recently it was the custom to take ailing children to this holed rock so that they might be cured.

---

[1] John Brand, *Popular Antiquities of Great Britain* (Bohn edition), Vol. III p. 261.

SACRED ROCKS AND STONES

A fire was lit and the clothing of a stripped child was passed through the hole from one woman to another and then the child was passed through.

When a member of a family was seriously ill a woman baked cakes at the holed rock and, having fired them on a stone placed in proximity to a wood fire, left them on the summit of the rock. If by next morning they had vanished it was believed that the patient would recover, but if they remained it was feared that the patient would die. A young south country doctor who was acting as a "locum" to a Dingwall doctor about twenty years ago attended a patient not far from the holed rock. On his second visit he found that the illness had taken a serious turn and he spoke gravely to the patient's mother, who puzzled him greatly by remarking, "He is sure to recover, doctor; the cakes were taken last night". The southerner was puzzled and asked what she meant. "Oh! it's just a saying we will have," came the evasive answer. The doctor consulted the writer, who suspected that the reference was to a folk custom, and he ultimately discovered that the cake-divination custom was often practised by women, assisted by children, who gathered dry sticks for the fire but were sent away before the cakes were baked and deposited. The local clergymen, doctors and school teachers and even the husbands of some of the women guilty of perpetuating the pagan custom were quite unaware of it. A somewhat similar custom was condemned by *Jeremiah* (vii, 18): "The children gather wood, and the fathers kindle the fire, and the women knead their dough, to make cakes to the queen of heaven."

Although some archæologists would have it that tradition knows nothing of the pagan sanctity attached to ancient standing stones, a haunting reverence clings to them in some parts of Scotland. Ill-luck is supposed to follow those who destroy, dislodge or remove the *clachan aoraidh*. The Rev. T. D. Miller,[1] referring to a megalith known in Gaelic as " the Stone of the Spotted Pig ", says that " last century the farmer of the Old Spittal removed the stone for the foundation of a dyke, but shortly after a murrain broke out among his cattle, and he thought it prudent to replace it ". Dr. George Henderson [2] found that " in the Highlands it is regarded as a source of danger to make use of pillared stones (*clachan carraghan*) in building human or other dwellings. Ill-luck or death follows any one who meddles with such ' druidical ' stones as are found in the numerous stone circles in Inverness-shire."

The writer had an interesting experience in the district known as the Kyle on the borders of Sutherland and Ross and Cromarty. Between Bonar Bridge and Altas he saw a mound at the corner of a field and near crofters' houses and went to examine it. The tops of megaliths protruded on its summit; the mound appeared to be a " heaped stone circle ". A crofter came out of one of the houses and, after being hailed in Gaelic, was asked if the relic had a name. He said it was called " Hillock of my wish " (Gaelic, *Torr mo ghuidhe*), and said he understood that people had been buried in it long ago. " I hope," he said, " you are not going to dig into the ' tor ', because they will be

---

[1] *Tales of a Highland Parish* (Glenshee), Perth, 1925, pp. 40-1.
[2] *Survivals in Belief Among the Celts*, pp. 198-9.

SACRED ROCKS AND STONES

saying that the man who does that will die within a year."

In further conversation he said that it was an old custom to wish wishes and make compacts upon the mound.

Memories of old customs linger in folk-beliefs regarding groups of megaliths. An Edinburgh archæologist who was measuring a stone circle in Moray asked a ploughman if there were any " stories " regarding it, and the reply was to the effect that if one came at midnight and walked around the circle three times " by the left " one would " raise the devil ".

Barren women visited certain stones or outcrops of rock, some of which had " cup marks ", at periods when the moon was " in growth " with desire to become mothers. " Child-getting " stones were formerly known in various parts of Scotland, and many of them have been broken up, buried or removed. On the slopes below Salisbury Crags, Arthur's Seat, Edinburgh, are the "slippy stanes", and children who have for generations slid down them appear to have been perpetuating the ancient " child-getting " custom.

Another custom kept alive by imitative children has been recorded by Sir Arthur Mitchell.[1] In Burghead Chapel yard a hollow resembling " cup marks " on ancient stones and rocks has been beaten out on a gravestone by young people by means of a beach pebble. They knew it as the "cradle stone", because when they struck it they put their ears to the hollow to hear the sound of a rocking cradle and the crying of a child. There is no record as to how this significant

[1] *The Past in the Present* (Edinburgh, 1880), pp. 263–5.

custom originated, but it may be that the gravestone had been "cup marked" before it was dressed and lettered. The Kilchoman sculptured stone has "cup marks" on its base, near which lies a stone of phallic shape. It may be that the mysterious cup marks on stones are relics of divination ceremonies connected with birth and death.

In the records of the Presbytery of Dingwall there is an interesting reference, dated 5th September, 1656, in connexion with the "superstitious practices" in the Loch Maree area. It was believed that

"future events in reference especiallie to lyfe and death, in takeing of Journeyis, was exspect to be manifested by a holl (hole) of a round stone quherein (wherein) they tryed the entering of their heade, which (if they) could doe, to witt be able to put in thair heade, they exspect thair returning to that place, and failing they considered it ominous."

Healing stones were formerly common. Dr. George Henderson had personal knowledge of "magic stones" being dipped in water to avert evil eye. In a book written by a Highland clergyman [1] is an account of a Free Church minister's denunciation of a "god stone" which was known as the "stitch stone" (pain stone). Mr. MacDonald writes:

"The stitch-stone was a charm supposed to give relief in cases of severe pain from sciatica up to acute pleurisy. It was common property, and always kept by the person who used it last till required by another. The last specimen of which I heard about 30 years ago was in Erradale, parish of Gairloch. Mr. Matheson, Free Church minister, got hold of it and took

---

[1] Rev. K. MacDonald, Applecross, *Social and Religious Life in the Highlands* (Edinburgh, 1902), p. 34.

it to the pulpit one day. At the close of the service he held it up before the congregation, remarking that the 'god of Erradale' was the smallest god of which he had ever heard or read. It was a small piece of flint stone, 3 or 4 inches long, found on the shore and highly polished by the action of the waves. . . . Mr. Matheson broke it in their presence and yet no dire results followed."

Some standing stones and cairns have long had associations with supernatural beings, or folk heroes who have been fused with them in the traditions of the folk. Our Cailleach, as we have seen, had connexions with megalithic remains. In the Coldingham area of Berwickshire a chambered cairn, demolished over a century ago, and a standing stone known as a " Pech ", or " Pecht ", stone were connected with the kelpie of Draedan burn, who is celebrated in a rhymed version of a folk-story:

" Grisly Draedan sat alane
By the cairn and Pech stane.
Said Billie wi' a segg sae stout
I'll soon drive grisly Draedan out.
Draedan leuchèd (laughed) and stalked awa'
Syne vanished in a babanqua (quagmire)."

This quagmire is now the drained and cultivated " Billie-mire ", or " Billy-mire ".

"Pecht" is the Lowland rendering of "Pict", or " Pect ". Not far distant from the " Pech stane " are the impressive ruins of a Pictish broch of the Romano-British period. According to the local tradition, it was occupied by " a freebooting giant who long carried on a successful system of depredation and, shut up in this, his place of power, effectually screened himself from the hands of justice ". The raiding Picts, or Pechts, who occupied the broch of " Eden's Ha' " were thus—like Arthur, Wallace and other later warriors—associated with the giants.[1]

---

[1] Alexander Allan Carr, *A History of Coldingham Priory* (London, 1836), pp. 9–12 and 20–1. "Segg" in the rhyme is a sedge-like weapon. "Babanqua" is probably "bobbing quag".

CHAPTER XIV

Sacred Wells and Trees

Magical influence of water—River pools and wells—Evil eye cure—Pagan wells Christianized—Pictish well reverenced as a god—Well near " Druid's Port "—Yew tree well—Well of the Cailleach—Wells associated with standing stones—Wishing wells—Culloden well offerings—Edinburgh wells—" New water " of " Well of Youth "—Well water protects baking—St. Mary's well water for dying persons—Sacred trees—Fortingal yew—Oracle birds—Hazel as milk tree and fire and lighting tree—Caltons of Edinburgh and Glasgow—The fairy boy of Leith—Highland fairy boys—Hazel as a god—Kentigern and the hazel—Rowan tree as " rock tree "—Sacred trees taboo—Trees as " soul bodies "—Trees growing from graves of lovers—Why houses are decorated at Christmas—Red berry protection—Druidical sacred groves in Galatia and Western Celtic area—Druidism and Cernunnos from Anatolia—Annual assemblies and courts—Scottish " nemets "—Cromarty tradition of Druidism—Last Judgment at druidical grove—Story of Sandy Wood—The " nemet " and the " Druid's Port ".

There still survives in rural Scotland a haunting belief in the efficacy of water as a source of magical influence in granting wishes, in warding off the attacks of supernatural beings and as a life-giver and therefore as a curative agency. Certain river pools are reputed to possess power and especially those under a bridge leading to a churchyard—" the bridge over which the dead and the living pass ". Water from such a pool may be used when performing ceremonies to cure an illness brought on by the sinister influence of " evil eye ". It is lifted in a wooden ladle and a charm is recited after a piece of silver has been dropped into the water. Then the sufferer is given three sips of the " silver water ", the remainder being sprinkled around him or her and around the fireside. The writer has personal knowledge of this ceremony and possesses a wooden ladle which was used when " silver water " was given to himself as a child to effect a cure of a sudden illness believed to have been caused by " evil eye ".

The " water of power " is more generally drawn from a particular well and especially one named after a saint. Many pagan holy wells were " taken over " by the early Christian missionaries who supplanted the Druids and even the deities, as did St. Mourie, whose name clings to Loch Maree and Isle Maree, and to whom bulls were sacrificed as late as the seventeenth century. Adamnan,[1] the abbot of Iona, tells that when St. Columba visited the province of the Picts he found that a well was " reverenced as a god ". Its water was " taboo " and supposed to cause those who drank of it or washed in it to become leprous or blind, but after St. Columba blessed it " many diseases were cured by the same spring ".

A well in Easter Ross which still retains a pre-Christian association is known in Gaelic as the " well of the black sword of Erin, facing the sun in the Druid's Port ".[2] Another, not far from it, is called the " well of the yew " and, according to the local lore, it cured the disease known as " white swelling " before the yew tree that flourished beside it was cut down.

[1] *Life of Columba*, Book II, Chapter X.
[2] W. J. Watson, *Place-Names of Ross and Cromarty*, p. 56. The Scottish " Erin " is referred to here.

SACRED WELLS AND TREES

Another well which was never Christianized is referred to in Sinclair's *Statistical Account of Scotland*.[1] It is situated in Keith parish in Banffshire near standing stones on " Card's Hill " (" artificer's hill "). The parish minister wrote of it:

" A little below this circle is a very fine fountain of excellent water called *Taber Chalich*,[2] or ' Old Wife's Well '."

The name really signifies " Well of the Cailleach ", the " Scottish Artemis ". People visited this well to make offerings, as they did also to another well in the neighbourhood and to a cascade known as the " Linn of Keith ".

The " Well of Virtues " at Castle Bay in Barra is similarly associated with standing stones and has long been credited with the cure of diseases. At Tullybelton (*Tulach Bealltuinn*, i.e. " Beltane Hill "), near Stanley, in the parish of Auchtergaven in Strathtay, a well was visited on Beltane morning (1st May). When the visitors had drunk of its water they walked around it " by the right " nine times and then walked around the standing stones beside it. Thus in pagan times certain groups of standing stones were associated with sacred wells, as were certain sacred trees.

Many sacred wells were regarded as " wishing wells " and are still referred to as such. Pins, pieces of money or food offerings were dropped into them or left beside them. Numbers of Inverness people still visit " Culloden Well " on the first Sunday of May and drop coins into it. The money thus collected is

---

[1] 1793, Vol. V, pp. 429–30.
[2] *Tobar Chaillich*, to be correct.

now given to Inverness Royal Infirmary. In Grange Road, Edinburgh, there is a wall-drinking fountain and the carved inscription " Penny Well " keeps alive the memory of a former custom associated with the spring from which the water supply is drawn. An Edinburgh " wishing well " is that of St. Anthony, near the ruins of the chapel of St. Anthony, below Arthur's Seat.

The water of some wells is reputed to be most effective when drunk at dawn. As we have seen, the Cailleach renewed her youth by drinking from a well at dawn before a bird chirped or a dog barked. Like the " new water " of the Nile, which comes when that river begins to rise in flood, the " new water " of the " Well of Youth " was supposed to possess " life-giving " qualities.

Water from a sacred well was used to protect a baking from supernatural beings, and especially the fairies, who were supposed to extract " the substance " from the oatmeal cakes or bannocks. The water was sprinkled upon and about the cakes as they were drying on " the cheeks " of the fireplace. Holy water was also sprinkled on the threshold and window-sills to keep away the demons. At Tarradale, Muir of Ord, Ross and Cromarty, is a spring called *Tobar Mhuire*[1] (" St. Mary's Well "). When a sick person asks for a drink of the water of this well, the request is taken as an indication that death is near. " She asks for a drink of *Tober Mhuire*," remarks the woman who acts as the nurse, and to all who hear her this means that the patient is aware that she is dying:

[1] Pronounced *Tober Voorie*.

Oh! my lips are sere and burning—
For thy water I'll be yearning
And yon road of no returning,
    Tober Mhuire.[1]

Sacred trees include the rowan (mountain ash), the holly, mulberry, the yew, the oak, the apple tree and the hazel. Iona, as we have seen, was associated with a druidical cult of the yew. At Fortingal in Perthshire is a very ancient yew that appears to have been in existence in pre-Christian times. Oracle birds were wont to haunt certain trees and there are stories of men or women enclosed in trees who were no doubt originally deities or ghosts.

The hazel was a sacred tree which was connected with the milk-yielding goddess because of the " milk " contained in its green nut, and with the deity of fire and therefore of lightning and thunder, because its wood was used to make fire by friction. Water diviners still use hazel twigs. The " hazel rod " was formerly used, as Brand notes, to detect veins of gold, lead, coal, &c. Hazel nuts are favoured at divination ceremonies practised at Hallowe'en.

A hazel-grove is in Gaelic *Calltuin* and there are " Caltons " in Edinburgh and Glasgow and elsewhere. The Edinburgh " Calton " was a fairy mound, and Sir Walter Scott in his *Minstrelsy of the Scottish Border* (Vol. I) quotes from Captain George Burton's *Pandæmonium, or the Devil's Cloister Opened* (1684), an account of a lad called " The Fairy Boy of Leith " who was wont to make weekly visits to the fairies under Calton

[1] My *Elves and Heroes*.

Hill and act as their drummer boy. He thus belonged to the class of musicians who, like the Strathspey fiddlers of the Inverness mound dance, provided music for the " little people ". There are many Highland stories of boys who were wont to associate with the fairies. A herd known as *Dòmhnull ruadh nan sìthichean* (" Red Donald of the Fairies ") was one of these. The fairies transported him often from a farm near Dalnacardoch in Perthshire to his father's house at Ardlàraich in Rannoch, to which he obtained entrance even when the door was barred at night. Another " fairy boy " was known in Benderloch, on the north side of the mouth of Loch Etive in Argyll, as " Callum Clever ". When sent on an errand he was carried very quickly for many miles by his fairy friends. The " Fairy Boy of Leith " story, collected and somewhat rationalized by an Englishman, was no doubt a variant of the " fairy boy " tales still current in the Highlands. Its chief interest is its record of the traditional association of supernatural beings with the hazel-grove hillock of Edinburgh. In early Gaelic the hazel was *coll* and in Keating's *History of Ireland* (Vol. I, Section 12) it is stated that " *Coll* (hazel) was god to MacCuill ". The hazel was a life-giving tree in the Irish elysium. From hazels growing above a pool red nuts fell into the water and were swallowed by the sacred salmon, which thus acquired its red spots.

A memory of the ceremonial use of hazel in producing "friction fire", or "new fire", is contained in Joceline's *Life of St. Kentigern* (Chapter VI). Kentigern, when a boy, took his turn as guardian of the sacred fire in the monastery, but certain of his jealous juvenile rivals extinguished it. He went, however, to a hazel tree and, drawing out a bough, prayed for "new light". A wonderful thing followed. Fire came from heaven, seizing the bough, and the youth knew that God had " sent forth his Light ".

A rowan tree on Cromarty Hill has, as indicated, long been known as the " rock tree ". Before boys went cliff-climbing they threw stones at this tree. When a stone darted sideways the thrower shouted, " The danger goes past". If, as it chanced, a stone came back towards the thrower, he returned homeward, believing that if he went climbing that day he would meet with some injury, if not death. In a hollow in this tree some fishermen were wont to deposit small white stones before setting out for the herring-fishing grounds at a distance from home. Their luck was supposed to be thus secured.

It was considered perilous to do any injury to a sacred tree or bush. M. Martin, writing regarding Loch Siant Well in Skye, says, " There is a small coppice near to the well, and there is none of the natives dare venture to cut the least branch of it for fear of some signal judgment to follow upon it."

There are traces of the ancient belief that certain trees were not only habitations of deities but " soul bodies " of individuals. In " The Sea Maiden " folk-tale three sons are born to the fisherman and three trees grow up behind his house. " When one of the sons dies," the fisherman is informed by the mermaid, " one of the trees will wither ".[1] Sir Walter Scott in his *Journal* (13th May, 1829) tells of an oak tree

[1] J. F. Campbell, *Popular Tales of the West Highlands*, Vol. II, Story IV.

growing beside a well in the grounds of Dalhousie Castle, near Dalkeith. "I saw the Edgewell tree," he writes, "too fatal, says Allan Ramsay, to the family from which he was himself descended." The belief prevailed that a branch fell from the tree before the death of a member of the family.

There are several ancient stories of trees growing from the graves of lovers and entwining their branches in loving embrace. In the Border ballad of " The Nut-brown Maid " the lovers perish:

> " Lord Thomas was buried without kirk wa',
> Fair Annet within the quire;
> And o' the tane there grew a birk,
> The other a bonnie brier.
>
> And aye they grew, and aye they threw,
> As they would fain be near;
> And by this ye may ken right weel
> They were twa lovers dear."

In the ballad of " The Douglas Tragedy " are the verses:

> " Lord William was buried in St. Marie's Kirk,
> Lady Margaret in Marie's quire;
> Out o' the lady's grave grew a bonnie red rose
> And out o' the knight's a brier.
>
> And they twa met, and they twa plat (pleated),
> And fain they wad be near;
> And a' the warld might ken right weel
> They were twa lovers dear."

Red berries plucked from the rowan or holly were

SACRED WELLS AND TREES 275

used to protect human beings and domesticated animals from evil influences. Houses were protected by decorating the doorways, windows and walls with branches of red-berry trees. Thus had origin the custom of the Christmas decoration of rooms.

A druidical sacred grove in which there was a stone shrine, a certain holy tree or a sacred well was anciently known as a " nemeton ", a name which in Irish Gaelic survives as " nemed " and in Scottish as " nemet ". The Celtic Galatæ who settled in Galatia in the third century B.C. had a " Drunemeton " (" chief nemeton ") in which the court of justice met and councils were convened. The Druids acted as judges and legislators. It may well be that Druidism was introduced into the Western Celtic area from Galatia, where, as we have seen, the Celts became converts to the cult of Attis and the " Great Mother " goddess of Pessinus. From Galatia, too, as a result of cult-blending appears to have come the horned god Cernunnos, who on the Gundestrup cauldron found in Jutland, the ancient country of the Cimbri, is associated with Asiatic fauna and flora and the Great Mother.[1]

In Gaul the annual druidical assembly was, as Julius Cæsar states, held in the land of the Carnutes nation. When the Gauls introduced the deified Augustus into their pantheon he was worshipped in the " Augustonemeton ". Professor W. J. Watson refers to " nemetons " in Gaul, including one sacred to the goddess Belisama. In Brittany there was a " wood of the nemet ". " Nemed " is rare in Irish place-names, but in Scotland there survive many " nemet "

[1] My *Buddhism in Pre-Christian Britain*.

place-names, especially in the aspirated forms of "Navity" or "Nevity" (*neimhidh*), "Nevyth", "Nevay" or "Neve". Rosneath is in Gaelic "Rosnevy" (*Ros-neimhidh*) and there are other "nemet" names in Clackmannan, Fife, Perthshire, Angus, Aberdeenshire, Banffshire, Inverness-shire, Ross and Cromarty and Sutherland.[1] There lingered well into Christian times the memory of druidical courts of justice at the old "nemets". At Cromarty a gravestone lying outside the old churchyard of St. Regulus is sacred to the memory of Alexander (Sandy) Wood, a man with a stutter, who had suffered a wrong at the hands of a neighbour of fluent speech. It was believed that the Last Judgment would be held at Navity, the druidical "nemet", and Wood was at his own request buried outside the churchyard so that when the dead arose at the last day he would be able to reach Navity and stutter his story to the Great Judge before the man who had wronged him could get over the churchyard wall. The wall has long been removed, but the churchyard is enclosed by a spiked railing even more difficult to climb. The lettered gravestone of Sandy shows that he died in the year 1690.

Navity slopes towards the beach on the southern shore of the Moray Firth, just outside the Cromarty Firth between the Eathie burn deep dell, which reeks of fairy-lore, and St. Bennet's wishing well, with overhanging bush still fluttering with rags in the year 1934. On the opposite side of the firth is "Druid's Port" (*Port an Druidh*), to the west of the fishing village of Shandwick. From the ridge of Navity Hill

---

[1] W. J. Watson, *History of the Celtic Place-Names of Scotland.*

one can see Inverness, where in the sixth century St. Columba came into contact with the Pictish Druid Broichan, from whose dictatorship the Christian missionary released King Brude and his senate.

CHAPTER XV

Festivals and Ceremonies

Beltane festival—No connexion with the god Baal—White or magical fires—House fires extinguished and relit—The *dealan-dé*—Heavenly fire—Dance of the new sun—Protection from fire—Feast of Beltane—Offerings to preservers and destroyers—Hallowe'en festival—Divination ceremonies—Pagan festivals and Christian festivals—Christmas and New Year's Day—The Gaelic year and months—Movements by right and left—Connexion with *Ursa Major* constellation—The spiral symbol—Spiral staircases in brochs and nuraghi—Celtic encircling ceremony—Vercingetorix and Cæsar—Encircling of chapels and houses—Cardinal points coloured—Purple most sacred colour—Pigments from Constantinople—St. Andrew legend—Wonder tales from Asia—The Indian rope trick story in Scotland and Ireland—Messages to the dead—The body, soul and shade—Ghosts of the living and the dead—Butterfly god—Second-sight—Folk cures.

The two great festivals in ancient Scotland were those of Beltane, the beginning of the " big sun " season, and Hallowe'en, the eve before the " little sun " season. Beltane, in modern Scottish Gaelic *bealltuinn* and early Gaelic *beltene*, has no connexion with the ancient god called " Baal " or " Bel ". The prefix " bel " appears to signify " bright " or " white " in the magical sense, so that Beltane may have referred originally to the fires kindled by friction of fire sticks. This " new fire ", supposed to come from heaven, was reputed to purify and protect and bring everything summed up in the term " luck "—good health, good fortune, increase, &c. Hence the pro-

FESTIVALS AND CEREMONIES

verbial, Gaelic saying: *eadar dà theine Bhealltuinn* ("between two Beltane fires"). Before the Beltane fires were lit with ceremony, all house fires had to be extinguished and brands were taken from the bonfires to relight them. A brand was kept whirling round about when being carried to a house, and was called *dealan-dé* ("brightness of the god"), a term also applied to the butterfly and to lightning (heavenly fire). On Beltane morning it was customary to assemble on an eminence to watch the dance of the "new sun", which was reputed to whirl round three times on rising above the horizon. Faces were washed in May dew for protection against "evil eye". There was dancing about the Beltane fires and luck was secured by leaping through the flames and smoke. Domesticated animals were driven over the embers for protection against all evil influences. Cakes baked at a fire were ceremonially eaten after portions had been cast into the fire as offerings or flung over shoulders. Liquors were freely drunk. Pennant in his *Tour through Scotland* describes a Scottish Beltane ceremony as performed in the latter part of the eighteenth century:

"They cut a square trench in the ground, leaving the turf in the middle. On that they make a fire of wood, on which they dress a large caudle of eggs, oatmeal, butter and milk, and bring besides these plenty of beer and whisky. Each of the company must contribute something towards the feast. The rites begin by pouring a little of the caudle upon the ground, by way of a libation. Everyone then takes a cake of oatmeal, on which are raised nine square knobs, each dedicated to some particular being who is supposed to preserve their herds, or to some animal the destroyer of them. Each person then turns his face to the fire, breaks off a knob and, flinging it over his shoulder, says, '*This I give to thee*', naming the being whom he thanks, '*preserver of my sheep*', &c.; or to the destroyer, '*This I give to thee (O fox or eagle), spare my lambs*', &c. When this ceremony is over they all dine on the caudle."

Hallowe'en is in Scottish Gaelic *Samhuinn* and in Irish *Samhainn*. The usual translation is "summer-end". Dr. Stokes, however, considered that *samain* meant "assembly".[1] Bonfires were lit as at Beltane and there were dances, feasting and a good deal of drinking. In the houses divination ceremonies were practised, and a number of these are detailed in Burns's "Hallowe'en" poem. It was believed that a general flitting of supernatural beings took place during the night, and houses had to be specially protected against them.

Ancient pagan festivals were Christianized and to the new Christian festivals which were introduced certain of the pagan ceremonies were transferred. To Christmas and New Year's Day passed ceremonies and customs originally connected with *Samhuinn* ("Hallowe'en"). Christmas is known in Gaelic as *Nollaig*, a name derived from the Latin *Natalicia* ("the Nativity"), or as *latha Nollaig mhóir* ("the day of big Nollaig"), while New Year's Day is *latha Nollaig bhig* ("the day of little Nollaig"), the seven days between Christmas and New Year being *Nollaig*.

The Gaelic name for "year" is *bliadhna*, which is of uncertain meaning. Spring is *earrach*, from *eàrr* ("end"), the old year ending with that season and the new beginning with Beltane (1st May); summer

---

[1] The Irish assembly and feast on 1st May was called *Cét-shamain*.

is *samhradh*, a name apparently connected with Sanskrit *sama* (" year ") and Zend *hama* (" summer "); harvest is *foghar* or *fogharadh*, which appears to mean " before winter "; winter is *geamhradh*, a name which has been connected with Sanskrit *himá* (" cold ") and Zend *zima* (" winter ").

The seasons are connected with the cardinal points as follows: spring (east), summer (south), autumn (west) and winter (north). The east is in front, the south on the right, the west behind and the north on the left. Thus the lucky movement " by the right " (*deiseil*) is that followed by the seasons. The opposite or unlucky movement is " by the left " (*tuaitheal*), which in Lowland Scots is called " widdershins " or " withershins ".

Although the movement " by the right " is usually referred to as " sunwise " or " by the sun ", it appears originally to have had a stellar significance. The constellation of *Ursa Major* (" the Great Bear "), also called " the Plough ", " Charles's Wain ", " the Dipper ", " the Farmer's Clock ", &c.,[1] points with its " tail " or " pole " eastward in spring, southward in summer, westward in autumn and northward in winter. The " lucky " movement " by the right " followed in coiling ropes, dealing out playing cards, approaching graveyards, stirring food in a pot, &c., is widely observed. Scottish fishermen before setting out for a fishing ground must have the boat turned " by the right ". In ancient times, as is gathered from Gaelic stories, warriors approaching a fort indicated

---

[1] The Gaelic name of the constellation is *grigleachan*, which is usually connected with *grian* (" sun "). *Ursa Minor* (" the Lesser Bear ") is *drag-bhod*.

that they were friendly by encircling it " by the right "; if they marched or drove "by the left", they indicated their hostility. The spiral staircases in the Pictish brochs and the Sardinian *nuraghi* were probably connected with the ceremony performed to ensure protection. Plutarch tells that, at the surrender of besieged Alesia in Gaul, the Celtic leader Vercingetorix appeared fully armed. " After he had taken some circuits about Cæsar, he dismounted, put off his armour and placed himself at Cæsar's feet." Among the " heathenish customs " referred to in the seventeenth century records of Dingwall Presbytery " were frequent approaches to some ruinous chappels and circulateing of them ". The ceremonial encircling of sacred wells and stone circles has already been referred to. Houses were protected by walking round them "by the right" while charms were recited. The writer has seen this custom practised in Argyll, the movement resembling the spiral-form symbol.

As in Egypt and Asia, the cardinal points ("airts") were coloured. The north is in Gaelic black, the east purple, the south white, and the west dun. There are also colours for the subsidiary points. Purple (Gaelic *corcur*, Welsh *porffor*) is thus the most sacred colour. It was obtained from the dog whelk, from which was also procured the purple of the Celtic illuminated manuscripts. In these manuscripts, however, as stated, imported pigments were used, including lapis lazuli for ultra-marine and malachite for green.

Now, the " clearing house " in Europe for Asiatic lapis lazuli was, as indicated, Constantinople, and it is of special interest to find that on the Pictish sculptured stones of the east coast of Scotland there are Byzantine art motifs, suggesting a cultural drift from the Near East along the ancient trade route of the Danube valley. The legend of St. Regulus carrying the relics of St. Andrew from Constantinople to Scotland may be a memory of the lapis lazuli trade. St. Andrews, where the St. Andrew cult became influential, was the seaport for the Continent, not only for south and eastern Scotland, but for the north of England, as Raine has shown in his *York*.[1]

Perhaps it was along this route that the pigment-carriers brought some of the wonder tales of the East.

We meet, for instance, with a version of the Indian rope trick story in the Islay blind fiddler's tale of " The Slim Swarthy Champion ".[2]

" Dust of Dust," the juggler and champion, " set a great ladder up against the moon," and caused to ascend it first a hare and a hound and then a lad and a girl. The hound was subsequently found to be eating the hare, and the juggler, using his hand, struck off the hound's head; the lad was kissing the girl, and the lad's head was struck off too. Afterwards the heads were restored.

An Irish version of this story given in *Silva Gadelica*, tells of a wandering " kern " who is really a god in disguise. He performed his " rope trick " before Teigue O'Kelly and " a general gathering and muster at his dwelling ". From a bag the juggler took a silken thread or cord and " so projected it upwards

[1] A. O. Anderson, *Scottish Annals*, p. 132, note 1.
[2] J. F. Campbell, *Popular Tales of the West Highlands*, Vol. I (1890 edition), pp. 297 *et seq.*

that it stuck fast in a certain cloud of the air ". Then he made a hare run up the cord. After the hare he sent up a hound and both animals vanished. Next he sent up a youth and after him " a winsome young woman ". The narrative continues:

" There for a long spell they were now altogether silent and the trick-man said, ' I fear me that up aloft there some bad work is forward '.

" ' Such as what?' asked the chief.

" ' That the hound would eat the hare and the lad make love to the lass.' "

The cord was then taken down, and the dog was found to be eating the hare and the lad making love to the lass.

Asiatic cultural influences, including wonder tales, evidently filtered into Western Europe, including the British Isles, long before Vasco da Gama made discovery of the sea route to India.

Other cultural influences can be associated with the migrations from the Continent of peoples of Celtic speech. An interesting example in this connexion is the custom of holding communication with the souls of the dead. Diodorus Siculus, drawing upon the lost writings of Posidonius, who visited the western Celtic area about 75 B.C., states that " upon the occasion of a burial many (Celts) cast upon the funeral pyre letters which they have written to their dead friends in the hope that the dead will read them ". A similar custom in the Highlands is referred to by Mrs. Grant of Laggan,[1] who, writing in the early part of the nine-

[1] *Essays on the Superstitions of the Highlands of Scotland* (London and Edinburgh, 1811), Vol. II, p. 106.

FESTIVALS AND CEREMONIES 285

teenth century, says that "people frequently send conditional messages to the departed". To a dying person they say:

"If you are permitted, tell my dear brother that I have merely endured the world since he left it; and that I have been very kind to every creature he used to cherish, for his sake."

Mrs. Grant adds:

"I have, indeed, heard a person of a very enlightened mind seriously give a message to an aged person to deliver to a child he had lost not long before, which she as seriously promised to deliver, with the wonted salvo, ' if she was permitted '."

This custom is not yet extinct. Indeed some Presbyterian clergymen in Scotland have of late expressed themselves in favour of praying that the departed may be informed of the loving thoughts regarding them which are entertained by the living.

In Scottish folk-lore we find traces of jumbles of religious notions regarding the mysteries of life and death which came in from various areas of origin at various periods and have blended with and been coloured by later concepts. One is reminded, for instance, of ancient Egyptian eschatology which insisted upon the separation after death of the component parts of an individual—the *ka*, the *bai* and the re-animated mummy—when we find Mrs. Grant of Laggan making the following statement about the Highland belief regarding body, soul and shade:

"While the body rested in the grave and the soul in some calm, intermediate dormitory appointed for its repose till the great day of final decision, there was a kind of wandering shade which was an unreal representative of both and hovered around its usual haunts or over the place of sepulture. Very much the accounts of those wandering shadows resemble those of the thin forms that flitted by Ulysses in the shadows below."

As in the land of the "green Osiris", we find in Scotland green supernatural beings and green ghosts like the "green ladies". J. F. Campbell[1] refers to a tale in which a king's daughter is educated by druids who "coloured her skin as green as grass". Green was an Otherworld colour and was favoured by fairies, the glaistig, &c. A ghost might appear attired in green or as a green light. Mrs. Grant of Laggan[2] tells of a lonely widow beside whose bed were seen nightly "six bright lights" and "a small greenish one". Seven children had predeceased the widow and the lights were their ghosts, who came to "cheer her dreams". The greenish light was the ghost of "one born untimely".

Deaths were foretold by lights seen on house roofs, at house doors, or moving towards a family burial plot in a churchyard. A light on a river, loch or the sea foretold a drowning.

There were in Scotland not only ghosts of the dead but also ghosts of the living. The latter usually hovered near the "human partner" in identical attire, or went on ahead and might be heard at a door or on a stair shortly before the "partner" arrived. Ghosts of the living might be met with wandering alone, and this was a sure indication that a sudden death was to take place. Some of these ghosts might be "attired in a shroud" and seen to carry a light known as "the

---

[1] *Popular Tales*, 1893 edition, Vol. IV, p. 267.
[2] *Op. cit.*, Vol. I, pp. 190 *et seq.*

FESTIVALS AND CEREMONIES 287

death candle ".[1] Ghosts of the living appeared in prophetic phantom funerals seen by individuals endowed with " second-sight ".

Ghosts did not always assume human form. Those of persons about to die or newly dead, or of persons lying asleep, might appear as birds, moths, butterflies, bees, cattle, dogs, cats, mice, horses, frogs, pigs, deer, &c. In Arran to dream of certain dogs is to dream of MacGregors, MacAlisters or MacDonalds. Other clan soul-forms are bees (Mackenzies), plovers (Curries), doves (MacKelvies), cats (MacNicols and MacNeishes), pigs (Cooks and MacMasters), mice (Bannatynes), bulls (MacNeils), rabbits (Mackinnons), frogs (Sillars), sheep (Kerrs), &c.[2] The clan soul-animal or insect was called *riochd nan daoine* (" sign ", " form " or " spirit " of the folk). Thus *an riochd mairbh* means " in the likeness of the dead ". Supernatural beings had, like human beings, their own particular soul forms. The goddess Bride had her serpent or bird form, Cailleach Bheur her bird, swine or deer form, and so on.

Bee-soul forms are referred to in various folk stories and the custom of " telling the bees " of a death in a family survived in the writer's boyhood in the north of Scotland.[3]

Souls in butterfly and moth forms are mentioned in the folk-lores of Scotland, Ireland, Wales, Cornwall and Brittany. Psyche, the Greek nymph, had butterfly wings and her name signified " soul ". Greek artists

[1] W. Grant Stewart, *Popular Superstitions* (Edinburgh, 1823), pp. 16 *et seq.*
[2] *Book of Arran*, edited by W. Mackay Mackenzie, p. 290.
[3] Hugh Miller, *My Schools and Schoolmasters*, Chapter VI; G. Henderson, *Survivals in Belief Among the Celts* (Glasgow, 1911), pp. 82 *et seq.*

frequently gave the soul a butterfly form. The Slavs, the Norse and the Italians believed there were butterfly souls. Souls or deities in butterfly form are met with as far east as China and Indonesia and among the Aztecs of pre-Columbian America.[1]

The god-form name of the butterfly is found in Scotland, but not in Wales, Isle of Man or Brittany. Scottish Gaelic butterfly god-names include *dealbhan-dé* ("image", "ikon" or "form of God"), *dearbadan-dé* ("manifestation of God"), *teine-dé* ("fire of God"), *eunan-dé* ("small bird of God"), *dealan-dé* ("brightness of God"),[2] *tarmachan-dé* ("God's ptarmigan"), and *amadan-dé* ("God's fool"). As we have seen, *dealan-dé* was also applied to lightning and the lighted brand from a Beltane fire which was kept whirling as it was being carried to a house to re-light the domestic fire.

Reference has been made to "second-sight", regarding which there is a very considerable literature.[3] "Second-sight" is still believed in throughout the Scottish Highlands, but there is much reticence regarding it, especially when questions are nowadays asked by non-natives. The commonest form of vision is the phantom funeral. In other instances the vision may be referred to as "telepathic", events at a distance being revealed in a temporary day-trance or in a dream.

---

[1] *Cornish Feasts and Folk-lore* (Penzance, 1890), quoted by W. Y. Evans Wentz, *The Fairy Faith in Celtic Countries* (London, 1911), p. 178; G. Henderson, *Survivals*, p. 79; Ralston, *Songs of the Russian People*, p. 118; my *Ancient Man in Britain*, pp. 191 et seq., and my *Myths of China and Japan*, pp. 225, 240, 241.

[2] Irish, *dalán-dé*.

[3] Norman Macrae in *Highland Second-Sight* (Dingwall, 1908) gives selections of the evidence from a number of sources.

Second-sight, according to Mrs. Grant of Laggan, is " a shuddering impulse, a mental spasm that comes unsought. . . . No one wishes for these mysterious visions, nor can anyone summon them at will." These usually " picture on the brain the approaching events that are to produce fear, wonder or sorrow. For gay visions seldom cheer the mind of the pensive visionary."[1]

Dr. Samuel Johnson similarly found during his Hebridean tour, as he has recorded, that " those who profess to feel it (second-sight) do not boast of it as a privilege, nor are considered by others as advantageously distinguished. They have no temptation to feign; and their hearers have no motive to encourage the imposture. . . . There is now a second-sighted gentleman in the Highlands, who complains of the terrors to which he is exposed." Johnson emphasizes that the " receptive faculty " is " neither voluntary nor constant. The appearances have no dependence upon choice; they cannot be summoned, detained or recalled. The impression is sudden and the effect often painful."

Some individuals may, according to the evidence, have only a single experience of " second-sight " in a lifetime. Others see no visions but have premonitions and prophetic or " telepathic " intuitions or " telepathic dreams ". The so-called " faculty " is supposed to exist in certain families in varying degrees of intensity.

" Blood-stoppers " have the reputation of causing blood to cease flowing from a wound by exercise of

[1] *Op. cit.*, Vol. II, pp. 34–5.

some power resembling hypnotism. Hereditary "curers" of various diseases are still known in the Highlands. Certain of them are undoubtedly mere quacks. It may be that in some authenticated instances of "cures" the sufferers have been victims of one or other of the neuroses that yield to the influence of the agencies of faith and suggestion.

INDEX

Aberdeenshire, pig bones in prehistoric grave, 66.
Aberfeldy, Peallaidh of, 234.
Achæans, Celts and, 5.
Africa, whirlwind lore of, and the Scottish, 202, 203.
Agamemnon, daughter of, sacrificed to Artemis, 136.
Ainu whirlwind lore, 203.
Alba, Scotland, 39. See *Scotland*.
Alexander the Great, Celts and Iberians visited, 67.
Alpine (Armenoid) race, 17.
Amber beads, inherited by wife of MacLaren chief, 259.
Anatolia, origin of pork taboo among Galatians, 66.
— pigs sacred or abominated in, 68 et seq.
Anderson, Dr. A. O., Blue Men, 92 et seq.
Anfred, Anglian prince, father of Pictish king, 33.
Angels, fallen, Aurora Borealis as, 92, 98.
— — Blue Men as, 87, 92, 98.
— — fairies as, 92, 98, 224.
Angles, Aidan fights against, 12, 13.
— Battle of Necktansmere, 13.
— Edwin supplants Ethelfrid, 12, 13.
— first invasion of Lowlands, 12, 13.
— mingled with Britons, 19.
— Oswald and Oswy refugees in Scotland, 13.
— Prince òf, father of Pictish king, 33.
— second occupation of Lowlands, 13.
Animals, sacred, on Scots sculptured stones, 62.
Annandale, rise of pork trade in, 55.
Annat, early religious settlement, 86.
Annie, Gentle, Cailleach as, 159 et seq.
Annis, Black, English Cailleach, 171.
Anwyl, Prof., grouped Celtic goddesses, 199, 200.
— — pig and Celtic Diana, 65.
Aphrodite, Bride and, 193.
Apollo, Egyptian mouse lore and, 78.
— Lord of Mice, Scottish mouse feast, 75 et seq.

Apollo, mouse feast and, 77.
Apple tree, mouse and, 80.
Arbroath fishers' aversion to swine, 50.
— hare superstitions, 81.
Argentocoxus, Caledonian leader, wife of, and Roman Empress, 34.
Argyll, Arthurian place-names in, 106.
— Blue Men and fallen angels, 92.
— Cailleach story in, 130, 131.
— Cailleach's bens in, 165.
— giant lore link with Lancashire, 114.
— Morvern giant, 109, 110.
— Scots settle in, 11, 12.
Argyll. See *Dalriada*.
Artemis, as lover and mother, 175.
— as wind-giver, 136.
— Bride and, 216.
— Cailleach and, 167, 168.
— connexions with trees and fish like Cailleach, 155.
— — water, wild vegetation and beasts like Cailleach, 155.
— deadly birds of, 155.
— fish connexion of, and Cailleach's, 153.
— goddess Bride and, 193.
— human sacrifices to, 149.
— loch monster requires human sacrifices like, 248.
— quail of, 146.
— river associations, 155.
— the Scottish, Cailleach Bheur as, 136 et seq.
Arthur, King, included among giants, 103 et seq.
— — Scots poets and, 104.
— — Thomas the Rhymer displaced as sleeping giant, 107.
— Stone, the Coupar Angus, 106.
Arthurian place-names in Scotland, Wales and England, 103 et seq.
Arthur's Bed, 105.
— Ben, Cobbler of Inveraray, 106.
— Cairn, Aberdeenshire, 106.
— Chair, in Northumberland, 104.
— — in Wales, 105.
— Face, rock called, 106.

291

INDEX

Arthur's Bed, Fountain, in Lanarkshire, 106.
— Grave, 105.
— Hall, 105.
— Oven, near Larbert, 106.
— Quiot, 105.
— Round Table, in Stirlingshire, 106.
— — names, 105.
— Seat, Cumberland place-name, 104.
— — (Edinburgh) and other Arthurian place-names, 103 et seq.
— — (Edinburgh), giant's sleep under, 106.
— — (*Suidhe Artair*) in Banffshire, 106.
— — the Dumbarton, 106.
— Stone, 105, 106.
— — in South Wales, 105.
— Table, 105.
— wife, Scots place-name, 104.
Aryan theory, 5.
Assyrians, pig taboo of, in Anatolia, 69.
Athach, giant or monster, 251.
Attis, Diarmaid as form of, 68, 70.
— Druidism and cult of, 275.
— pig taboo and cult of, 66 et seq.
Auchmithie, fisher superstitions, 50.
— hare superstitions, 81.
" Auld Wife's Lifts ", Cailleach and, 167, note 1.
Aurora Borealis as fallen angels, 92, 98.
— — " Everlasting Battle " of, 222.
Ayrshire, Carrick poet with Highland accent, 29.
— harvest hare, 83.

Babanqua (quagmire), 265.
Babylon, Celts and Iberians visited, 67.
Babylonia, Otherworld of, 6.
Badenoch, " Wife of Laggan " folk-tale, 131, 132.
— Wolf of, as a giant, 103.
Banffshire, giant lore, link with Lancashire, 114.
— — story, 110 et seq.
— Green Lady (ghost) story, 242, 243.
Banshee, as *Fuath*, 239.
— as ghost, 240.
— bird forms of, 239.
— fairy queen and, 196.
— physical defects of, 208.
— washer of the ford, 239.
Baobhan sìth, blood-thirsty demon in girl form, 236, 237.
Barra, Kewach lore, 113.
— pork taboo in, 54.
Battle, the Everlasting, fairies of air and sky fight, 222.
— — giants wage, 100.
Beauly, giant story, 102.
Beaumont and Fletcher, mouse medicine, 79, 80.

Bede, arrival of Picts, 36.
— northern and southern Picts, 35.
— Pictish language, 30.
— — marriage customs, 33.
— — namesake of, 30, 31.
Bee, soul as, 287.
Beira, Cailleach as, 163. See *Cailleach*.
Beithir, The, lightning, thunderbolt or serpent demon, 247.
Beltane, big sun arrives, 278.
— ceremonies of, 279, 280, 281.
— new fire of, 278, 279.
— no connexion with god Baal or Bel, 278.
— sacred fire-brand, 279.
— walking around well and standing stones, 269.
Ben Arthur, Loch Long, 106.
— Cruachan, Cailleach as well-guardian on, 154.
— Ledi, Dorsetshire parallel, 114.
— — giant of, 102, 103.
Benderloch, Cailleach and, 151.
Bens, Cailleach's connexions with, 141, 144, 152, 154, 164, 167, 173, 174, 193.
Beowulf, Scottish, 118 et seq.
— epic, Grendel story and Scottish versions, 134, 135.
— — old British lore in, 135.
— — Skye folk and Grendel section of, 119 et seq.
Bernicia, country of Brigantes, 19.
Biasd Bealach Odail, Skye monster, 250, 251.
Big Ears, cat demon, 246.
Birds, Banshee as raven or hoodie crow, 132, 148, 236, 239.
— boar's bird form, 59.
— Bride and Cailleach as, 287.
— Bride's birds, 193.
— Cailleach as gull, cormorant, eagle, heron, &c., 125 n., 146, 147, 148.
— deadly birds of Artemis, 155.
— Glaistig and, 241.
— hoodie crow and raven as forms of demon, 236.
— Strathpeffer sacred eagle, raven or falcon hawk, 62.
— tabooed by ancient Britons, 81.
Black, north is, 282.
Blakeborough, R., Yorkshire fishers' aversion to swine, 52.
Blood covenant, mouse-feast and, 77.
— stoppers, 289.
Blue Men, bardic contests with, 88, 89, 90.
— captured in Morocco, 92 et seq.
— culture blending, 98.
— evidence of, ignored, 7.
— fairies and aurora borealis and, 92, 98.
— in Ireland, 94.
— lore of, 85 et seq.

INDEX

Blue Men, modern representatives south of Morocco, 95.
— poem on, 91.
— seal lore and, 87, 98.
— skin-staining custom, 95.
— tradition and, 3, 4, 92 et seq.
Blue Sultan, the, 95.
— yarn, Cailleach's, 152, 153.
Boadicea, divination by hare, 83.
Boar, ancestor theory, 63.
— Artemis and, 147.
— Attis-Diarmaid myth, 68.
— Celtic Diana and, 65.
— Diarmaid's hunt of, 147, 148.
— Inverness boar stone, 60, 61, 62.
— protected by Cailleach, 148.
— sacred or lucky, 59 et seq. See *Pork Taboo* and *Swine*.
— Set and Osiris in boar forms, 70.
— tusk of, in prehistoric Highland grave, 66.
Boars, Islands of, Orkneys as, 62.
Boers, mouse medicine, 80.
Bone, worm from Cailleach's, becomes dragon, 150, 151.
Bones, Black Lad of, 150.
Boswell, James, pig sacrifice to sea-horse, 62.
Boulder, Cailleach as, 144, 154.
— oracular bird on, 148.
Boulders, flung by giants (Fomorians), 100 et seq.
Breadalbane, ghosts in animal form, 243.
Bride, a beneficent goddess, 187 et seq.
— Artemis and, 216.
— as " aid woman " at birth of Christ, 190.
— associated with serpent, 188, 189.
— birds of goddess, 193.
— Cailleach and as birds, 287.
— Christ as foster-son of, 190.
— cock-fighting and fishers' custom on day of, 193.
— dandelion milk-yielding plant of, 190.
— early lamb nourished by, 190.
— fusion of with St. Bridget, 190.
— Hathor and, 216.
— invoked at birth, 190.
— links with classical goddesses, 193, 194.
— magic wand of, 191.
— milk-yielding plants and, 190.
— oat-straw " baby " and Bride's eve ceremonies, 191.
— plant milk of, 216.
— Rhea and, 193.
— serpent of, and the dragon, 188, 189.
— winter imprisonment of, 193.
Brigantes, 35 .
— Angles mingled with, 19.
Bristol, giant's cave at Clifton, near, 115.
Brittany, hare taboo in, 83.
— no Blue Men in, 97.

Brittany, soul forms in, 287.
Brochs, absent from Ireland, Wales and England, 36.
— Eden's Hall broch folk-lore, 265.
— Picts as builders of, 36.
— Sardinian *nuraghi* and, 36.
Brollachan, son of Fuath, 238.
Bronze Age, descendants of people of, in Scotland, 25.
Brownies, 229, 230, 231.
Bryce, Professor T. H., pigs in prehistoric Scottish graves, 65.
— — race types in Scotland, 23 et seq.
Buchan, pig bones in prehistoric grave, 66.
Bull, sacred Scottish, 62.
Burghead, cradle stone, 263.
Burns, Robert, race type, 28.
Burt, Captain, on Scots treatment of pig, 44, 45.
Butterflies, sacred names of, 288.
Byzantine culture drifts, 283.
Byzantium, cultural connexion of, with Scotland, 40.

Cæsar, Julius, Celtic leader encircles, 282.
— — Dualism in Gaul, 32, 33.
— — food taboos in Britain, 81.
Cailleach (pronounced *cál'ydch*; *ch* guttural), animal forms of, 287.
— animals of, 147–9, 151, 152, 167, 175, 247.
— apple taken from, 158.
— Artemis and, 136 et seq., 167, 168.
— as a *fuath*, 233.
— as bridge builder, 164.
— as cause of south-westerly gales, 159 et seq.
— as deep-sea wader, 165.
— as inhospitable housewife, 166, 167.
— as lightning and thunder bringer, 165, 166.
— as " loathly hag " 138, 139.
— as loch wader, 165, 166.
— as lover and mother like Artemis, 175.
— as Mala Lia', the keeper of swine, 147 et seq.
— assistants of, ride wolves and pigs, 152.
— associated with winter, 137.
— as water dragon, 131, 157, 158, 250.
— Banffshire well of, 269.
— becomes a boulder, 144, 154.
— *beur* wives, 137.
— birds and, 125 n., 132, 146, 148, 241, 287.
— birth from bones, 150.
— " Black Annis " of Leicestershire and, 171.
— Black Demeter and, 174.
— " black goddess " as prototype of, 155.
— blue-black face and forehead eye of, 139.

INDEX

Cailleach, Bride and, as birds, 287.
— cairn of, 144, 146–7, 164, 167.
— cat form of, 131, 132.
— cattle and byre of, 151.
— cave gruagach and, 241.
— cheese vats of, 151.
— Christian influence in lore of, 164.
— connexions of, 167, 168.
— — with holly and whins, 155.
— — with reeds, beside lochs, 137.
— Corryvreckan connexion, 141, 142.
— Cup of Victory stolen by, 158.
— Cyclopean deity, 174.
— dance associated with, 167, 168.
— day of, was former New Year's Day, 143.
— deer deity theory, 146, 167, 168.
— — protected by, 152.
— disease carried by, 146.
— fish connexion of, and that of Artemis, 153, 155.
— forests burned by, 166.
— " Gentle Annie " form, 159 et seq.
— ghost of, 147.
— " gizzen briggs " female, 162.
— Glaistig acts like, 176, 177.
— Greek, Babylonian and ancient Egyptian links, 174.
— gull, cormorant, eagle and heron forms, 146.
— Gyre Carlin as " Nicnevin ", 150.
— Gyre carling as, 149.
— Gyre carling as a sow, 149.
— herds of in Glen Nevis and Sutherland, 152.
— heron form of, 146, 147.
— holly tree connexion, 250.
— human sacrifices demanded by, 159.
— in Fin (Fionn) story, 135.
— in Finlay the Changeling folk-tale, 124 et seq.
— local names of, 136.
— loch creator, 153, 154.
— Loch Lomond formed by, 165.
— Loch Tay and, 154.
— longevity of, 162, 163.
— Long Meg and, 115.
— magic wand of, in Finlay the Changeling story, 127 et seq.
— magic wand or rod of, 140, 167.
— magic wand in the Sea Maiden story, 131, 132.
— megalithic remains and, 265.
— memory of human sacrifices, 149.
— Milton's " blue meager hag ", 171.
— Morgan le Fay and, 172.
— Morrigan and, 152.
— mother of giants comes from sea, 135.
— mountain builder, 164.
— mountain connexions, 141, 144, 152, 154, 164, 167, 173, 174, 193.
— myths of, 141 et seq.

Cailleach, myths of, in Isle of Man, 145.
— new water as life-giver to, 270.
— Norse, Swedish and Danish links with, 172.
— Norse theory, 169.
— origin of name of, 137.
— raven and hoodie-crow birds of, or forms of, 132, 148.
— red as protection against, 153.
— reptile forms of, 131, 150–1, 157–8, 250.
— river-ford demon, 159.
— rocks of, 161, 162.
— Rumanian link with, 173.
— sea-form and Sumerian and Egyptian deities, 157, 158.
— sea-form of, 156 et seq.
— serpent revival and, 250.
— shape changing of, 125, 130, 131, 132.
— sheep and goats of, in Mull cave, 151.
— slain by Diarmaid, 148, 149.
— spring period named after, 161.
— storms raised by, 142, 143.
— summary of activities and connexions, 174, 175.
— Tarbat wind controller, 162.
— theory of Caledonian connexion, 169.
— Thomas the Rhymer legend, 138, 139.
— visit to Fionn, &c., 138.
— well guardian, 153, 154.
— Well of Youth near Loch Ba, 162, 163.
— William the hunter spies on, 152, 153.
— witches acquired lore of, 147.
— worm from bone of, becomes loch dragon, 150, 151.
Cairn, demon and, 265.
— Cailleach and, 144, 146–7, 164, 167.
— Glaistig's or Cailleach's, 176, 177.
— Merlin's grave, 106.
— vows taken on, 258.
Caithness, unlucky to name clergyman or pig at sea, 51.
Caledonians, dualism of, 35.
— Galgacus, general of, 10.
— giant of Ben Ledi, 102, 103.
— husband selection by female, 34.
— intellectual life of, 7.
— muscular fighting men, 21.
— Picts absorbed, 35.
— Picts successors of, 11.
— reached Scotland from Continent, 36.
Calton, fairies under the Edinburgh hill named, 271, 272.
— " fairy boy " of Leith, 271, 272.
— (hazel grove), at Edinburgh and Glasgow, 271.
Camden, Arthur Seat, Edinburgh, mentioned by, 104.
Campbell, J. F., boar tusk in prehistoric grave, 66.
— — fairies as spirits, 224.

INDEX

Campbell, J. F., *Fuath* and water, 233.
— — Kewach lore, 113.
— — Rev. J. G., Cailleach and thunder, 165.
— — Cailleach as bridge builder, 164.
— — Cailleach's cattle, 151.
— — Cailleach's great age, 162, 163.
— — demons of vampire type, 237.
— — devil and pig or horse, 52.
— — fairies and ghosts, 221.
— — fairies small, 207.
— — fairy " airt ", 200.
— — fairy queen, 196.
— — fallen angels lore, 92.
— — *Fuath*, 233.
— — Glaistig and goat, 184, 185.
— — Glaistig lore, 178.
— — *Glaistig* theory, 240, 241.
— — Kewach lore, 113.
— — " lucky pig ", 58.
— — milk offerings to dead, 218.
— — Muileartach theory of, 156.
— — noiseless movements of fairies, 208.
— — Serpent slaying, 250.
— — spring gales, 142.
Campbells, pig and the, 54.
Caoineag, the death foreteller, 239, 240.
Cardinal points, Gaelic colours of, 282.
— — prominent in many mythologies, 120.
— — Scottish lore regarding, 119, 120.
Carham, battle of, 13, 14.
Carlin. See *Gyre Carlin*.
Carmichael, Dr. Glaistig lore, 177.
— — Bride ceremonies, 191, 192.
— — fairies and ghosts, 221, 222.
— — fairies as fallen angels, 224.
— — fairy lore, 207 *et seq.*
— — Fuath lore, 233.
— — Glencoe massacre lore, 239, 240.
— — installation stone of MacDonalds, 257, 258.
— — King Geigean, 244.
— — milk offerings, 218, 219.
— — reindeer in Scotland, 205.
— — spring gales, 142, 143.
— — Urisk lore, 185 *et seq.*
— — water fairies, 206, 207.
Cashen, W., Manx giant lore, 116.
Cat, Cailleach in form of, 131, 132.
— clan, no cat carvings, 63.
— fertilizes pear tree, 80.
Cats, demons in forms of, 245, 246.
— (Picts) place-names of, 33.
— sacrifice of in *Taghairm* ceremony, 245, 246.
Cattle, ghosts as, 243.
Caves, English giants in, 115.
— giants in, 122 *et seq.*, 107, 112, 113.
— Irish giants in, 116.
— no Scottish fairies in, 203.
Cear, the (" blood one "), 244.
Ceasg, mermaid, 251.

(E 859)

Celtic, Alexander the Great visited by Celts, 67.
— alleged mental leanings called, 5.
— civilization Homeric, 5.
— Continental Celts, Gauls and Galatae, 4.
— differences in pantheons and faiths, 6.
— doctrine of metempsychosis, 6.
— early settlers in Britain ate pork, 65.
— fairy lore and Teutonic gloom, 197, 198.
— Gaulish Diana and boar, 65.
— Gundestrup cauldron and culture drifting, 67, 68.
— Irish pig lore, 72, 73.
— La Tène settlements and salt mines, 65.
— " lucky boar ", 64, 65.
— mercenary Celtic warriors in Near East, 67.
— messages sent to departed and modern customs, 284, 285.
— migrations of Celts with wives and families, 26.
— modern term " Keltic ", 4.
— no homogeneous folk-lore or religion, 5, 6.
— no people in Britain or Ireland named Celts, 4.
— not a racial term, 4.
— origin of Galatian pork taboo, 66, 67.
— otherworld beliefs, 6.
— pork taboo, 7, 41 *et seq.*
— pork trade with Italy, 65.
— Scots folk-lore and, 4.
— Scots taller and fairer than Irish, Welsh or Bretons, 28.
— Votadini, Brigantes, Damnonii, &c., in Scotland, 35.
Cernunnos, Druids and cult of, 275.
— god of Gundestrup cauldron, 68.
— imported from Galatia, 275.
— St. Kentigern and cult animals of, 68.
Chairs, hills as, for giants, 99 *et seq.*
Chaucer, fairy lore of, 196, 197, 198.
— Loathly Hag story, 139.
Childe, Professor V. Gordon, Caledonians and Belgae, 36.
China, whirlwind lore, 203.
Christmas, origin of house decorations, 275.
Clan Codrum, descended from seals, 87.
— ghosts, 287.
Coldingham, demons of, 265, 266.
Colignon, Dr., race resistance to intrusions, 19.
— — race survivals, 18.
Colour symbolism, cardinal points coloured, 282.
— green as fairy colour, 212, 286.
— green glaistig, 178.

20

296   INDEX

Colour symbolism, green ladies, 242, 243.
— green light, 286.
— green ointment, 226.
— green table, 225.
— stone colours, 222.
Columba, at Brude's court, 31.
— required interpreters in Highlands, 31.
Connel Ferry, Cailleach's goats, 151.
— Cailleach rocks, 162.
— goddess of Loch Etive, 90.
Constantinople, culture drifts from, 282, 283.
— Swedish merchants in, 93.
— trading connexions of with Scotland, 40.
Cormorant, Cailleach as, 146.
Cornwall, giants' caves, 115.
— giant lore of and the Scottish, 133, 134.
— soul forms in, 287.
Cow, man in hide of, in *Taghairm* ceremony, 247.
Crete, mother goddess of and Cailleach, 174.
— race survivals in, 19.
Cro-Magnons, in Scotland, 17.
— survivals in France, 18.
Cromarty, archaic fisher dialect, 160, 161.
— Cailleach as " Gentle Annie ", 159 *et seq.*
— cursing stone, 255.
— giant cobblers, 101, 102.
— giant lore, 101, 102.
— Last Judgment at Navity near, 276.
— Pictish place-name, 102.
— pigmentation evidence from, 27, 28.
— " rock tree " ceremony and offerings, 273.
— spitting stone and rock tree, 259.
— Thomas the Rhymer lore in, 107.
Cromarty Firth, as Sykkersund (" safe sound "), 160.
Cruithne, the Irish, Britons not Picts, 37.
Cuchulainn, fairies and, 212, 213.
— in Skye, 39.
— milk as healer, 218.
Cuckoo, a fairy bird, 204.
Cup of Victory, 158, 159.
Curers, the Hereditary, 289.
Cursing stones, 255.
Cybele, Bride and, 194.

Dalriada, Dunadd wild-boar figure, 61, 62.
— Irish translated old British names in, 32.
— Pictish dualism in, 32.
— pork taboo in, 58.
— pork taboo in Lorne, 46.
— Scots settle in, 11, 12.
Dalyell, J. G., Scots prejudice against swine, 44, 72.
— — swine rents, 57.

Damnonii of Scotland and English and Irish branches, 35, 36.
Dance, the ceremonial Cailleach, 167, 168.
Danes, conquests in England and Ireland, 14.
Danish Cailleach, 172.
Dawson, Warren R., mouse medicine, 79.
Dead, associated with fairies, 221 *et seq.*
— swine and the deified, 69 *et seq.*
Death candle, 285, 286.
Deer, as " cattle of fairies ", 204, 205.
— Cailleach protector of, 152.
— ghosts as, 243.
— reindeer in Scotland, 205.
— sacred stag, 62.
Deira, 19, 20.
Deiseil, " by the right ", the friendly and lucky movement, 281, 282.
Delattre, Floris, sadness of Teutonic mythology, 198.
Demeter, Cailleach and the Black, 174.
Demons, Banshee, 239.
— *baobhan sìth* as hoodie crow or raven, 236, 237.
— *beithir* of cave or corrie, as serpent, lightning or thunderbolt, 247.
— black urisks, 245.
— *Bòchdan* as headless man, goat, dog, &c., 251.
— *caoineag*, 239, 240.
— cat forms of, 245, 246.
— *cear* (" blood one ") and *cearb* (" killing one "), 244.
— Draedan and Billie, 265, 266.
— Draedan of burn and babanqua (quagmire), 265.
— *fachan* and *athach*, 251.
— Fraoch story, 249.
— *Geigean*, 244.
— ghosts as glaistig or banshee, 240.
— Glen Etive monster with one eye, one leg and one hand, 251.
— Loch Morar monster, 247, 248.
— monsters of lochs and passes, 250, 251.
— rock and underground *frid*, 244.
— rowan tree guardian, 249.
— sacrifices to loch monsters, 248, 249.
— St. Columba's methods of worsting, 232, 233.
— salmon as form of water demon, 249.
— Skye forms of, 250, 251.
— *Taghairm* ceremony, 245, 246, 247.
— urisk, shellycoat, brounger, smiter and clootie, 234, 235.
— vampire-like furies, 236, 237.
— water-horse in animal and human forms, 237, 238.
— white serpents, 249.
Devil, as " big black pig ", 52.
— as giant, 103.
— cards as " books " of, 52.

INDEX 297

Devil, Glaistig as " she devil ", 177.
— horse and, 52.
— Peallaidh as, 234.
— pig and, 52.
Diana, the Celtic and the boar, 65.
Diarmaid, fatal boar hunt of, 147, 148.
— Kewach slain by, 113.
— myth of Attis and, 68, 70.
Dingwall, giant lore, 101.
— sacred rock near, 260.
Dio Cassius, Boadicea and hare, 83.
Diodorus Siculus, mouse lore, 78.
Dog, Glaistig as, 177, 184.
— supernatural, 243, 244.
Dogs, as enemies of giants, 122 et seq.
— ghosts as, 243, 251.
Dolmen as " giant's load ", 116.
Dornoch Firth, giant story, 101.
— " gizzen brigs ", 162.
Dorsetshire, giant figure in, 115.
— stone-putting giants, 114.
Dragon, Bride's serpent and, 188, 189.
— Cailleach and, 131, 250.
— Cailleach becomes, 150, 151, 157-8, 250.
— Cailleach's link with Asia, 151.
— serpent and, 249 and note 2.
— water monster and, 249.
Druid Wands, Finlay gets from giant's cave, 127 et seq.
— used by Cailleach, 140, 141, 167, 168, 178, 191.
Druidism, theory of Galatian origin of, 275.
Druids, Broichan as king's guardian or as priest-king, 40.
— Cernunnos cult and, 275.
— nemets of, 275 et seq.
Druid's Port, 268, 276.
Dual organization in Gaul, 32, 33.
— the Pictish, 32 et seq.
Duald mac Firbis, Blue Men of Morocco narrative, 92 et seq.
Dualism, Pictish and exogamy, 33, 34.
Dumbarton, Thomas the Rhymer as sleeping giant, 107.
Dumfriesshire, beginning of pork trade in, 54, 55.
— pig scares in, 47 et seq.
— " witchcraft " of first pork curer, 55.
Dumna, goddess of deep, 253.
— " Long Island " called, 253.
Dun, west is, 282.
Dunbar, William, " Arthur Sate ", 104
— — Cailleach of thunder, 165.
— — calls Carrick poet Highland, 29.
Dundee, giant stone of, 103.

Eagle, Cailleach as, 146.
Easdale, giant of, 103.
Edderton, giant of, 101.

Edinburgh, Arthur's Seat and giant lore, 103 et seq.
— Calton (hazel grove) of, 271, 272.
— fairy hill of, 271, 272.
— St. Anthony's pig, 64.
— " slippy stanes ", 264.
— spitting-on-stone custom, 259.
— wishing and pin wells, 270.
Edwin, King, Ethelfrid slain by, 12, 13.
Eels, Dr. Johnson on Scots prejudice against, 46.
— Glaistig eater of, 178.
— Scottish prejudice against, 80, 81.
Egypt, Cailleach and reptile deities, 157, 158.
— fierce goddess of, 174.
— milk offerings to mummy, 218.
— mouse as " life giver ", 78.
— nail tree in, and the Scottish, 213, 214.
— Osirian paradise of, and Scots fairyland, 7, 223.
— Pharaoh's soul in whirlwind, 202.
— Pictish law of succession like that of, 34.
— race link with Britain, 27.
— race types in, 18, 19.
— Set-Osiris myth and the pig, 70.
— sky world of, 6.
— treatments of pig in, 73, 74.
Eigg, Kewach of, 113.
Eildon hills, giant of, 103.
— hills, sleepers under, 108.
Elves, fairies and, 197, 198.
England, Cailleach as " blue hag " and " Black Annis ", 171.
— Cornish giant lore and Scottish, 133, 134.
— Danish conquest of, 14.
— giant figures in, 115, 116.
— — lore of, 114 et seq.
— giants' caves of, 115.
— hare and fowl taboos in ancient, 81.
— hare eaten in pre-Celtic times, 83.
— mouse medicine in, 78, 79.
— no Pictish brochs in, 36.
— pig prejudice in north-east of, 41.
— " swine-eaters " of, 42.
— whale-fishing giant in, 114.
— whirlwind lore, 202.
Ethelfrid, King, battle of Degsastan, 12.
— — Edwin overthrows, 12, 13.
" Everlasting Battle, The ", giants (Fomorians) wage, 100, 222.
Evil eye, prayer for protection against, 231.
— water-off-silver cure, 267, 268.
Eye colours in Scotland, 24, 25.

Fachan, one-handed monster, 251.
Fairies, a complete republic, 195, 196.
— a small race, 207.
— abduction stories, 224, 225.
— always come from west, 120.

Fairies, annual assemblies of in island, 213.
— as deities, 211 et seq.
— as " departed souls ", 227.
— as " fallen angels ", 224.
— as invisible beings, 208.
— as noiseless beings, 208.
— as " spirits in prison ", 224.
— as " the mothers ", 199.
— as tree spirits, 212, 214, 215.
— baking protected against, 208.
— blending of those of folk-belief and literature, 195 et seq.
— Border ballads lore, 199.
— Brownies and, 229.
— caves not occupied by, 203.
— changelings, 209.
— chiefly women, 198, 199, 200.
— child's experience with fairy woman, 222, 223.
— confusion of witches with, 210.
— Cuchulainn and, 212.
— " cup of Mary ", 215.
— dead among the, 223, 224, 225.
— dead with in underworld, 6.
— deer as " cattle " of, 204, 205.
— descriptions of, 207, 208.
— dwellings of, 203.
— Egyptian and Scottish, 213, 214.
— elves and, 197, 198.
— English poets transformed, 196, 197.
— " everlasting battle " waged by, 222.
— eye salve makes them visible, 225, 226.
— " fairy boy of Leith ", " Red Donald ", and " Callum Clever ", 271, 272.
— fairy milk goddess, 215, 216.
— *frid* inside rock, 244.
— ghosts travel with, 221, 222.
— gifts from, 210.
— goddess groups and, 199, 200.
— Greek nymphs in whirlwinds like, 201, 202.
— hazel as milk tree, 217.
— herb protection against spells of, 209.
— host called " sluagh ", 221.
— houses protected against, 209.
— human beings stolen by, 209.
— human prototypes theory, 210.
— Inverness milk famine caused by, 219, 220, 221.
— iron and red substances protections against, 209.
— lights in groves, 214.
— " loireag ", a water fairy, 206, 207.
— longevity of, 211, 212.
— Lowland variety, 207.
— male gruagach, gunna, and old man of barn, 229 et seq.
— meal and milk offerings to, 208, 209.
— milk offerings to the " loireag ", 218, 219.

Fairies, milk stolen by, 218 et seq.
— non-human in folk-tales, 223, 224.
— physical defects of, 208.
— prayer for protection against, 231.
— queen of as hag, 138, 139.
— queen of, imported, 195, 196.
— raids of, 209.
— second sighted individuals see, 225.
— Thomas the Rhymer and queen of, 199.
— tree goddess gives milk of wisdom to women, 214, 215.
— war in heaven, 224.
— water fairies, 205, 206.
— Welsh and English lore, 226, 227.
— west the " airt " of, 200.
— whirlwind travellers, 200 et seq.
— worship of, in Ireland, 200.
Fairyland, animals in, 204.
— dead in, 223 et seq.
— like Osirian paradise, 223.
— migrating birds in, 204.
— Scottish, an underworld, 203, 204.
— supernatural lapse of time in, 227 et seq.
Festivals, Christmas and New Year's Day, 280.
— Scottish, 278 et seq.
Ferdiad, in Skye, 39.
Fianna, Cailleach robs Cup of Victory, 158, 159.
— lore imported into Scotland from Ireland, 112.
— slain Cailleach becomes dragon, 150, 151.
Fideal, personification of loch-grass, 235, 236.
Fife, giant of Norman's Law, 103.
Finlay the Changeling, Skye folk-tale and *Beowulf*, 119 et seq.
— — Argyll and Badenoch versions, 130 et seq.
Fionn, as chief sleeping giant, 107, 108.
— as sleeping giant in Skye, 107.
— Kewach conflict, 112.
— Thomas the Rhymer displaced as sleeping giant, 107, 108.
Fish, Artemis and Cailleach connected with, 153.
— Artemis connected with, 155.
— Glaistig fond of, 178.
— taboo in Scotland, 80, 81.
Fishers, aversion to swine, 41, 50 et seq.
— " Gentle Annie " lore of, 159 et seq.
— hare superstitions, 81, 82.
Flemings, in early Scots burghs, 15.
Flintshire, Arthurian lore, 105.
Flodden, big Scots at, 21, 22.
Folk-lore, Celtic theory, 4 et seq.
— plundering of Scottish, 7.
— race influences and, 4.
Fomorians, Arthurian lore and, 103 et seq.

INDEX

Fomorians, as family gods, 109.
— as Hebridean pirates, 117.
— boulders flung by, 100 *et seq.*
— " everlasting battle " of, 100.
— Finlay the Changeling folk-tale, 119 *et seq.*
— giants as, 99 *et seq.*
— in Irish mythology and Scots folk-lore, 118.
— Irish giant forms, Loch Neagh, 117.
— Kewach (Ciuthach) Hebridean lore, 112, 113.
— meaning of " fomór ", 117.
— naming of, 117.
— north the cardinal point of, 120.
— Red Etin, 149.
— sleeping under hills, 106 *et seq.*
— vulnerable moles of, 109 *et seq.*
— Welsh giant flings quoit into Ireland, 116.
— " Wolf of Badenoch " among, 103. See *Giants.*
Forres, spitting stone, 259.
Fortingal, ancient yew at, 271.
— sacred mouse stone, 80.
Fraoch, monster story, 249.
Frazer, Sir J. G., independent origin theory, 97.
— whirlwind lore, 202.
Frid, the, milk offered to, 244.
— pipers and, 244.
— rock dweller, 244.
Fuath, as water spirit, 233.
— Banshee as, 239.
— Brollachan as son of, 238.
— Peallaidh as, 234.
— urisk as, 234.
— various monsters called, 233.

Galatia, as source of Druidism, 275.
— Gaulish language in, 67.
— origin of Celtic pork taboo in, 66, 67.
— spread of pork taboo from, 67 *et seq.*
Galgacus (Calgacus), Caledonian general, 10.
Gall-Gaels, 16.
Galloway, harvest hare, 82, 83.
— King Kenneth mac Alpin from, 12.
— MacDougalls and MacDowells, 15.
Gaul, Celtic Diana and boar, 65.
— language of, in Galatia, 67.
— pig bones in prehistoric graves, 66.
— pig god of, 65.
Geigean, King, death revels, 244.
Ghosts, animal forms of, 287.
— as green light, 286.
— bird, butterfly, moth, bee and animal, 287.
— clans with different, 287.
— deer and cattle as, 243.
— dog form of " green lady ", 243.

Ghosts, dogs as, 243.
— green, 286.
— green, in Banffshire story, 242, 243.
— headless man, goat, dog, &c., 251.
— hunters and dogs as, 243, 244.
— lights as, 286.
— of the living, 286.
Giants, Arthurian lore and, 103 *et seq.*
— boulders flung by, 100 *et seq.*
— called " devils ", &c., 102, 103.
— caves of in England, 115.
— dogs as enemies of, 122 *et seq.*
— Eden's Hall broch giant, 265.
— English like the Scottish, 144 *et seq.*, 134, 135.
— English figures of, 115, 116.
— " everlasting battle " of, 100 *et seq.*
— Finlay the Changeling folk-tale, 119 *et seq.*
— hills of, in Scotland, 99 *et seq.*
— Irish and megalithic remains, 116, 117.
— Isle of Man lore, 116.
— Long Meg's circle and Scottish Cailleach, 115.
— mother of, stronger than husband or sons, 124 *et seq.*
— Red Etin, 149.
— sleeping, 106 *et seq.*
— souls of, in stone, egg, fish, tree, &c., 113.
— treasure of includes magic wands, 127 *et seq.*
— Welsh lore, 116.
— whale-fishers, 110, 114.
— widespread Scottish stories of, 100, 102.
— " Wolf of Badenoch " among, 103. See *Fomorians, Kewach.*
Giant's grave, Irish stone circle as, 116.
— — on Welsh hill, 116.
— graves, 115.
— ring, an Irish, 117.
Gibraltar, in Blue Men narrative, 94.
Gildas, arrival of Picts, 36.
Gilltrax, Pictish place-name, 102.
Glaistig, animal forms of, include dog, mare, foal, sheep and goat, 177, 184.
— as deep-sea wader like Cailleach, 179, 180.
— as demon of ford, 181.
— as " familiar " of pirate, 180, 181.
— as family guardian, 178.
— as ghost, 240, 241.
— as half-woman, half-goat, 177.
— as house builder, 182, 183.
— as long-haired gruagach, 179.
— as " she devil ", 177.
— associated with domesticated animals, 184.
— as wailer for dead, 179, 181.
— Banffshire story of, 110 *et seq.*
— birds and, 241.

INDEX

Glaistig, bridge-builder like Cailleach, 176, 177.
— child of, 241.
— converts cows into stones, 178.
— curse of, 183.
— ferry story of, 183, 184.
— fond of children, 178.
— fond of fish, 178.
— fond of lonely people, 179.
— green form of, 178.
— green ghosts and, 242.
— Lochaber Kennedy legend, 181.
— MacMhuirich and, 241.
— magic wand of, 178.
— milk offerings to, 179.
— rapid movements of, 180.
— trickster like Queen Mab, 183, 184.
— water imp, 177.
— yew tree refuge of, 178.
Glasgow, Cailleach standing stones near, 115.
— Cailleach stones near, 167.
— Calton (hazel grove) of, 271.
— god Cernunnos and St. Kentigern, 68.
— St. Kentigern and sacred white boar, 59, 60.
Glen Nevis, Cailleach's herds in, 152.
Glencoe, Massacre of, spirit warning, 239, 240.
Glennie, John Stuart, Arthurian theories of, 104.
Goat, devil as, 184.
— Glaistig and, 177, 240, 241.
— lame, 185.
— Urisk's connexion with, 185.
Goats, Cailleach and, 151.
— ghosts as, 251.
Goddesses, "black goddess" in Scotland, 155.
— Bride a beneficent deity, 187 *et seq.*
— Celtic groups of, and the fairies, 199, 200.
— Dumna of the Deep, 253.
— fierce female deities in Greece, Babylonia, &c., 173, 174.
— great mother of Pessinus on Celtic cauldron, 275.
— Loch Etive's "foul one", 90 and note 2.
— Maid of the Wave, 252. See *Artemis, Bride, Cailleach, Demeter, Kore, Persephone.*
Golden Bough, the, independent origin theory, 97.
Gold sword in Skye folk-tale and Beowulf epic, 127.
— swords in Beowulf epic and Skye story of Finlay, 119, 134, 135.
Goose, tabooed by ancient Britons, 81.
Gortlich, Inverness-shire, Fraser giant of, 109.

Grant, Mrs., Cailleach and wells, 154.
— Mrs. (of Laggan) messages to departed, 284, 285.
— — second sight.
— Mrs. K. W., Cailleach and Norway, 169.
— — Cailleach in Rumania, 173.
— — Cailleach lore, 151.
— — Cailleach myths, 141 *et seq.*
Great mother, Anatolian, 67, 68.
— "mother son" and, 67, 68.
Greece, Arcadian pork taboo, 73.
— Lamia, the Gello, Black Demeter and Cailleach, 173, 174.
— magic hammers, 168.
— pig sacrifices in, 72.
— soul forms in, 287, 288.
— treatment of pig in, 69 *et seq.*
— whirlwind nymphs and fairies, 201, 202.
Green ladies (ghosts), 242, 243.
Gregor, Rev. Walter, hare superstitions, 81, 82.
— — pig superstitions, 52.
Groves, the sacred, Druids and, 275 *et seq.*
Gruagach, as cave monster, 241.
— Glaistig as the female, 179.
— male type, 229.
— milk offered to, 230.
— sea, 240, 241.
Gull, Cailleach as, 146.
Gundestrup cauldron, Druidism and, 275.
— — evidence of culture drifting, 67, 68.
Gunna, a fairy, 230.
Gyre Carlin, Indian sacrifice reference, 150.
— Red Etin and, 149.
— same as Cailleach, 149.
— sow form of, 149.

Hair colours in Scotland, 24, 25.
Hakon, King, Hebridean campaign, 15.
Hallowe'en, ceremonies of, 280.
— little sun of, 278.
Handfasting, in Scotland and Wales, 34, 35.
Hare, Boadicea's ceremony, 83.
— eaten in Ireland, 83.
— eaten in pre-Celtic England, 83.
— harvest, 82, 83.
— "St. Monacella's lambs", 84.
— Scottish superstitions, 81, 82.
— tabooed by ancient Britons, 81.
— tabooed in Brittany, 83.
— tabooed in Wales, 83, 84.
— witches, assumed form of, 82.
Harold Fairhair, 93.
Harvest hare, in Scotland and on Continent, 82.
Hawes, H. B., race survivals in Crete, 19.
Hazel, as a god, 272.
— as milk-yielding sacred tree, 271.

INDEX

Hazel, as source of fire, 272, 273.
— in Gaelic paradise, 272.
— milk in nuts of, 272.
Hebrides, descendants of Norse in, tabooed pork, 58.
— ghosts as dogs, 243, 244.
— Hakon's campaign in, 15.
— King Gilli, 20.
— Magnus Bareleg seizes, 14.
— " mother sow ", 63, 64.
— Norse evacuation of, 15.
— Norse in, 14.
Henderson, Dr. George, magic stones, 264, 265.
— — " mother sow ", 63, 64.
— — stone superstitions, 262.
— Robert, pig scares in Dumfriesshire, 47 et seq.
— — rise of Dumfriesshire pork trade, 54, 55.
Herodotus, Egyptian pork taboo, 73.
Heron, Cailleach as, 146, 147.
Hillock of my Wish, 262, 263.
Hills, giants and, in Scotland, 99 et seq.
History, ancient life in folk-tales, 3.
— methods of novelists in folk-tales, 3.
Homeric civilization, Celts and Achæans, 5.
Honey and milk, Greek incantation, 202.
Hoodie crow, as form of demon, 236.
— Banshee as, 239.
— Cailleach and, 148.
Horn blower, G. D., Egyptian nail tree, 214.
Horse, Glaistig as foal or mare, 177.
— hoof marks, Arthurian, 105.
— sacred, sacrifice of pig to, 62.
— sacred Scottish, 62.
— shoes, Argyll place-name, 143, 144.
Horse's leap, Tiree place-name, 144.
Hull, Miss Eleanor, Irish Cailleach lore, 169, 170, 171.
— — Irish pig lore, 72, 73.
Human sacrifices, Artemis and Cailleach and, 136, 149.
— " Black Annis " and, 171.
— Gyre carling and, 149.
— loch monster requires, 248, 249.
— Maid of the Wave required, 252.
— Muileartach demands, 159.

Iceland, Kewach in, 113.
Independent origin theory, Blue Men and, 96 et seq.
— history of, 96 et seq.
— workings of mind of man, 97.
India, births on sacrificial platform, 150 and note 2.
— milk goddess of, 216.
— rope trick, story of, in Ireland and Scotland, 283, 284.

Indo-European theory, 5.
Indo-Germanic theory, 5.
Inverness, boar stone near, 60, 61, 62.
— fairy ball in Tomnahurich, 228.
— fairy milk famine in, 219, 220, 221.
— offerings dropped in Culloden well, 269, 270.
— St. Columba's visit to Pictish King Brude, 31.
— Thomas the Rhymer and Fionn as sleeping giants at, 107.
— three giants of, 102.
Iona, pre-Christian Yew cult in, 98.
Ireland, Blue Men in, 94.
— Britons who settled in, 39.
— Cailleach in, 169, 170, 171.
— Cruithne of, not Picts but Britons, 37.
— Danann deities not in Scotland, 31.
— Danann pantheon of, 118.
— deities and cardinal and subsidiary points, 120.
— demons as " mouse lords ", 80.
— fairy worship in, 200.
— Fianna lore reached Scotland from, 112.
— grey eye of, rare in Scotland, 25.
— hare eaten in, 83.
— healing milk in, 218.
— Hebridean surnames in, 15 and note 2.
— Indian rope trick in, 283, 284.
— Isles of Blest, 6.
— Loch Neagh giant, 117.
— Lugaid and Scottish mouse feast, 75 et seq.
— magic swine in, 72.
— no genuine Picts in, 38.
— no Pictish brochs in, 36.
— no pork taboo in, like Scotland, 41.
— no supernatural Blue Men in, 97.
— pig lore of, 72, 73.
— pig sacrifice in, 62, 63.
— Ptolemy place-name theory in, 37.
— Scots folk-lore and, 7.
— soul forms in, 287.
— warriors and prophetesses trained in Scotland, 39.
Islands, demons or deities and priestesses in, 98. See Iona and Shiant Isles.
— of Blest, 6.
Islay, Cailleach's bridge, 164.
— Cailleach's hill in, 164.
Isle of Man, fairies as spirits in, 224¡
— St. Patrick and Cailleach, 145.
Italy, Celtic pork trade with, 65.

James VI, food prejudices of, 42, 43¡
Japan, whirlwind lore, 203.
Jarlshof, Shetland, Picts arrived at during Bronze Age, 36.
Jeremiah, cakes to queen of heaven, 261.
Johnson, Dr. Samuel, pig sacrifice, 62.
— pork and eel taboos in Scotland, 44–46.

INDEX

Johnson, Dr. Samuel, second sight, 289.
Jollie, Mrs. E. T., mouse medicine among Boers, 80.

Keats, John, the elfin-storm, 202.
Keightley, T., Lowland fairies, 207.
Kelpie, a river demon, 238.
— lore of, 238.
— water horse and, 238.
Keltic. See *Celtic*.
Kendrick, T. D., Norse chronology, 93.
Kennedy, Walter, a Carrick Highlander, 29.
Kenneth mac Alpin, as King of Picts, 12.
— claim to Pictish throne, 35.
Kewach, slain by Oscar, 112.
— Hebridean giant, 112, 113.
Kilmorack, giant story, 102.
Kintail, giant story, 101.
Kirk, Rev. Robert, fairies as spirits, 227.
Kore-Persephone, Bride and, 193.

Lancashire, giant lore links with Scotland, 114.
— giants' graves, 114.
Lancelot, as giant slayer, 115.
Lang, Andrew, independent origin theory, 97.
Language, barrier of, between Pictland and Ireland, 31.
— bi-lingual period in Dalriada, 32.
— Gauls and Galatians conversed after seven centuries, 67.
— " Ingliss " in Lothian, 13.
— Pictish and Gaelic, 38, 39.
— Pictish language non-Gaelic, 30, 31.
— St. Columba's interpreters in Highlands, 31.
Languages, national traditions and, 9, 10.
Largs, skirmish of, 15.
Leeds, giant of hill at Armley, 114.
Leicestershire, " Black Annis " as Cailleach, 171.
— giant's grave in, 114, 115.
Leith, " Fairy Boy " of, 271, 272.
— St. Anthony and swine, 64.
— shellycoat of, 235.
Lesmahagow, pork taboo in, 46.
Leverhulme, Lord, Lewis pig scheme, 54.
Lewis, Kewachs of, 112.
— Miss Mary L., giant lore of Wales, 116.
— Morrison " brehons " of, 215.
— pork taboo in, 54.
— sea-god of, 252, 253.
Lightning, demon of, 247.
Lights, ghosts as, 286.
Lindsay, Sir David, Arthur referred to by, 104.
— Gyre carling and Red Etin, 149.
Loathly Hag, the, Chaucer's version of story of, 139.

Loch Awe, Cailleach and, 153, 154.
— Ba, Cailleach and well near, 162, 163.
— Eck, Cowal, Cailleach and, 154.
— Etive, goddess of, 90.
— Lomond, Kewach of, 113.
— Maree, fairy island and wishing tree and well, 213.
— Morar monster, 247, 248.
— Ness, Cailleach and, 153, 154.
— — giant story, 102.
— Tay, Cailleach and, 154.
Lochaber, Glaistig Kennedy legend, 181.
Lochiel, silver shoe lore, 246.
Lochs, monsters of, 250, 251.
Lockerbie, rise of pork trade in, 55.
Lorne (Dalriada) pork taboo in, 46.
Lowlands, Broad-heads in east, 25.
— Carrick as a Gaelic area, 29.
— English language spreads in, 13.
— Gaelic in Lothian, 29, 30.
— pork taboo in, 42.
— two English occupations of, 12, 13.
Lucian, treatment of pig in Near East, 68.
Luckington, giant's cave, 115.
Lugh, Irish god, comes from north-east, 120.
Luideag, Skye monster, 251.
Lycia, pig and deified dead, 69.
Lyon King of Scotland, 259.

Macbain, Dr. A., *Shony*, sea-god, 253.
M'Bain, J. M., fishers' aversion to swine, 5.
— hare superstitions, 81.
MacGregor, Rev. Alex., pork taboo, 53.
— — prayer for protection against fairies and evil eye, 231.
— Rev. Walter, pig-lore, 71.
Mackay, J. G., Cailleach and Caledonians, 169.
— Cailleach and fish, 153.
— Cailleach and matriarchal customs, 161, note 1.
— Cailleach deer deity theory, 146.
Mackenzie, Dr. W. Mackay, Scots types in famous battles, 21.
MacLeod, Mr. Malcolm, Skye folk-tale, 119.
Magic hammers, in Greek myth, 168.
Magic wand, Bride had a, 191.
— Cailleach uses, as weather controller, 139 *et seq*.
— Glaistig has, 178.
— in Finlay the Changeling story, 127 *et seq.*
— in " the Sea Maiden " story, 132, 133.
— iron club of Gyre Carling, 149.
Magnus Bareleg, 15.
— Hebridean son of, 20.
Maid of the Wave, a sea-goddess, 252.
— as giver of children, 252.

INDEX

Maid of the Wave, story of hero and, 252. See *Mermaids*.
Mala Lia', Cailleach as in Glen Glass story, 147 *et seq.*
Malcolm II plants Gaelic colonies in Lowlands, 13, 14.
Man, Isle of, giant lore of, 116.
Martin, M., abductions by fairies, 224.
— Bride ceremony, 191.
— installation cairn, 258.
— sea-god " Shony ", 252, 253.
— *Taghairm* ceremony, 246, 247.
Mediterranean race, 17.
Megalithic remains, Cailleach and, 167.
— Cailleach becomes a boulder, 144.
— courts as stone circles, 257.
— giants and, 115, 116, 117.
— standing stone becomes warrior when struck by magic wand, 130.
— standing stones reverenced, 262, 263.
Merlin's grave, on the Tweed, 106.
Mermaids, 251, 252. See *Maid of the Wave*.
" Merry Dancers ", as fallen angels, 92, 98.
Mesopotamia, Labartu of and Black Annis, 174.
— Tiamat and Cailleach, 157, 158.
Metempsychosis, Celtic belief in, 6.
Milk, Christ as baby washed in, 217.
— demons in vessels containing, 232, 233.
— goddess Bride and milk-yielding plants, 190.
— Greek incantation, 202.
— hare steals from cows, 82.
— hazel the milk tree in Scotland, 217.
— healing from, 218.
— honey and, as elixir, 217.
— Indian and other goddesses as givers of, 216, 217.
— in fairy lullaby, 204, 205.
— " lame goat " with great supply, 185.
— latex as, 216.
— oblations of, poured on hills, 219.
— offered to dead, 218.
— offered to Egyptian mummies, 218.
— offered to fairies, 208, 209.
— offered to Glaistig, 179.
— offered to gruagach, 230.
— offered to urisk, 185.
— offerings of, to the *fridean*, 244.
— Roman cult, 216, 217.
— source of wisdom, 215, 216.
— Zeus fed on honey and, 216, note 1.
Milky Way, 217 and note 1.
Miller, Hugh, Cailleach as mountain maker, 164.
— — fairies non-human, 223.
— — giant lore, 101.
— — green ladies (ghosts), 242, 243.
— — independent origin theory, 96.
— — " Me-mysel' " story, 167.

Miller, Hugh, Tarbat wind-controller, 162.
— Rev. T. D., stone superstitions, 262.
Milton, Cailleach and blue hag of, 171.
Mithra, cult of, reached Western Europe and Britain, 67.
Mole, Cailleach dragon's, 150, 151.
Moles, the Vulnerable, 109 *et seq.*
Morar, Loch, monster of, 247, 248.
Moray Firth, fishers' aversion to swine, 50.
Morocco, in Blue Men narrative, 94.
— modern Blue Men in, 95.
Morrigan, milk as healer, 218.
— the Irish goddess, comes from northwest, 120.
Mountains, Cailleach as shaper of, 164.
— Cailleach's bens, 164. See *Cailleach*.
Mouse as medicine in Egypt and Britain, 78 *et seq.*
— brothers, ancient Scottish custom, 77.
— feast, in Scotland and Near East, 75 *et seq.*
— — pork taboo and, 77, 78.
— fertilizes apple tree, 80.
— lords, as demons in Ireland, 80.
— lore of, connexion with sun and new water, 78.
— medicine, Boers used, 80.
— names, 77, 78.
— standing stone of, 80.
Muileartach, as a *fuath*, 233.
— as old woman in folk-tale, 158.
— Cailleach sea-form, 156 *et seq.*
— demands human sacrifices, 159.
Mull, Cailleach and well near Loch Ba, 162, 163.
— Cailleach's bridge, 164.
— Cailleach's deer, 152.
— Cailleach in, 151.
— Cailleach wades deep loch in, 165, 166.
— Glaistig in, 178.
— " lucky pig " in, 58.
Munlochy, giant story, 100.
— sleeping giants in cave, 107.
Murray, Miss Margaret, fairies and witches, 210.

Nationality, more influential than racial leanings, 9, 10.
Nemets, as sacred groves, 275 *et seq.*
— Druidical holy places in Galatia, Gaul and Briton, 275 *et seq.*
— last judgment in Cromarty " Navity ", 276.
Nennius, arrival of Picts, 36.
New Grange, Danann deities and, 116.
Newhaven, fisher superstitions, 51.
" Nimble Men " (Aurora Borealis), 92, 98.
" No-man " stories in Greek and Gaelic, 167.
Nordic race, 17.

304　INDEX

Nordics, rare in fertile belt of Scotland, 25, 26.
Normans, influence of, in Scotland, 14, 15.
Norse, as allies of anti-Norman Highlanders, 15.
— Blue Men of Morocco, 92 *et seq.*
— Cailleach and connexion with, 169.
— Cailleach ballad, 172.
— Gall-Gaels and, 16.
— ghostly hunters and dogs, 243, 244.
— Hebridean as king of, 20.
— Hebrides evacuated by, 15.
— knew Orcs and Cats were Picts, 33.
— Magnus Bareleg's campaigns, 14.
— Scots descendants of, and pork taboo, 58.
— Scottish element, 13, 14.
— sea-god *Shony*, 253.
— soul forms, 288.
— women not allowed in warships or forts, 20.
North, giants come from, 120.
Northumberland, " Arthur's Chair " in, 104.
Norway, Scots folk-lore and, 7.　See *Norse*.

Oak, as wishing tree, 213, 214.
— Black Annis and, 171.
Orcas, Cape, Pictish place-name of fourth century B.C., 37.
— early place-name, 253.
Orcs (Picts), place-names of, 33.
Orkney, Blue Men narrative and, 93 *et seq.*
— broad-heads in, 26.
— ethics of Earls of, 20.
— giant lore, 100.
— in Roman period, 11.
— " Isles of Boars ", 62.
— Magnus Bareleg seizes, 14.
— Norse in, 14.
— pork eaten in prehistoric times, 63.
— " Sow Day ", 62.
Oscar, Kewach conflict, 112.
Osiris, 7.
— boar form of, 70.
— paradise of, and Scots fairyland, 223.
— pig taboo and, 73, 74.
Oswald, Anglian prince, Gaelic culture, 33.
Oswy, Anglian prince, Columban education of, 33.

Pausanias, origin of Celtic pork taboo, 66.
Peallaidh, as devil in Lewis, 234.
— demon or god, 234.
— rock footprint of, 234.
— shellycoat and, 234.
— urisk and, 234.
Penrith, giant's cave near, 115.
Perthshire, mouse stone in, 80.

Perthshire, Peallaidh in, 234.
— whirlwind fairies in, 201.
Pictones of Gaul, Scottish Picts and, 38.
Picts, agriculturists and seafarers, 36.
— an Aberdeenshire Bede, 30, 31.
— Angle the father of king of, 33.
— arrival of, at Jarlshof, Shetland, 36.
— as broch builders, 36.
— boar ancestor theory, 63.
— broad-heads among, 26.
— Caledonians absorbed by, 35.
— Cape Orcas of fourth century B.C., 37.
— connexion with Pictones of Gaul, 38.
— Cruithne of Ireland not, 37.
— Dalriada subdued by, 11, 12.
— Druids influential among, 40.
— dualism of, 32 *et seq.*
— dynasty of, 11.
— fathers of kings of, were often aliens, 33, 34.
— Gaelic nobles supplant nobles of, 12.
— Gilltrax place-name, 102.
— hegemony in Scotland passes to, 11.
— inheritance through females, 33 *et seq.*
— in northern Scotland in fourth century B.C., 37.
— intellectual life of, 7.
— Inverness and Dunadd boar figures and, 60 *et seq.*
— Kenneth mac Alpin as king of, 12, 35.
— language of, was P-Celtic, 30, 31.
— law of succession like that of ancient Egyptians, 34.
— marriage customs, 33 *et seq.*
— migration to northern Scotland, 36.
— mother-right, 33.
— no cat clan carvings, 63.
— Norse, Welsh, Old English and Old Scots names of, 38.
— northern and southern, 11.
— northern, St. Columba converts, 40.
— Orc and Cat clans and place-names, 33.
— Pecht stones, 265, 266.
— Saxons as allies of, 11.
— southern, converts of St. Ninian, 39.
— well worshipped as god by, 268.
Pinkie-cleuch, big Scots at, 21.
Pliny, mouse lore, 78.
Plutarch, Celtic mercenaries, 67.
Plymouth, giant figures near, 115, 116.
Pork taboo, Anatolian and Scottish aspects of, 68 *et seq.*
— ancient Egyptian, 73, 74.
— Arcadian (Greece) and the Scottish, 73.
— Attis cult and, 66 *et seq.*
— Attis cult-drift theory, 68.
— Barra's two pigs, 54.
— Ben Jonson on King James's prejudice, 43.
— black divination pig, 60.
— boar tusk in north Highland grave, 66.

INDEX 305

Pork taboo, borrowing from Jews theory, 44.
— Cailleach associated with swine, 148, 149.
— Captain Burt on, 44, 45.
— Celtic Diana rides on boar, 65.
— Celtic pig god, 65.
— Celtic pork trade on Continent, 65.
— Christian missionaries as pork eaters, 57, 58.
— Dalyell on Scots prejudice against swine, 44.
— decline of, in Dumfriesshire, 54, 55.
— devil as " big black pig ", 52.
— " devil's mark " on pig, 52.
— Dr. Samuel Johnson on, 44–46.
— Dumfriesshire pig scares, 47 et seq.
— ebbing prejudice, 54.
— evidence of cult-drifting, 67, 68.
— Fife horror of swine, 50, 51.
— fishers' aversion to swine, 41, 50 et seq.
— forest rents for swine feeding, 57.
— Greek pig sacrifices, 72.
— Greek treatment of pig, 69 et seq.
— Hebridean Norsemen and, 58.
— in Dalriada (Lorne) and Lanarkshire of Britons, 46.
— in Scotland, 41 et seq.
— introduction of Mithra cult and Galatian pig cult, 67.
— Inverness boar stone, 60, 61, 62.
— Irish pig lore, 72, 73.
— " Jewish Scots " in English song, 44.
— Lord Leverhulme and, 54.
— " lucky pig ", 58 et seq.
— monks and barons kept swine, 57.
— " mother sow ", 63, 64.
— mouse feast and, 77, 78.
— origin of, in Galatia, 66 et seq.
— Orkney " Sow Day ", 62.
— Pictish boar ancestor theory, 63.
— pig and deified dead, 69.
— pig as " Sandy Campbell ", 54.
— pig in good and evil senses, 64.
— " Pig of Truth ", 73.
— pig sacrifices in Hebrides and Ireland, 62, 63.
— pigs' bones in prehistoric graves, 65, 66.
— pork as cause of disease, 53.
— pork eaten in prehistoric Orkney, 63.
— pork medicine, 71.
— Prestonpans miners regard pig as unlucky, 51, 52.
— revival of, in Skye, 70, 71.
— sacred pig and devil pig, 71.
— St. Anthony's association with swine, 64.
— St. Kentigern and sacred white boar, 59, 60.
— sanctity and abhorrence of swine in Scotland and elsewhere, 56 et seq.

Pork taboo, Scots boar figures indicate no horror of pig, 62.
— Shakespeare's reference, 43.
— shape-changing boar, 59.
— Skyeman's prayer, 53.
— swine and the dead, 69 et seq.
— swine blood and lard as medicine, 71, 72.
— theory of Biblical origin, 56, 57, 58.
— unlucky swine, 71.
— " vomiting last year's pig ", 53, 54.
— Welsh pig lore, 73.
— Yorkshire fishers' aversion to swine, 52.
Prestonpans, miners' aversion to swine, 51, 52.
Ptolemy, place-names of, survivals in Scotland, 37.
Purple, east is, 282.
Pytheas, Scottish place-names, 253, 254.

Raasay, Cailleach in, 153.
— pig sacrifice to horse demon of loch in, 62.
Races, Alpine, Mediterranean, Norman and Palæolithic, 17.
— Angle as father of Pictish king, 33.
— Angles invade Lowlands, 11, 12.
— Angles mingled with Britons, 19.
— Anglian royal refugees in Scotland, 13.
— big Scots at battles of Flodden, Solway Moss and Pinkie-Cleuch, 21, 22.
— breeding out of intruders, 19.
— Britons and Scots in Lowlands, 13.
— Caledonian type, 21.
— Celtic not a racial term, 4, 5.
— Cromarty pigmentation evidence, 27, 28.
— cultural influences on, 9, 10.
— Danes in England and Ireland, 14.
— dark tall Scots, 26.
— Earl Thorfinn dark, 20.
— English and Pictish Bedes, 30, 31.
— ethnics of Orkney earls, 20.
— European types, 17.
— first English occupation of Lowlands, 12, 13.
— Flemings and Lowlanders in north burghs, 15.
— food supplies in early Scotland, 21, 22.
— Gaelic colonies in Lowlands, 13.
— Gall-Gaels, 16.
— Hebridean settlers in Ireland, 15.
— influences of environment, 9.
— Irish grey eye rare in Scotland, 25.
— languages and, 9, 10.
— MacDougalls not Danes, 15.
— Magnus Bareleg's campaigns, 14.
— nationality and, 9, 10.
— Nordic type rare in fertile belt, 25, 26.
— Normans in Scotland, 14.
— Norse customs regarding women, 20.

306 INDEX

Races, Norse element in Scotland, 13, 14.
— Norse evacuation of Hebrides, 15.
— Norse names in Hebrides, 15.
— Norsemen as allies of anti-Norman Highlanders, 15.
— Picts and Irish Cruithne, 37.
— Picts and Pictones, 38.
— pigmentation problem, 26 et seq.
— proto-Egyptians and ancient Britons, 27.
— resistance to intrusions, 19.
— St. Kilda type, 27.
— Saxons as allies of Picts, 11.
— Scots cranial and pigmentation statistics, 23 et seq.
— Scots taller and fairer than Irish, Welsh or Bretons, 28.
— Scots tallest people in Europe, 22.
— Scottish physical characters, 17 et seq.
— Scottish types, 16 et seq.
— second English occupation of Lowlands, 13.
— skull shapes and temperament, 8.
— survivals in France, Egypt, Crete, &c., 18 et seq.
— Thorfinn, Earl of Orkney, half a Scot, 14.
Raglan, Lord, view on tradition, 3.
Ramsay, Dean, Fife horror of swine, 50.
Ramsay, Sir W. M., Anatolian treatments of pig, 68 et seq.
Raven, as form of demon, 236.
— Banshee as, 239.
— Cailleach and, 148.
Red berries, protection from, 275.
Reid, Professor R. W., pig's bones in prehistoric grave, 66.
Religion, Celtic faiths differed, 5, 6.
— dead among fairies, 6.
— Scottish, Irish and Welsh faiths, 6, 7.
— Sky-world and Isles of Blest, 6.
— Transmigration of souls, 6.
Rhea, Bride and the goddess, 193.
Rhodesia, mouse medicine in, 80.
Rhys, Sir John, fairies chiefly women, 198, 199.
Ripley, W. Z., Scottish physical characters, 22, 23.
River Ness, St. Columba and monster in, 233.
— spirits, Cuachag, the Nethy spirit and river cow, 233, 234.
Rivers, Cailleach of ford, 159.
— power in pools of, 267.
Robertson, Rev. C. M., demon lore, 236.
— Dr. W., independent origin theory, 96.
Rock, sacred, cakes offered at, 261.
— — children cured at, 260.
— — getting answer at, 260.
— — near Dingwall, 260.
— — oracle bird near, 260.

Romans, Caledonian marriage customs and that of, 34.
— campaigns in Scotland, 10, 11.
— Hadrian's wall captured, 11.
— Mithra cult, 67.
— Picts and pun of, 38.
— Picts, Scots and Saxons allied against, 11.
Rome, Celtic pork trade with, 65.
— god Terminus, 257.
— milk cult of, 216, 217.
Rona, Cailleach in, 153.
Rowan tree, demon guardian of, 249.
Rumania, Cailleach link with, 173.

Sacrifices. See *Human Sacrifices*.
St. Andrew, cult of, 283.
St. Anthony, association of, with swine, 64.
St. Bridget, goddess Bride and, 190.
St. Columba, converts northern Picts, 40,
— expulsion of demons, 232, 233.
— gets Iona from Picts, 12.
— Pictish Druids, 277.
— pork not tabooed by, 57.
— River Ness monster, 233.
— well Christianized by, 268.
St. Jerome, Galatians could converse with Gauls, 67.
St. John, C., Cailleach story, 146, 147.
St. Kentigern, cult animals of Cernunnos, 68.
— gets fire from hazel, 272, 273.
— sacred white boar, 59, 60.
St. Kilda, physical characters of natives of, 27.
St. Martin, pig sacrifice at festival of, 62, 63.
St. Monacella, hares as lambs of, in Wales, 83, 84.
St. Mungo. See *St. Kentigern*.
St. Ninian, conversion of southern Picts, 39.
— pork not tabooed by, 57.
St. Patrick, in Cailleach lore, 145.
Samson, Ben Ledi giant called, 103.
Saxons, as allies of Picts, 11.
Scotland, alien intrusions rare in, 10.
— Angles in Lowlands for eighty-two years, 13.
— Anglian princes refugees in, 13.
— Anglo-Saxons in Lowlands for forty-one years, 13.
— animal figures on sculptured stones in, 62.
— Attis cult-drift to, 68.
— Ayrshire formerly regarded Highland, 29.
— big fat men at Flodden, &c., 21, 22
— black-and-white divination pigs, 59, 60.
— blond types of, 23–25.
— Blue Men, 3, 4, 7.

INDEX

Scotland, Blue Men and independent origin theory, 96 et seq.
— — in restricted area of, 97.
— — lore, 85 et seq.
— boar figures in, and Greek and Anatolian customs, 62.
— Britons of Strathclyde, 12, 13.
— broad-heads in, 24 et seq.
— Byzantine culture reaches, 283.
— Caledonian and Roman marriage customs, 34.
— — dualism, 35.
— Caledonians muscular, 21.
— Celtic theory and folk-lore, 4.
— cranial and pigmentation statistics, 23 et seq.
— cultural connexions of, with Scotland, 40.
— Dalriada, 12.
— Dalyell on prejudice against swine in, 44.
— dead associated with fairies in, 6.
— destiny of soul, 5, 6.
— different pig cults in, 56 et seq.
— — treatments of pig in, as in Near East, 68 et seq.
— Dr. Johnson on Scots eel taboo, 46.
— Druidical *nemet* place-names in, 275, 276.
— Dumfriesshire pig scares, 47 et seq.
— emigration reduced stature of, 23.
— Ethelstane invasion of Lowlands, 13.
— fair Celts in, 26.
— fairy lore of, 199 et seq.
— fallen angels in folk-lore, 87, 92, 98.
— festivals of, 278 et seq.
— Fianna lore from Ireland, 112.
— first Anglian intrusion, 12, 13.
— fishers' superstitions, 50 et seq.
— food prejudices of James VI, 42, 43.
— fowl and fish taboos, 80 et seq.
— Gaelic in Lothian in twelfth century, 29, 30.
— giant lore of, 99 et seq.
— handfasting in, 34.
— hare 'superstitions, 81 et seq.
— — taboo, 81 et seq.
— harvest hare, 82, 83.
— Indian rope trick story in, 283, 284.
— Inverness boar stone, 60, 61, 62.
— Irish Danann deities not in, 31.
— — grey eye rare in, 25.
— — heroes trained in Skye, 39.
— " Islands of Boars ", 62.
— " Jewish Scots " in English song, 44.
— mac William claimants to throne of, 14, 15.
— Magnus Bareleg invades, 14.
— Malcolm Canmore's successors, 14.
— messages to departed, 284, 285.
— milk and honey elixir, 217.

Scotland, " mother sow ", 63, 64.
— mouse and apple tree; cat and pear tree, 80.
— — brothers in, 77.
— — feast in, 75 et seq.
— — medicine in, 78.
— Near East mouse-cult reached, 80.
— no Irish Danann pantheon in, 118.
— no people named Celts in, 4.
— Nordics in, 26.
— Normans enter, 14.
— Norse as allies of Highlanders, 14.
— — element in, 13, 14.
— — evacuation of Hebrides, 15.
— northern and southern Picts, 11.
— Orc and Cat place-names, 33.
— origin of pork taboo, 66 et seq.
— Orkney " sow day ", 62.
— Pictish and ancient Egyptian laws of succession, 34.
— — dualism in, 32 et seq.
— — dynasty, 11, 12.
— — language P-Celtic, 30, 31.
— — law of succession changed by Kenneth II, 35.
— — marriage customs, 33 et seq.
— Picts and Pictones of Gaul, 37, 38.
— — as leading people in, 11 et seq.
— — migrated to northern Scotland, 36.
— pig as luck bringer, 59.
— — bones in prehistoric graves, 65, 66.
— pigmentation, evidence of, 26 et seq.
— plundering of folk-lore of, 7.
— pork eaten in prehistoric Orkney, 63.
— — in Lanarkshire, 46.
— — in Lorne, 46.
— — taboo in, 41 et seq.
— prehistoric types in, 24.
— Ptolemy's place-names in, 37.
— racial types in, 16 et seq.
— Roman period in, 10, 11.
— sacred mouse-stone in Perthshire, 80.
— — white boar, 59, 60.
— sanctity and abhorrence of swine in, 56 et seq.
— Saxons as allies of Picts, 11.
— Scandinavian surnames in, 15.
— Scots and Picts, 11, 12.
— — dynasty supplants Pictish, 12.
— Shakespeare's witches and swine, 43.
— soul forms in, 287.
— " star clock " of farmers, 281.
— swine and the dead in, and in Near East, 69 et seq.
— tall, dark people in, 21 et seq., 26.
— witch lore of late introduction, 210.
Scott, Michael, 249.
— Reginald, urisk lore, 187.
— Sir Walter, Edgewell tree, 273, 274
— — elves and fairies, 198.

Scott, Sir Walter, "fairy boy of Leith" story, 271, 272.
— — Scottish pork taboo, 42.
— — shellycoat lore, 234, 235.
— — the "mother witch", 149.
— — Thomas the Rhymer legend, 138, 139.
— — Thomas the Rhymer and sleepers, 108.
Sea deities, sea-horse sacrifice, 62.
Seal folk, Blue Men and, 87, 98.
— Clan Codrum and, 87.
Seasons, Great Bear constellation and, 281.
Seats, hills as, for giants, 99 et seq.
Second sight, 288, 289.
Serpent, Bride and, 188 et seq.
— deathless, 250.
— lightning and, 247.
— should be slain, 250.
— white, 249. See *Dragon*.
Set, boar form of, 70.
Severus, Emperor, wife of, and Caledonian customs, 34.
Shakespeare, William, fairies of, 196, 197.
— witches and swine, 43.
Sheep, Cailleach and, 151.
— Glaistig and, 177.
Shellycoat, as smiter, brounger and clootie, 235.
— Brollachan and, 238.
— like Peallaidh and the urisk, 234.
— lore of, 234, 235.
— river spirit, 235.
Shetland, broad-heads in, 26.
— Norse in, 14.
— Picts arrived during late Bronze Age, 36.
— — introduced Iron Age in, 36.
Shiant Isles, annat in, 86.
— Blue Men and, 85 et seq.
— Blue Men wintered in, 95.
— Christian hermits in, 98.
— origin of name, 85 et seq.
Shony, sea-god, 252, 253.
Sigurd, Earl, mother of Irish and wife Scottish, 20.
Silver, crooked sixpence to shoot witch-hare, 82.
— water off, as cure for evil eye, 267, 268.
— Well, in Isle of Man, 145.
Skara Brae, prehistoric pork eaters, 63.
Skye, baby killed by pig in, 70, 71.
— Fionn as sleeping giant in, 107.
— giant story, 101.
— Irish warriors trained in, 39.
— monsters of, 250, 251.
— non-Gaelic language in, 31.
— pork taboo in, 53.
— — and eel prejudice in, 45, 46.
— urisks in, 186.

Skye, weather controlling stone, 256.
Sligachan, Cailleach in, 153.
Smith, Professor G. Elliot, independent origin theory, 96, note 1.
— — proto-Egyptians and British Neolithic peoples, 27.
— — race survivals in Egypt, 18, 19.
Solway Moss, big Scots fight at, 21.
Soul, destiny of, Celtic faiths, 6, 7.
Soul body, the giant's, 113.
Souls, bee and butterfly forms of, 287, 288.
— communications sent to, 284, 285.
Spenser, fairy lore of, 196.
Stag, sacred Scottish, 62.
Standing stone, becomes warrior when struck by magic wand, 130.
Standing stones, Cailleach and, 167, note 1.
— giants and, 116. See *Megalithic remains*.
Stars, Great Bear indicates seasons, 281.
Stewart, W. Grant, fairies in whirlwinds, 201.
— — fairies non-human, 223.
— — fairy republic, 195, 196.
— — protection against fairies, 209.
— — water fairies, 205, 206.
Stokes, Whitley, pig lore, 63.
Stone, boundary stones, 257.
— Burghead cradle stone, 263.
— Cailleach and, 144, 146, 154, 167, 265.
— ceremonial movements around, 269.
— child-getting stones, 263, 264.
— coronation stone, 257, 259.
— courts at circles, 257.
— cup-marked stones, 263, 264.
— cure stone, pain stone and "god stone", 264, 265.
— cursing, 255.
— divination stone, 264.
— Glaistig turns cows into, 178.
— god Terminus, 257.
— haunting reverence of megaliths, 262, 263.
— healing stones, 264, 265.
— Lord of Isles' installation stone, 257, 258.
— MacLaren chief's stones of office with amber beads for wife, 259.
— magic power in, 255 et seq.
— megaliths, cairns and supernatural beings, 265.
— Morgan le Fay becomes, 172.
— mouse name of Perthshire megalith, 80.
— souls in, 256.
— spitting ceremonies, 259, 260.
— "telling it to the stones", 257.
— trees associated with megaliths, 269.
— weather controlling by means of, 256.
— worship or bowing stones, 256. See *Boulder*, *Megaliths* and *Rock*.

INDEX

Strathclyde, Britons of, 12, 13.
Strathpeffer, giant link with Leeds, 114.
— giant of Knockfarrel, 101.
— sacred bird on sculptured stone, 62.
Succellos, Gaulish pig-god, 65.
Sullivan, Dr., Celtic pork trade, 65.
Sunwise, " by the right " in Gaelic, 281.
Sussex, " The Long Man of Wilmington ", 116.
Sutherland, Cailleach's herds in, 152.
— pork taboo story, 53, 54.
Sweden, merchants of, in Constantinople, 93.
Swedish Cailleach, 172.
Swine, associated with deified dead, 69 et seq.
— bird form of demon pig, 59.
— blood of, cures warts, 71, 72.
— bones of, in prehistoric Scottish graves, 65, 66.
— Cailleach and Gyre Carling and, 148, 149, 152.
— Celtic trade in, 65.
— Continental Celts breeders of, 65.
— divination pigs, white and black, 59 et seq.
— first pig seen in Dumfriesshire, 47 et seq.
— Greeks and, 69 et seq.
— magic pigs in Ireland, 72.
— Near East treatment of, 68 et seq.
— Orkney " sow day ", 62.
— " Pig of Truth ", 73.
— sacred white boar, 59, 60.
— St. Anthony and, 64.
— sanctity and abhorrence of in Scotland and elsewhere, 56 et seq.
— Set and Osiris and, 70.
— shape-changing boar, 59. See *Pork Taboo.*
Sykkersund (" safe sound "), Cromarty Firth called, 160.

Taghairm, bumping ceremony, 246, 247.
— cat sacrifice, 245, 246.
— Lochiel performs, 246.
— man in cow's hide, 247.
— meaning of, 247.
Tain, giant story, 101.
Temperaments, no national, 8.
Teutonic gloom, 198.
— race, 17.
Thomas the Rhymer, as sleeper under Dunbuck Hill, Dumbarton, 107
— as sleeping giant, 107 et seq.
— Eildon Hills sleepers, 108.
— fairy queen as hag, 138, 139.
— in elfland, 199.
— in Inverness fairy story, 228 et seq.
Thorfinn, Earl, grandmother, Irish, 20.
Thunderbolt, demon of, 247.

Thunder goddess, Cailleach as, 165, 166.
Tiree, Kewach in, 113.
— long life of Cailleach, 163.
— sea-gruagach, 240, 241.
Tocher, Dr., ethnics of Scotland, 23 et seq.
Tradition, ancient forerunners of historical novelists, 2, 3.
— " Blue Men " and, 3, 4, 7.
— Caledonians and Picts in, 7.
— history and, 2 et seq.
— Lord Raglan on, 3 and note 1.
Transmigration of souls, Celtic belief in, 6.
Tree, fairy goddess of tree, 214, 215.
— spirits, fairies as, 212.
Trees, Artemis and Cailleach connected with, 155.
— associated with standing stones, 269.
— Druid groves, 275. See *Nemets.*
— nail trees of Scotland and Egypt, 213, 214.
— " rock tree " ceremony, 273.
— rowan and holly berries protect houses, &c., 274, 275.
— sacred, 267 et seq.
— — danger of cutting, 273.
— — oak tree connexion with family, 273, 274.
— — rowan, yew and hazel, 271 et seq.
— — souls in, 273, 274.
— wishing, 213.
Tuaitheal, " by the left ", the unfriendly and unlucky movement, 281, 282.
Tylor, E. B., independent origin theory, 97.
Tytler, P. Fraser, Scottish herds of swine, 57.

Urisk, as *fuath*, 234.
— as house or family familiar, 185, 186.
— as satyr-like lord of mountains, 187.
— associated with Glaistig, 187.
— black forms of, 245.
— Brollachan and, 238.
— goat connexion, 185.
— haunts of, 185, 186, 187.
— lore of, 234.
— milk offerings to, 185.
— shellycoat and, 234.
— terrifying stories told by, 186.
— waterfalls of, 185.

Varro, Celtic pork trade, 65.
Victoria, Queen, wishing tree offering, 213.
Viking Age, Blue Men narrative, 92 et seq.
— chronology of, 93.
Votadini, 35.

Wales, Arthurian place-names in, 104 et seq.
— destiny of souls in, 6, 7.
— eye salve makes fairies visible, 226, 227.

Wales, female fairies in, 198, 199.
— giant of, flings "quoit" into Ireland, 116.
— handfasting in, 35.
— hare tabooed in, 83, 84.
— no Blue Men in, 97.
— no Pictish brochs in, 36.
— no pork taboo in, like Scotland, 41.
— pig lore of, 73.
— Scots folk-lore and, 7.
Wallace, Sir William, giants named after, 103.
Wands, the magic, in Finlay the Changeling story, 127 et seq. See *Magic Wands*.
Water fairies, 205, 206, 207.
— horse, in animal and human forms, 237, 238.
— horse, Kelpie and, 238.
— magic power in, 267 et seq.
Watson, Mrs. W. J., Cailleach lore, 140.
— — demon lore, 237.
— — Glaistig lore, 176 et seq.
— — spring gales, 142, 143.
— Prof. W. J., ancient place-names, 253.
— — *Fuath* lore, 233.
— — Kewach lore, 112, 113.
— — Loch Etive goddess, 90, note 2.
— — mouse and standing stone, 80.
— — "mouse lords", 80.
— — Nemet place-names, 275 et seq.
— — Peallaidh and devil, 234.
— — Ptolemy place-names in Scotland, 37.
— — Scots Arthurian place-names, 105, 106.
— — Shiant Isles and annats, 86 et seq.
— — *Taghairm* ceremony, 247.
— — tree fairies, 212.
— — yew cult, 98.
Well of Youth, in Mull, 162, 163.
Wellox (MacGregor), Kelpie worsted by, 238, 239.
Wells, associated with standing stones, 269.

Wells, Cailleach as guardian of, 153, 154.
— Cailleach's well, 269.
— Christianizing of pagan, 268.
— diseases cured by, 268 et seq.
— god-well, 268.
— new water life-giving, 270.
— offerings dropped in, 269, 270.
— sacred, 267 et seq.
— St. Mary's Well and dying persons, 270, 271.
— Well of Youth, 270.
West, cardinal point of fairies, 120.
Whirlwinds, Biblical symbolism, 203.
— Chinese, Japanese and Polynesian lore, 203.
— fairies and demons in, 200 et seq.
— Greek nymphs in, like fairies, 201, 202.
— Pharaoh's soul in, 202.
— widespread lore of supernatural beings in, 202, 203.
White, south is, 282.
Widdershins, "by the left", the unlucky movement, 281, 282.
Wild huntsman, 243, 244.
William-sit-down, in Cailleach story, 166.
William the Lyon, castles and burghs established by, 15.
Wishing hillock, 262, 263.
Witches, Cailleach lore acquired by, 147.
— fairies and, 210.
— hare forms of, 82.
"Wolf of Badenoch, The" (Prince Alexander Stewart), as a giant, 103.
Wolf, the sacred, 62.
Wolves, Cailleach and, 152.
Worm, soul form as, 150, 151.

Yew cult, Iona and, 98.
— sacred, 271.
— Well of the, 268.
Yorkshire, fishers' aversion to swine, 52.
— pig bones in prehistoric graves, 65.

Zeus, milk and honey given to, 216, note 1.

Lightning Source UK Ltd.
Milton Keynes UK
UKHW041914041119
352900UK00004B/73/P